Judicial Behavior and Policymaking
An Introduction

★ ★ ★

Robert J. Hume, PhD
Fordham University

ROWMAN & LITTLEFIELD
Lanham • Boulder • New York • London

Executive Editor: Traci Crowell
Assistant Editor: Mary Malley
Senior Marketing Manager: Kim Lyons
Interior Designer: Pro Production Graphic Services
Cover Designer: Enterline Design Services

Credits and acknowledgments for material borrowed from other sources, and reproduced with permission, appear on the appropriate page within the text.

Published by Rowman & Littlefield
A wholly owned subsidary of The Rowman & Littlefield Publishing Group, Inc.
4501 Forbes Boulevard, Suite 200, Lanham, Maryland 20706
www.rowman.com

Unit A, Whitacre Mews, 26-34 Stannary Street, London SE11 4AB, United Kingdom

British Library Cataloguing in Publication Information Available

Library of Congress Cataloging-in-Publication Data
Names: Hume, Robert J., author.
Title: Judicial behavior and policymaking : an introduction / Robert J. Hume, Ph.D., Fordham University.
Description: Lanham : Rowman & Littlefield, 2018. | Includes bibliographical references and index.
Identifiers: LCCN 2017040639 (print) | LCCN 2017041492 (ebook) |
   ISBN 9781442276055 (electronic) | ISBN 9781442276031 (cloth : alk. paper) |
   ISBN 9781442276048 (pbk. : alk. paper)
Subjects: LCSH: Judicial process—United States. | Political questions and judicial power—United States. | Judges—Political activity—United States.
Classification: LCC KF8775 (ebook) | LCC KF8775. H86 2018 (print) |
   DDC 347.73/5—dc23
LC record available at https://lccn.loc.gov/2017040639

♾ ™ The paper used in this publication meets the minimum requirements of American National Standard for Information Sciences—Permanence of Paper for Printed Library Materials, ANSI/NISO Z39.48-1992.

Printed in the United States of America

Brief Contents

Detailed Contents

★ ★ ★

Figures, Tables, and Textboxes

★ ★ ★

FIGURES

TABLES

TEXTBOXES

Judicial Process Boxes

Methodological Notes

Preface

THIS TEXTBOOK IS about judicial behavior and policymaking. My objective is to cover these subjects as a political scientist would, reviewing what social science research can teach us about what motivates judges and how court decisions shape society. It is not, primarily, a book about judicial process. As a political scientist, I am interested more in questions about power than process or doctrine. I want to know why judges make the choices that they do, who has the power to influence judicial decision making, and what the consequences of court decisions are.

The textbook will also familiarize readers with the methods that political scientists use to answer these questions. You will learn about how researchers derive hypotheses from theories about judging and then analyze them using quantitative and qualitative methods. You will have the opportunity to review actual data that political scientists use and make your own conclusions about how well or poorly the data support their hypotheses. By learning to think like a political scientist, you will gain a better understanding of what we know about judicial behavior and policymaking, instead of what we imagine to be true.

I write this book at a time when judging has become highly politicized. When I began my formal study of the courts over two decades ago, it seemed radical to say that judges are motivated by their policy preferences. Now, it sometimes seems more radical to suggest that the law might matter to judges after all. The confirmation process for U.S. Supreme Court justices is more contentious than ever. Recently the Senate delayed the confirmation of the late Justice Antonin Scalia's successor for over a year to secure the appointment of a more ideologically compatible nominee. State judicial elections have also become contentious, with donors and interest groups pouring huge sums into these contests. So much of our discourse about judging has become so politicized that it is a good time to reflect on what we actually know about what judges do, how much discretion they have, and how they use that discretion.

I developed this textbook for the Judicial Politics course that I teach annually at Fordham University, so I would like to begin by thanking my undergraduate students in that course for reading draft chapters and providing comments during the past two years of development. The textbook is for them, and my future students, to help them to better understand the field of judicial politics and how professional political scientists conduct research about the courts.

Many others have also helped with the development of this textbook. I am particularly grateful to Traci Crowell and Mary Malley at Rowman & Littlefield, who have been enthusiastic champions of this project from the start. I received comments and assistance on drafts from Ida Bastiaens, Zein Murib, Chris Bonneau, David Klein, Lydia Tiede, Andrew H. Sidman, and Richard Vining. The book is much stronger because of their contributions.

I thank Michael Bailey for generously sharing data for two of the figures in chapter 3. The data were originally used in Michael A. Bailey and Forrest Maltzman, *The Constrained Court: Law, Politics, and the Decisions Justices Make* (Princeton University Press, 2011). Portions of chapter 7 are adapted from Robert J. Hume, *Courthouse Democracy and Minority Rights: Same-Sex Marriage in the States* (Oxford University Press, 2013).

I also extend special thanks to my wife, Shannon, and children, Megan and Sean, for their patience and support as I completed this project.

A textbook of this nature can only exist because of the work of innumerable political scientists who have come before me and continue to perform outstanding research about the judiciary every day. There are too many of these scholars to mention here, but it is important to recognize their contributions and to thank them for all that they have done to establish and sustain the field of judicial politics. The pages that follow are a celebration of their work.

1

Judges as Policymakers

THE EYES OF the nation were on the U.S. Supreme Court. It was June 28, 2012, the last day of the Court's term, when the justices often make landmark decisions, and this year's case promised to be momentous. At stake was the constitutionality of the Affordable Care Act, commonly known as "Obamacare." The legislation was President Barack Obama's signature accomplishment and the centerpiece of his fall reelection campaign. The Court's ruling would have consequences for millions of uninsured Americans who stood to benefit from the law's provisions.

When Chief Justice John Roberts began reading his opinion from the bench, it looked like the justices would strike down Obamacare. The chief justice's initial remarks were critical of the Affordable Care Act, particularly the individual mandate, which required Americans to purchase health insurance or pay a penalty. Journalists outside of the courthouse initially—and wrongly—reported that the justices had ruled that the mandate was unconstitutional.[1] The confusion was understandable because Chief Justice Roberts did not, in fact, accept the Obama administration's primary argument that the mandate was a valid exercise of Congress's constitutional power to regulate interstate commerce.[2] Roberts announced that the commerce clause did not authorize Congress to compel Americans to purchase health insurance.

But then Roberts pivoted. "That is not the end of the matter," he said.[3] Despite rejecting the Obama administration's primary argument, Roberts stated that the individual mandate was still constitutional on the basis of the taxing and spending clause—the Obama administration's secondary rationale—which previous courts had rejected. "The Affordable Care Act's requirement that certain individuals pay a financial penalty for not obtaining health insurance may reasonably be characterized as a tax," the chief justice said. "Because the Constitution permits such a tax, it is not our role to forbid it, or to pass upon its wisdom or fairness."[4]

The decision was sensational, not just because of what the Court had ruled, but because of who had supported the outcome. It turned out that Chief Justice Roberts had provided the crucial fifth vote needed to uphold the statute. A conservative Republican justice had just saved the major legislative accomplishment of a Democratic president, and he had gone out of his way to do it. What no one could figure out was why. The episode touched upon a central puzzle in judicial politics: What explains judicial behavior? What led Chief Justice Roberts to vote as he did? Did he believe the law compelled him to side with the Obama administration? Or did he think that it was simply good strategy to avoid charges of judicial activism? Did Chief Justice Roberts personally support the law, despite his conservative background? All three explanations were possible, but none was immediately obvious from the opinion.

More generally, the health care decision highlighted the key role that the judiciary plays in making policy in the United States. As the French political thinker Alexis de Tocqueville once remarked after visiting the United States in the 1830s, "There is hardly a political question in the United States which does not sooner or later turn into a judicial one."[5] Americans turn to courts to ratify major legislative acts such as the Affordable Care Act, and we permit courts to overturn these acts, even when they enjoy broad public support. Judges tell us what our rights are, what laws our elected representatives can pass, and what these laws mean. In fact, you might be surprised at just *how much* judges make policy—not just Supreme Court justices, but *all judges*, at all levels of the American judiciary. Throughout this textbook, you will learn about how judges make policy and the effects that judicial policy choices have on American society.

The first chapter introduces you to the idea of judges as policymakers. As you will see, judges vary in the amount of discretion that they have to make policy, but all judges have at least some discretion, and the choices that they make touch upon most aspects of our lives. When a trial judge determines the length of a prison sentence or accepts a plea deal, the judge is making policy. When a lower federal court judge decides that a Supreme Court precedent does not apply to a new set of facts, the judge is making policy. When a state supreme court justice rules that the right to marry includes same-sex couples, the judge is making policy. Because judges have so much power, the politics of judging—inside and outside the courthouse—is often contentious.

Political scientists and other scholars who study the courts disagree about what influences judicial behavior. Some scholars believe that judges are motivated by policy goals much like other government officials, but another school of thought maintains that judges are professionals who are guided by legal principles. Still other scholars have found that social background characteristics, such as gender and race, influence judging. In subsequent chapters, we will explore these different theories in greater detail and evaluate the evidence for them.

A common explanation for Chief Justice Roberts's vote in the health care case was that he was acting strategically in response to pressures from outside of the Court. Specifically, Roberts was trying to avoid being labeled as an activist judge for striking down the president's most important legislative accomplishment during an election year. Linda Greenhouse, the former Court reporter for the *New York Times*, called the chief justice's vote "a deeply pragmatic call" that "saved the Supreme Court from the stench of extreme partisanship."[6] Jeffrey Toobin of CNN agreed, calling the vote "a singular act of courage" by which Roberts "insulates himself from charges of partisanship for the foreseeable future."[7] The implication was that Chief Justice Roberts cared about how his decision would be received and voted in a way that would deflect controversy from the Court. The Chief Justice was, in effect, playing politics.

We are unlikely to gain clearer insights into why Roberts voted the way he did until much later, after the current justices retire and scholars gain access to their private papers. When that day comes, we may very well learn that the conventional wisdom was wrong and that the chief justice really did think his decision made for good law, and not just good politics. For now, what is clear is that Chief Justice Roberts had discretion to make policy and he used his discretion to make a choice that had ramifications for American law, public policy, and even the presidential election. In this respect, the chief justice was not unique, but a typical judge.

JUDGES AS POLICYMAKERS

All judging requires making choices. It requires judgment. If it were possible to answer legal questions by following a formula, then it would not be necessary to hire people to do it. We could just let computers decide. However, most of us would disapprove of letting a machine determine whether we have to pay a traffic ticket or tell us what the terms of child custody arrangements should be. We would not want a computer to assign a prison sentence, to interpret a statute, or to define our rights, because we understand that every case is a little bit different, requiring human judgment to determine how the law applies in each circumstance.

In this book, I define **policy** broadly to include any authoritative directive made by a government institution, such as a court. By *making policy*, I mean that judges have genuine choice about what directives to make, which is to say that judges are not mechanically following rules set out in statutes, precedents, and other legal authorities. Judges use their discretion to determine how to apply the law to the unique set of facts before them. These policy choices might be significant, such as determining whether to overturn an act of Congress, or they might be more modest, like fixing bail. Yet, all of these behaviors represent policy choices.

The amount of discretion that judges have to make policy depends on where the judges are located within the judicial hierarchy. A basic overview of this hierarchy appears in Figure 1.1. Generally speaking, the higher that judges are in the hierarchy, the more discretion they have to make policy. The U.S. Supreme Court, at the top of the judicial hierarchy, has the most discretion, with supervisory authority over the entire federal judiciary and over state judges on questions of federal law. Among the reasons that the justices have so much discretion is that they choose which cases they want to decide out of the thousands of requests that come to them. Typically, the justices take cases in which the law is not clear, meaning that there are good arguments on both sides and therefore a real choice about where to move the law.

The resolution of other cases is left to lower courts, with the U.S. courts of appeals serving as the courts of last resort for most federal cases. Lower-court judges are supposed to follow the Supreme Court's precedents, but the reality is that many ambiguities in federal law are unresolved by the Supreme Court, leaving it to the judges on the courts of appeals, or "circuit courts," to fill in the gaps. In the absence of controlling precedent, circuit judges have discretion to decide questions of federal law based on their own interpretations of the legal authorities.

State courts do not get the same attention from political scientists that federal courts do, even though most civil and criminal

Figure 1.1   Structure of the United States Judiciary

U.S. Supreme Court
9 justices, appointed by the
President and confirmed by the
Senate for life terms; has final
authority on matters of federal law.

only on matters
of federal law

U.S. Courts of Appeals
12 geographic circuits (including
one for the District of Columbia)
plus a special Federal Circuit;
judges are appointed by the
President and confirmed by the
Senate for life; judges typically
decide cases on 3-judge panels.

State Supreme Courts
50 state supreme courts, selected
and retained through a variety of
mechanisms (e.g., appointment,
election, and merit selection);
have final authority on matters
of state law.

Intermediate Appellate Courts
Only 41 of the 50 states have
intermediate appellate courts.

U.S. District Courts
94 geographic districts,
sometimes several per state, as
well as other specialty courts
(e.g., U.S. Bankruptcy Courts);
judges are appointed by the
President and confirmed by the
Senate for life.

State Trial Courts
May have general jurisdiction or
limited jurisdiction (e.g., traffic
courts, small claims courts);
structure varies by state; selection
and retention methods also vary
(e.g., appointment, election,
merit selection).

Federal Judiciary   **State Judiciary**

litigation occurs there, but like federal courts these tribunals can have
a substantial impact on law and policy. State supreme courts have
the final say over the meaning of state constitutions, and in some
states these courts have proved to be more innovative than the U.S.
Supreme Court. For example, the California Supreme Court decided

that California's state constitution required the state to permit inter-racial marriages twenty years before the U.S. Supreme Court ruled that antimiscegenation laws also violated the federal constitution.[8] Similarly, the Supreme Judicial Court of Massachusetts interpreted its state constitution to make Massachusetts the first state to provide full marriage equality to same-sex couples.[9] In these areas, state supreme courts were policy innovators long before the U.S. Supreme Court seriously considered these alternatives.

Trial judges, at the bottom of the hierarchy, are the most con-strained because they are supposed to apply legal policies set by their judicial superiors. However, trial judges are not without discretion, and their use of it can have startling consequences. For example, in November 1997, a jury in Cambridge, Massachusetts, convicted a nineteen-year-old British *au pair*, Louise Woodward, of second-degree murder after the baby she was caring for died, apparently of "shaken baby syndrome."[10] Woodward was a sympathetic defendant, but few expected the trial judge, Hiller B. Zobel, to throw out the jury's verdict and reduce it to a manslaughter conviction, releasing her on time served. "Viewing the evidence broadly, as I am permitted to do," Judge Zobel wrote, "I believe that the circumstances in which Defendant acted were characterized by confusion, inexperience, frus-tration, immaturity and some anger, but not malice." Judge Zobel believed that the baby's death, while tragic, had been an accident.

Cases like these are only the most prominent examples of judges acting as policymakers. Day in and day out, judges make choices about all sorts of matters, ranging from traffic tickets to deporta-tions to contracts and torts. In the process, judges function not merely as interpreters of law but as sources of law. The choices that judges make can have as much influence over the direction of law and policy as the actions of other government actors, if not more.

JUDICIAL ACTIVISM

Many people resist the idea that judges make policy because they have been told that **judicial activism** is a cardinal sin of judging. For decades, politicians have told us that "activist judges" abuse their power by making policy on issues ranging from abortion and criminal procedure to campaign finance law. In his 2010 State of the Union address, President Obama blasted the Supreme Court for its decision in *Citizens United v. Federal Election Commission*.[11] "Last week the Supreme Court reversed a century of law that I believe will open the floodgates for special interests—including foreign corporations—to spend without limit in our elections," he told an audience that included a number of sitting justices. "I don't think American elections should be bankrolled by America's most powerful interests, or worse, by foreign entities. They should be decided by the American people."[12] The president was accusing the justices of *activism*—making policy choices that should be left to the American people or their representatives in Congress.

President Obama was not the first president to accuse the Supreme Court of activism. In the 1930s President Franklin D. Roosevelt criticized the justices for striking down portions of his New Deal plan. "In the last four years the sound rule of giving statutes the benefit of the doubt has been cast aside," he said in a public radio address. "The Court has been acting not as a judicial body, but as a policy-making body."[13] Similarly, Richard Nixon made judicial activism a major theme of his 1968 presidential campaign, stating that his judicial nominees "would be strict constructionists who saw their duty as interpreting law and not making law."[14] Since that time, this rhetoric has been a particularly prominent feature of Republican presidential campaigns (see Box 1.1), although, as the examples above demonstrate, candidates from both parties use it.[15]

For the most part, professional political scientists do not take the phrase *judicial activism* very seriously. It is a term that politicians use more frequently than social scientists do. Politicians use *judicial activism* primarily to criticize court decisions that they dislike. The irony is that these politicians do not want judges to stop making policy at all. They just want them to make different choices. Conservative politicians describe as "activist" court decisions favoring abortion, same-sex marriage, and the rights of the accused, but liberal politicians will say that these decisions are *just* or *fair*. For their part, liberal politicians charge activism when courts strike down campaign finance laws or increase state power, but conservatives will say that these decisions are needed to restore the appropriate constitutional balance of power.

Charges of judicial activism also arise when judges interpret legal texts using methods that other people think are invalid. For the most part, legal texts do not provide instructions to judges about how they should be interpreted, and reasonable people will disagree about what the words and phrases mean. When it comes to constitutional interpretation, supporters of **originalism** believe that constitutional words and phrases should be interpreted based on what people thought the words meant at the time that they were written. In contrast, supporters

TEXTBOX 1.1 | **Republican Presidential Rhetoric about the Supreme Court, 1968–2016**

Republican presidents and presidential candidates have been particularly vocal critics of judicial activism since at least the 1960s, when candidate Richard Nixon criticized the liberal decisions of the Warren Court. Below are sample comments.

"There are other requirements I would make of nominees to the high court which the people have a right to know. They would be strict constructionists who saw their duty as interpreting law and not making law. They would see themselves as caretakers of the Constitution and servants of the people, not super-legislators with a free hand to impose their social and political viewpoints upon the American people."

Richard M. Nixon, November 2, 1968

"I want judges of the highest intellectual standing who harbor the deepest regard for the Constitution and its traditions—one of which is judicial restraint."

Ronald Reagan, October 21, 1985

"I don't have any litmus test. But what I would do is appoint people to the Federal bench that will not legislate from the bench, who will interpret the Constitution."

George H. W. Bush, October 13, 1988

"I want people on the bench who don't try to use their position to legislate from the bench. We want people to interpret the law, not try to make law and write law."

George W. Bush, March 28, 2002

"My nominees will understand that there are clear limits to the scope of judicial power and clear limits to the scope of federal power."

John McCain, May 6, 2008

"I will nominate judges who know the difference between personal opinion and the law. It is long past time for the Supreme Court to return the issue of abortion back to the states, by overturning *Roe v. Wade*."

Mitt Romney, October 8, 2011

TEXTBOX 1.1 | **Continued**

"I am looking to appoint judges very much in the mold of Justice Scalia. I'm looking for judges—and I've actually picked twenty of them—so that people would see, highly respected, highly thought of and actually very beautifully reviewed by just about everybody. But people that will respect the Constitution of the United States. And I think that this is so important."

Donald Trump, October 9, 2016

of a **living constitution** approach believe that constitutional language should be interpreted based on what people think that these words mean today. Disagreements over how to interpret the Constitution can lead to differences over how to resolve cases and to charges of activism.

For example, consider how differences over constitutional interpretation might generate disagreements over whether the death penalty is constitutional. Originalists would look at the language of the Eighth Amendment, which prohibits "cruel and unusual punishments," and ask whether people thought the death penalty was cruel or unusual at the time the amendment was ratified, in 1791.[16] Because executions were common in the 1790s, originalists would say that the Eighth Amendment could not have been meant to prohibit the death penalty. Supporters of the living constitution approach, however, would try to understand what is cruel or unusual based on how people understand the concept today. Judges who take this approach might look to trends in state laws, public opinion data, and even international law to arrive at the contemporary understanding of "cruel and unusual punishments."

Originalists would say that judges are being activist when they try to keep the Constitution current with the times. Originalists think that the most appropriate way to update the Constitution is to amend it, using the procedures outlined in Article V, and that the living constitution approach gives judges too much power to change the Constitution's meaning.[17] However, critics of originalism would say that nothing in the Constitution requires the text to be interpreted based on originalist principles. The Constitution describes broad concepts, such as "cruel and unusual punishments," but it does not endorse any particular conception of what these concepts mean. Critics maintain that originalism advances a method of constitutional interpretation that is not necessarily supported by the document.

WHY JUDGES MAKE POLICY:
SOURCES OF UNCERTAINTY IN LAW

Judges have discretion to make policy for many reasons. As I discuss below, laws are often written in general language, they must be applied to new facts, and they frequently come into conflict with each other, creating ambiguities in the law that judges must resolve to decide cases. The category of what constitutes "law" is expansive, but in this textbook I refer primarily to **statutes**, which are written by legislatures, and **constitutions**, which are broad frameworks of government. I also refer to **regulations** promulgated by administrative agencies and **precedents** authored by courts, which present many of the same interpretive problems.

Laws Are Written in General Language

The first reason that judges encounter uncertainty in the law is that legal texts are frequently written in broad, ambiguous language that leaves room for interpretation. The Constitution, for example, gives Congress the power "to regulate commerce," but it does not specify what "commerce" is.[18] The First Amendment protects "speech" without clarifying whether "speech" is limited to verbal or written forms of expression or includes expressive conduct, such as flag burning or exotic dancing.[19] When confronted with vague or general language in an authoritative legal text, judges need to make choices about how to apply the law.

You might be surprised at just how ambiguous much of the law can be on matters that affect us every day. For example, New York State penal law states that a person is guilty of "jostling," a class A misdemeanor, "when, in a public place, he intentionally and unnecessarily places his hand in the proximity of a person's pocket or handbag."[20] Few would disagree with punishing individuals who intentionally rifle through another's purse. But what does the law mean by placing a hand "in the proximity" of the purse? And what counts as "intentional" or "unnecessary" jostling? One commentator offered a hypothetical situation:

> You lose your balance as the A train stops short, brushing against the newspaper and bag of a fellow commuter as you regain your footing.

Have you just stumbled, or have you committed a class A misdemeanor, Jostling? Were a police officer to apply the statute's vague wording and arrest you, and a judge to agree with the officer's interpretation, you could be facing up to one year in prison.[21]

One might hope that judges would not put people in jail for brushing up against other passengers on the subway. However, when the penal code is unclear, people may disagree about what conduct is forbidden. It is up to judges to determine how to resolve these types of ambiguities when applying laws to concrete circumstances.

Laws are unclear for a number of reasons. Legislators might choose to write statutes broadly to give judges flexibility about how to apply them to new factual circumstances. Statutes might also lack clarity as part of legislative compromises. If, to become law, a bill requires the support of hundreds of legislators, sometimes the only way to get enough votes is to write a bill in general language that will appeal to a large coalition. Legislators might also choose general language if the actors who will implement the statute have greater expertise in the subject matter. In administrative law, for example, legislators frequently write statutes in general terms with the expectations that administrative agencies will fill in the gaps. In this way, policy experts at organizations such as the Food and Drug Administration and the Nuclear Regulatory Commission can draw upon their technical knowledge to make better policies than Congress would achieve by acting alone. Courts must then determine whether agencies have exercised their discretion appropriately when implementing the statutes.

Additionally, legislators might choose to write statutes broadly to serve their self-interest. If legislators care about getting reelected— and most of them do—they will avoid including details in statutes that will offend key constituents. As David Mayhew observed in his classic work on Congress, "Position-taking politics may produce statutes that are long on goals but short on means to achieve them."[22] A vaguely written statute permits members of Congress to claim credit for addressing a problem (such as reducing crime or improving health care) while avoiding blame for a solution that might alienate voters. "The electoral requirement is not that he make pleasing things happen," Mayhew explains, "but that he make pleasing judgmental statements."[23] Whatever the reason for the lack of clarity in the law, the ambiguities that arise provide opportunities for judges to make policy. Judges cannot avoid the responsibility of deciding the cases before them. Someone has to win and someone has to lose. If the sources of law do not provide a clear answer, then judges need to decide how to resolve the uncertainty.

Laws Must Be Applied to New Facts

Another source of uncertainty in the law is that legal texts must be applied to new facts that the drafters might not have anticipated. Every case is unique, so every case raises questions, to a greater or lesser degree, about how judges are to apply the law to the particular factual circumstances before them. As time passes and society changes from the time when laws were enacted, questions become more difficult about how to apply these laws to new situations. The issue commonly arises in constitutional interpretation, in which judges must determine how to apply constitutional language that is hundreds of years old to new situations and new technologies, such as text messaging, thermal imaging devices, and the internet. Needless to say, the Constitution says nothing directly about these technologies, so the justices must make choices about how to resolve constitutional questions concerning them.

The Supreme Court encountered this problem in 2010, when the justices had to decide whether the Constitution barred California from passing a law prohibiting the sale of violent video games to minors.[24] The Constitution does not say anything about video games, but the First Amendment does protect free speech, and a majority of the justices thought that video games were analogous to other forms of protected expression. "Like the protected books, plays, and movies that preceded them," Justice Antonin Scalia wrote, "video games communicate ideas—and even social messages—through many familiar literary devices (such as characters, dialogue, plot, and music) and through features distinctive to the medium (such as the player's interaction with the virtual world). That suffices to confer First Amendment protection."[25]

Other justices were not so sure that the analogy to other media was appropriate. Justice Samuel Alito thought that the interactive nature of video games made them a unique medium that warranted heightened regulation. "Persons who play video games . . . have an unprecedented ability to participate in the events that take place in the virtual worlds that these games create," he wrote.[26] The experience of simulating violent acts in these worlds was not comparable to watching a film or reading a Choose Your Own Adventure book. "If the technological characteristics of the sophisticated games that are likely to be available in the near future are combined with the characteristics of the most violent games already marketed," he wrote, "the result will be games that allow troubled teens to experience in an extraordinarily personal and vivid way what it would be like to carry out unspeakable acts of violence."[27]

Another landmark case in which the justices had to consider how to apply old constitutional language to new technologies concerned the Fourth Amendment and police surveillance. The Fourth Amendment protects us against "unreasonable searches and seizures," but the language of the amendment suggests that we are only secure in our "persons, houses, papers, and effects."[28] Charles Katz was arrested after the police tapped into a telephone booth he was using to transmit illegal wagering information. It was unclear whether the police could wiretap a public phone booth without a warrant because the Fourth Amendment says nothing directly about phone booths or wiretapping. Previously the Supreme Court had ruled that if there was no physical trespass of protected spaces such as houses—which are mentioned in the amendment—then the police could intrude on people's privacy without a warrant.[29]

A majority of the Court in *Katz v. United States* disagreed. "The Fourth Amendment protects people, not places," Justice Potter Stewart wrote for the majority.[30] What mattered was not where the search had occurred but whether Katz expected his conversations to be private. The majority believed that by closing the door of the phone booth, Katz had established an expectation of privacy into which it was unreasonable for the police to intrude.

The majority in *Katz* made a choice to extend Fourth Amendment protections to new forms of police surveillance by emphasizing the personal nature of Fourth Amendment rights, a choice that others on the Court considered a departure from the original understanding of the amendment. In dissent, Justice Hugo Black suggested that it posed no great interpretive challenge to determine how the founders would have treated wiretapping. "Tapping telephone wires, of course, was an unknown possibility at the time the Fourth Amendment was adopted," he wrote. "But eavesdropping (and wiretapping is nothing more than eavesdropping by telephone) was . . . and, if they had desired to outlaw or restrict the use of evidence obtained by eavesdropping, I believe they would have used the appropriate language to do so in the Fourth Amendment."[31] Justice Black thought that it was better, when faced with a new technology, to choose an interpretation of the text that more closely approximated the original understanding.

In both of these cases, judges needed to determine how to apply old legal texts to new, unanticipated circumstances, and in both cases they did so by making analogies to other, more familiar situations that the judges had encountered before. Yet, in choosing these analogies, the judges once again encountered uncertainty: Which comparisons are truly analogous? How far should these analogies extend? Within these ambiguities, judges find discretion to make policy.

Laws Come into Conflict with Each Other

A third reason for uncertainty in the law is that laws come into conflict with each other. Judges might find, for example, that several legislative statutes cover the same issue, or that a higher court has made conflicting pronouncements on the same legal question. Because the law is not written by a single person, but by groups of people across multiple institutions over time, it is inevitable that conflicts will arise and that judges must make choices about how to apply conflicting authorities to the cases before them.

What happens, for example, when acts of Congress conflict with the U.S. Constitution? The Supreme Court in *Marbury v. Madison* (1803) assumed that judges should resolve these conflicts. "It is emphatically the province and duty of the Judicial Department to say what the law is," wrote Chief Justice John Marshall. "If two laws conflict with each other, the Courts must decide on the operation of each."[32] Chief Justice Marshall believed that the judicial power, which was vested in the federal judiciary by Article III, included **judicial review**, the power of courts to evaluate the policies of other government institutions and invalidate them because they are inconsistent with the Constitution. (See case excerpt at the end of the chapter.)

Chief Justice Marshall's assertion of judicial review was particularly bold because he used it to evaluate the policies of coequal branches of government, specifically the president and Congress. There is a clearer constitutional basis for judicial review of the policies of subordinate institutions, such as state governments, because the Supremacy Clause of Article VI states that, "This Constitution . . . shall be the supreme law of the land; and the judges in every state shall be bound thereby, anything in the constitution or laws of any state to the contrary notwithstanding."[33] The Supremacy Clause provides a foundation for **vertical judicial review**, evaluating the policies of subordinate institutions, but a much less clear foundation for **horizontal judicial review**, evaluating the policies of coequal institutions.

Nevertheless, Marshall believed that horizontal judicial review was necessary. "If both the law and the Constitution apply to a particular case," he wrote, "so that the Court must either decide the case conformably to the law, disregarding the Constitution, or conformably to the Constitution, disregarding the law, the Court must determine which of these conflicting rules governs the case. This is of the very essence of judicial duty."[34] Judges would be avoiding their responsibility to decide cases if they did not determine which of the competing sources of law governed the cases before them.

Today, most people accept that it is the responsibility of judges to resolve these types of conflicts. However, at the time of *Marbury*, there was considerable disagreement about whether judges should review the policies of coequal branches. Among the most prominent critics of judicial review was Thomas Jefferson. In an 1819 letter to Judge Spencer Roane, Jefferson denied that judges possess the power of judicial review, writing, "My construction of the Constitution is . . . that each department is truly independent of the others, and has an equal right to decide for itself what is the meaning of the Constitution in the cases submitted to its action."[35] Jefferson's **departmental theory** maintained that each branch, or department, of the national government was equal and that judges should not second-guess the policies of other branches.

Judges in the years after *Marbury* were also divided over judicial review. In *Eakin v. Raub* (1825), John Bannister Gibson of the Pennsylvania Supreme Court argued that when an act of Congress conflicts with the Constitution, it is the role of the judge to defer to Congress's interpretation.[36] "I am of the opinion," he wrote, "that it rests with the people, in whom full and absolute sovereign power resides, to correct abuses in legislation, by instructing their representatives to repeal the obnoxious act." According to Gibson, if the American people believed that Congress had interpreted the Constitution incorrectly, then it was the responsibility of the people, not judges, to correct the mistake, either by instructing their representatives or voting them out of office. (See case excerpt at the end of the chapter.)

After two centuries of experience, Americans have become accustomed to judicial review, and we trust judges to exercise this power responsibly.[37] However, there is little doubt that judicial review has increased the power of judges to make policy. By accepting judicial review, we have given judges the power to decide on the constitutionality of legislation and the scope of our rights. Critics like Jefferson and Gibson would have left this responsibility to us.

AN OVERVIEW OF THIS BOOK

This textbook introduces you to the subject of judicial behavior and policymaking, drawing upon leading political science research to help you better understand how judges exercise their discretion to make policy. You will compare different theories of judicial behavior and learn about how other actors, including the public, influence the choices that judges make. We will also consider how judicial policies influence American society. Much of the political science literature on these subjects focuses on the U.S. Supreme Court, so that tribunal is a major focus of this volume. However, each chapter also discusses how the theories apply to other courts, such as the U.S. courts of appeals, state supreme courts, and trial courts.

Part I of the textbook describes the leading theories of judicial behavior, beginning in chapter 2 with the **attitudinal model**, which is the dominant theory of judicial behavior and the starting premise for political scientists who study the courts. The attitudinal model holds that, when judges have discretion, they are guided primarily by their personal values and ideologies. As you will see, the model applies best to the U.S. Supreme Court, but there is also evidence that it explains the behavior of judges on other courts as well. We will examine the theoretical justifications for the attitudinal model, evaluate some of the evidence for it, and consider its key implications. The chapter also includes an overview of **social background theory**, which suggests that judicial behavior is shaped by a judge's personal traits and experiences.

Chapter 3 turns to the **legal model**, which holds that legal principles influence judicial behavior. Much contemporary research on the legal model acknowledges that judges' sincere policy preferences influence their decision making, but supporters of the legal model maintain that judges are also professionals who seek to advance legal goals and values. The challenge has been to identify how and when legal principles are most likely to affect judicial behavior. While all judges use legal language to justify their decisions, it is by no means clear that these justifications are what actually lead judges to behave as they do. Legal justifications might be rationalizations for choices that are based on ideology or other motives. You will learn about disagreements that scholars have had over how to measure the influence of legal principles on judicial behavior and you will evaluate some of the evidence that these scholars have collected.

The third major theory of judicial behavior, the **strategic model**, is the focus of chapter 4. This model suggests that judges do not make decisions in isolation but are influenced by the behavior of other actors on and off the court. For example, Supreme Court justices must work with other justices on the Court to assemble the five votes needed for a majority. The justices might also pay attention to other actors outside of the Court, such as members of Congress, if they are concerned about implementation or the possibility that the elected branches will take steps to curb judicial power. These strategic considerations and others will be explored.

Part II of the textbook situates judicial behavior and policymaking within a broader political context, exploring in greater depth how other actors, including the public, influence judicial behavior, and examining the impact of judicial policy choices on society. The focus of chapter 5 is on judicial selection and retention. The process of selecting judges is controversial because it affects who gets to be a judge and, by extension, what policy choices judges are likely to make. In this chapter, we look at the various methods of selection and retention used for federal and state courts and consider their implications for judicial behavior. You will learn that there are strengths and weaknesses to each of the systems, but all of them permit at least some amount of public influence over the judiciary. The research presented in this chapter has fueled a sometimes contentious debate over whether judicial elections should be so widely adopted.

Chapter 6 elaborates further on the relationship between courts and the public. Because most state judges are elected in some manner, they have incentives to be responsive to public opinion. Yet, even federal judges, who are not directly accountable to the public, are attentive to public preferences in some circumstances. The chapter examines the relationship between judging and variations in the public mood before considering how certain litigants, known as repeat players, have systematic advantages over others who participate in the legal system. This chapter will also include a discussion of the influence of interest groups and lawyers on judging.

Finally, chapter 7 concludes the textbook by exploring the impact of courts and considering whether judges are likely to change their behavior depending on how they expect interpreting and implementing groups to react to their decisions. As you will see, reform groups frequently turn to courts to achieve significant social reform, but the ability of judges to achieve this reform on their own is mixed. We will discuss efforts by the black civil rights movement and the women's rights movement to achieve social reform with the U.S. Supreme

Court, as well as more recent efforts by supporters of marriage equality in state courts. As you will see, the impact of judges is variable, and their capacity to influence policy is determined at least in part by how courts are structured and how resistant their decisions are to being overturned.

METHODOLOGICAL NOTE: STUDYING JUDICIAL POLITICS SCIENTIFICALLY

This textbook examines the judiciary through the lens of political science. Like other social sciences, political science is concerned with making empirical statements about human behavior, institutions, and processes. **Empirical statements** describe how the world *is*, while **normative statements** focus on how the world *should be*. For example, someone making a normative statement about the judiciary might say that the U.S. Supreme Court *should* overturn *Roe v. Wade* (1973), while someone making an empirical statement would investigate whether the justices *are likely to overturn it*. Political scientists are not primarily interested in making normative statements because these claims cannot be investigated with the tools of science. They depend on human values. Political scientists prefer to describe the world based on observable evidence. While empirical findings can and do influence normative debates about law and policy, the focus of social science is on description, not prescription.

As a discipline, **political science** is broadly interested in studying power, or in what Harold Lasswell described as "who gets what, when, how."[38] Many of the questions that political scientists study about the courts focus on dimensions of power: Why do some litigants win and others lose? Which judge writes the **majority opinion** and what shapes its content? Who gets to be a judge, and how are these judges retained? What resources do other actors have to curb judicial power? All these questions are variations on "who gets what, when, how."

Political scientists are guided by **theories**, which are collections of statements or principles that, in the social sciences, explain human behavior, institutions, and processes. In the judicial behavior literature, the three leading theories are the attitudinal model, the legal model, and the strategic model. As mentioned above, the attitudinal model maintains that judges are guided by their sincere policy preferences. The legal model holds that legal principles guide judicial behavior. The strategic model states that judges are constrained by other actors who prevent them from acting sincerely. We will examine these theories in depth in later chapters.

From a theory, political scientists develop **hypotheses**, which are testable implications of the theory that typically involve the relationship between at least two variables. A **dependent variable** (Y) is a phenomenon about the political world that a political scientist would like to explain, while an **independent variable** (X) is another phenomenon that a political scientist believes can explain the variation in the dependent variable:

$$X \quad \rightarrow \quad Y$$

(independent variable)   (dependent variable)

For example, a political scientist who is seeking to test the attitudinal model might propose that judicial ideology explains how judges vote on the merits:

$$X \quad \rightarrow \quad Y$$

(judicial ideology)   (votes on the merits)

Political scientists would then look for evidence to determine whether their hypotheses are supported or not. To collect this evidence, political scientists employ a wide range of methodologies. **Qualitative methods** draw upon interviews, archival research, and field work to explain political behavior and processes in detail, while **quantitative methods** use data to identify broad trends in behavior. Regardless of the method used, the logic of political analysis is the same. Researchers look at the available evidence to determine the extent to which their hypotheses are supported by the evidence, and the extent to which they are not supported.

There are a number of high-quality sources of data that judicial politics scholars use to conduct their research. Online search engines such as LexisNexis and Westlaw have made it considerably easier to examine large volumes of cases. Scholars also make use of databases assembled by other social scientists. Among the most prominent is the Supreme Court Database, originally developed by Harold Spaeth and available online at http://scdb.wustl.edu/. The website includes full versions of the database for professional researchers and analysis tools for nonexperts to mine data. Another excellent resource for nonexperts is the Stat Pack released every year by *SCOTUSblog*, with statistics from the Supreme Court's previous term (available at http://www.scotusblog.com/reference/stat-pack/).

It is not necessary to be well versed in political science methodologies to read this textbook, but it is helpful to understand how political scientists approach the subject of judicial politics. Above all, political scientists want to describe judicial behavior and processes as accurately as possible. They present as much evidence as they can so you can verify that the statements they make are correct. Throughout this textbook, you will encounter statistics, as well as excerpts from cases and judges' off-the-bench remarks, so that you can reach your own conclusions about judicial politics.

RESOURCES

Political scientists who conduct research on the courts draw upon a number of publicly available databases. Below is a selection of the resources they use.

- **The Supreme Court Database.** The Supreme Court Database, originally compiled by Harold Spaeth, is a comprehensive database of Supreme Court decisions from 1946. A newly released legacy database includes data from earlier terms as well. The website includes full versions of the database for professional researchers, as well as analysis tools for nonexperts to mine data. Available at http://scdb.wustl.edu/.
- **ScotusBlog Stat Pack.** Compiled each term by ScotusBlog.org, the Stat Pack is a user-friendly, easily interpretable collection of data about Supreme Court terms, dating back to 1995. Available at http://www.scotusblog.com/reference/stat-pack/.
- **Court of Appeals Database.** The Court of Appeals Database, originally compiled by Donald Songer but subsequently expanded by Ashlyn Kuersten and Susan Haire, provides comprehensive data on a sample of decisions from the U.S. courts of appeals, dating from 1925 to 2002. Available at http://artsandsciences.sc.edu/poli/juri/appct.htm.
- **State Supreme Court Data Project.** The State Supreme Court Data Project includes data on 21,000 state supreme court decisions from 1995 to 1998, covering four hundred judges and all fifty states. Available at http://www.ruf.rice.edu/~pbrace/statecourt/.

DISCUSSION QUESTIONS

1. Commentators were surprised when Chief Justice John Roberts upheld the Affordable Care Act, President Obama's signature legislative accomplishment. What do you think explains Chief Justice Roberts's decision? Do you agree with commentators who described the chief justice's behavior as strategic?
2. Do you think it is ever appropriate to characterize judicial behavior as *activist*? What types of decisions would you consider to be activist, and why?
3. Which approach to constitutional interpretation do you think is better, *originalism* or the *living constitution* approach? Why do you support one perspective more than the other?
4. Do you agree with Chief Justice John Marshall in *Marbury v. Madison* (1803) that it is the responsibility of judges to resolve legal conflicts even if it means striking down legislative acts? Is it better for judges to defer to legislators, as John Bannister Gibson proposes in *Eakin v. Raub* (1825)?

KEY TERMS

policy
judicial activism
originalism
living constitution
statutes
constitutions
regulations
precedents
judicial review
vertical judicial review
horizontal judicial review
departmental theory
attitudinal model

social background theory
legal model
strategic model
empirical statements
normative statements
political science
majority opinion
theories
hypotheses
dependent variable
independent variable
qualitative methods
quantitative methods

NOTES

1. Brian Stelter, "CNN and Fox Trip Up in Rush to Get the News on the Air," *New York Times* (June 29, 2012), A16.
2. U.S. Const., art. 1, § 8 ("The Congress shall have Power . . . To regulate Commerce . . . among the several States").

3. *National Federation of Independent Business v. Sebelius*, slip op. at 31 (2012).

4. Id., at 44.

5. Alexis de Tocqueville, *Democracy in America: A New Translation by George Lawrence*, J. P. Mayer, ed. (New York: Anchor Books, 1969), 270.

6. Linda Greenhouse, "A Justice in Chief," *Opinionator: Exclusive Online Commentary from the New York Times*, June 28, 2012, available at http://opinionator .blogs.nytimes.com/2012/06/28/a-justice-in-chief/.

7. Jeffrey Toobin, "To Your Health," *New Yorker*, July 9, 2012, available at http://www.newyorker.com/talk/comment/2012/07/09/120709taco_talk_toobin.

8. Compare the California Supreme Court's decision in Perez v. Sharp, 32 Cal.2d 711 (1948), with the U.S. Supreme Court's decision in Loving v. Virginia, 388 U.S. 1 (1967).

9. See the Opinions of the Justices to the Senate, 802 N.E.2d 565 (Mass. 2004), which clarified the mandate of Goodridge v. Dept. of Public Health, 798 N.E.2d 941 (Mass. 2003).

10. Carey Goldberg, "In a Startling Turnabout, Judge Sets Au Pair Free," *New York Times*, November 11, 1997.

11. Citizens United v. Federal Election Commission, 558 U.S. 310 (2010).

12. "Obama's State of the Union Transcript 2010: Full Text." January 27, 2010. Available from *Politico*, http://www.politico.com/story/2010/01/obamas -state-of-the-union-address-032111.

13. Franklin D. Roosevelt, "Defending the Plan to 'Pack' the Supreme Court," (March 9, 1937), in *FDR's Fireside Chats*, ed. Russell D. Buhite and David W. Levy (Norman: University of Oklahoma Press, 1992), 88.

14. E. W. Kenworthy, "Nixon, in Texas, Sharpens His Attack," *New York Times*, November 3, 1968, A1.

15. For Richard Nixon, see E. W. Kenworthy, "Nixon, in Texas, Sharpens His Attack," *New York Times*, November 3, 1968, A1; for Ronald Reagan, see Bernard Weinraub, "Reagan Says He'll Use Vacancies to Discourage Judicial Activism," *New York Times*, October 22, 1985, A1; for George H. W. Bush, see "The Presidential Debate; Transcript of the Second Debate between Bush and Dukakis," *New York Times*, October 14, 1988, A14; for George W. Bush, see Elisabeth Bumiller, "Bush Vows to Seek Conservative Judges," *New York Times*, March 29, 2002, A24; for John McCain, see Juliet Eilperin, "McCain Says He Would Put Conservatives on Supreme Court," *Washington Post*, May 7, 2008, A9; for Mitt Romney, see Mitt Romney, "Remarks at Values Voter Summit," *CQ Transcriptions*, October 8, 2011; for Donald Trump, see "Transcript of the Second Debate," *New York Times*, October 10, 2016, available at https://www.nytimes .com/2016/10/10/us/politics/transcript-second-debate.html?_r=0.

16. U.S. Const., amend. VIII ("Excessive bail shall not be required, nor excessive fines imposed, nor cruel and unusual punishments inflicted.").

17. U.S. Const., art. V ("The Congress, whenever two thirds of both Houses shall deem it necessary, shall propose Amendments to this Constitution, or, on the Application of the Legislatures of two thirds of the several States, shall call a Convention for proposing Amendments, which, in either Case, shall be valid to all Intents and Purposes, as Part of this Constitution, when ratified by the Legislatures

of three fourths of the several States or by Conventions in three fourths thereof, as the one or the other Mode of Ratification may be proposed by the Congress").

18. U.S. Const., art I, sec. 8.

19. U.S. Const., amend. I.

20. N.Y. Pen. Law § 165.25: Jostling.

21. Leah Robinson, "Opponents of Over-Policing Target 'Vague Laws,'" *CityLimits.Org*, available at http://www.citylimits.org/blog/blog/143/opponents -of-over-policing-target-vague-laws#.UYAK2KPD-_A.

22. David R. Mayhew, *Congress: The Electoral Connection* (New Haven, CT: Yale University Press, 1974), 134.

23. Id., 62.

24. Brown v. Entertainment Merchants Association, 131 S.Ct. 2729 (2011).

25. Id., at 2733.

26. Id., at 2749.

27. Id., at 2750.

28. U.S. Const., art IV.

29. Olmstead v. United States, 277 U.S. 438 (1928).

30. Katz v. United States, 389 U.S. 347, 351 (1967).

31. Id., at 366 (Black, J., dissenting).

32. Marbury v. Madison, 5 U.S. 137, 177 (1803).

33. U.S. Const., art. VI, cl. 2.

34. *Marbury*, at 178.

35. Thomas Jefferson, "Letter to Judge Spencer Roane" (September 6, 1819), in *The Portable Thomas Jefferson*, ed. Merrill D. Peterson (New York: Viking Press, 1975), 563.

36. Eakin v. Raub, 12 Sargent & Rawle 330 (PA. 1825) (Gibson, J., dissenting).

37. For an overview of the consistently high levels of public confidence in the Supreme Court, see Gregory A. Caldeira and James L. Gibson, "The Etiology of Public Support for the Supreme Court," *American Journal of Political Science* 635 (1992): 36.

38. Harold D. Lasswell, *Politics: Who Gets What, When, How* (New York: Whittlesey House, 1936).

CASE ANALYSIS

Marbury v. Madison, 5 U.S. 137 (1803)

*In Marbury v. Madison (1803), Chief Justice John Marshall held that courts possess the power of **judicial review**, the ability to evaluate the policies of other government institutions. What do you think? Do you agree with Marshall that judges must exercise the power of judicial review? Or is it more appropriate for judges to defer to the choices made by other branches?*

CHIEF JUSTICE MARSHALL delivered the opinion of the court:

The question whether an act repugnant to the Constitution can become the law of the land is a question deeply interesting to the United States, but, happily, not of an intricacy proportioned to its interest. It seems only necessary to recognise certain principles, supposed to have been long and well established, to decide it.

That the people have an original right to establish for their future government such principles as, in their opinion, shall most conduce to their own happiness is the basis on which the whole American fabric has been erected. The exercise of this original right is a very great exertion; nor can it nor ought it to be frequently repeated. The principles, therefore, so established are deemed fundamental. And as the authority from which they proceed, is supreme, and can seldom act, they are designed to be permanent.

This original and supreme will organizes the government and assigns to different departments their respective powers. It may either stop here or establish certain limits not to be transcended by those departments. . . .

Between these alternatives there is no middle ground. The Constitution is either a superior, paramount law, unchangeable by ordinary means, or it is on a level with ordinary legislative acts, and, like other acts, is alterable when the legislature shall please to alter it.

If the former part of the alternative be true, then a legislative act contrary to the Constitution is not law; if the latter part be true, then written Constitutions are absurd attempts on the part of the people to limit a power in its own nature illimitable.

Certainly all those who have framed written Constitutions contemplate them as forming the fundamental and paramount law of the nation, and consequently the theory of every such government must be that an act of the Legislature repugnant to the Constitution is void. . . .

If an act of the Legislature repugnant to the Constitution is void, does it, notwithstanding its invalidity, bind the Courts and oblige them to give it effect? Or, in other words, though it be not law, does it constitute a rule as operative as if it was a law? This would be to overthrow in fact what was established in theory, and would seem, at first view, an absurdity too gross to be insisted on. It shall, however, receive a more attentive consideration.

It is emphatically the province and duty of the Judicial Department to say what the law is. Those who apply the rule to particular cases must, of necessity, expound and interpret that rule. If two laws conflict with each other, the Courts must decide on the operation of each.

So, if a law be in opposition to the Constitution, if both the law and the Constitution apply to a particular case, so that the Court must either decide that case conformably to the law, disregarding the Constitution, or conformably to the Constitution, disregarding the law, the Court must determine which of these conflicting rules governs the case. This is of the very essence of judicial duty.

If, then, the Courts are to regard the Constitution, and the Constitution is superior to any ordinary act of the Legislature, the Constitution, and not such ordinary act, must govern the case to which they both apply.

Those, then, who controvert the principle that the Constitution is to be considered in court as a paramount law are reduced to the necessity of maintaining that courts must close their eyes on the Constitution, and see only the law.

This doctrine would subvert the very foundation of all written Constitutions. It would declare that an act which, according to the principles and theory of our government, is entirely void, is yet, in practice, completely obligatory. It would declare that, if the Legislature shall do what is expressly forbidden, such act, notwithstanding the express prohibition, is in reality effectual. It would be giving to the Legislature a practical and real omnipotence with the same breath which professes to restrict their powers within narrow limits. It is prescribing limits, and declaring that those limits may be passed at pleasure.

That it thus reduces to nothing what we have deemed the greatest improvement on political institutions—a written Constitution, would of itself be sufficient, in America where written Constitutions have been viewed with so much reverence, for rejecting the construction. But the peculiar expressions of the Constitution of the United States furnish additional arguments in favour of its rejection.

The judicial power of the United States is extended to all cases arising under the Constitution.

Could it be the intention of those who gave this power to say that, in using it, the Constitution should not be looked into? That a case arising under the Constitution should be decided without examining the instrument under which it arises?

This is too extravagant to be maintained.

In some cases then, the Constitution must be looked into by the judges. And if they can open it at all, what part of it are they forbidden to read, or to obey?

There are many other parts of the Constitution which serve to illustrate this subject.

It is declared that "no tax or duty shall be laid on articles exported from any state." Suppose a duty on the export of cotton, of tobacco, or of flour, and a suit instituted to recover it. Ought judgment to be rendered in such a case? ought the judges to close their eyes on the Constitution, and only see the law?

The Constitution declares that "no bill of attainder or *ex post facto* law shall be passed."

If, however, such a bill should be passed and a person should be prosecuted under it, must the Court condemn to death those victims whom the constitution endeavours to preserve?

"No person," says the Constitution, "shall be convicted of treason unless on the testimony of two witnesses to the same overt act, or on confession in open court."

Here the language of the Constitution is addressed especially to the Courts. It prescribes, directly for them, a rule of evidence not to be departed from. If the Legislature should change that rule, and declare one witness, or a confession out of court, sufficient for conviction, must the constitutional principle yield to the legislative act?

From these and many other selections which might be made, it is apparent, that the framers of the Constitution contemplated that instrument as a rule for the government of courts, as well as of the Legislature.

Why otherwise does it direct the judges to take an oath to support it? This oath certainly applies in an especial manner to their conduct in their official character. How immoral to impose it on them if they were to be used as the instruments, and the knowing instruments, for violating what they swear to support!

The oath of office, too, imposed by the Legislature, is completely demonstrative of the legislative opinion on this subject. It is in these words:

"I do solemnly swear that I will administer justice without respect to persons, and do equal right to the poor and to the rich; and that I will faithfully and impartially discharge all the duties incumbent on me as according to the best of my abilities and understanding, agreeably to the Constitution and laws of the United States."

Why does a judge swear to discharge his duties agreeably to the Constitution of the United States if that Constitution forms no rule for his government? If it is closed upon him and cannot be inspected by him?

If such be the real state of things, this is worse than solemn mockery. To prescribe or to take this oath becomes equally a crime.

It is also not entirely unworthy of observation that, in declaring what shall be the supreme law of the land, the Constitution itself is first mentioned, and not the laws of the United States generally, but those only which shall be made in pursuance of the Constitution, have that rank.

Thus, the particular phraseology of the Constitution of the United States confirms and strengthens the principle, supposed to be essential to all written Constitutions, that a law repugnant to the Constitution is void, and that courts, as well as other departments, are bound by that instrument.

CASE ANALYSIS

Eakin v. Raub, 12 Serg. & Rawle 330
(Supreme Court of Pennsylvania, 1825)

In Eakin v. Raub *(1825), Justice John Bannister Gibson of the Pennsylvania Supreme Court directly challenged Chief Justice John Marshall's arguments in favor of judicial review. According to Justice Gibson, what should judges do when they are confronted with potentially unconstitutional laws? Do you find his alternative persuasive? Why or why not?*

JUSTICE GIBSON, dissenting:

I am aware, that a right to declare all unconstitutional acts void . . . is generally held as a professional dogma; but, I apprehend rather as a matter of faith than of reason. I admit that I once embraced the same doctrine, but without examination, and I shall therefore state the arguments that impelled me to abandon it, with great respect for those by whom it is still maintained. But I may premise, that it is not a little remarkable, that although the right in question has all along been claimed by the judiciary, no judge has ventured to discuss it, except Chief Justice Marshall, and if the argument of a jurist so distinguished for the strength of his ratiocinative powers to be found inconclusive, it may fairly be set down to the weakness of the position which he attempts to defend. . . .

The constitution and the right of the legislature to pass the act, may be in collision. But is that a legitimate subject for judicial determination? If it be, the judiciary must be a peculiar organ, to revise the proceedings of the legislature, and to correct its mistakes; and in what part of the constitution are we to look for this proud pre-eminence? Viewing the matter in the opposite direction, what would be thought of an act of assembly in which it should be declared that the Supreme Court had, in a particular case, put a wrong construction on the constitution of the United States, and that the judgment should therefore be reversed? It would doubtless be thought a usurpation of judicial power. But it is by no means clear, that to declare a law void which has been enacted according to the forms prescribed in the constitution, is not a usurpation of legislative power. . . .

But it has been said to be emphatically the business of the judiciary, to ascertain and pronounce what the law is; and that this necessarily involves a consideration of the constitution. It does so: but how far? If the judiciary will inquire into any thing beside the form of enactment, where shall it stop? There must be some point of limitation to such an inquiry; for no one will pretend, that a judge would be justifiable in calling for the election returns, or scrutinizing the qualifications of those who composed the legislature. . . .

But the judges are sworn to support the constitution, and are they not bound by it as the law of the land? In some respects they are. In the very few cases in which the judiciary, and not the legislature, is the immediate organ to execute its provisions, they are bound by it in preference to any act of assembly to the contrary. In such cases, the constitution is a rule to the courts. But what I have in view in this inquiry, is the supposed right of the judiciary, to interfere, in cases where the constitution is to be carried into effect through the instrumentality of the legislature, and where that organ must necessarily first decide on the constitutionality of its own act. The oath to support the constitution is not peculiar to the judges, but is taken indiscriminately by every officer of the government, and is designed rather as a test of the political principles of the man, than to bind the officer in the discharge of his duty: otherwise it were difficult to determine what operation it is to have in the case of a recorder of deeds, for instance, who, in the execution of his office, has nothing to do with the constitution. But granting it to relate to the official conduct of the judge, as well as every other officer, and not to his political principles, still it must be understood in reference to supporting the constitution, only as far as that may be involved in his official duty; and, consequently, if his official duty does not comprehend an inquiry into the authority of the legislature, neither does his oath. . . .

But do not the judges do a positive act in violation of the constitution, when they give effect to an unconstitutional law? Not if the law has been passed according to the forms established in the constitution. The fallacy of the question is, in supposing that the judiciary adopts the acts of the legislature as its own; whereas the enactment of a law and the interpretation of it are not concurrent acts, and as the judiciary is not required to concur in the enactment, neither is it in the breach of the constitution which may be the consequence of the enactment. The fault is imputable to the legislature, and on it the responsibility exclusively rests. In this respect, the judges are in the predicament of jurors who are bound to serve in capital cases, although unable, under any circumstances, to reconcile it to their duty to deprive a human being of life. To one of these, who applied to be discharged from the panel, I once heard it remarked, by an eminent and humane judge, "You do not deprive a prisoner of life by finding him guilty of a capital crime: you but pronounce his case to be within the law, and it is therefore those who declare the law, and not you, who deprive him of life.". . .

But it has been said, that this construction would deprive the citizen of the advantages which are peculiar to a written constitution, by at once declaring the power of the legislature, in practice, to be illimitable. I ask, what are those advantages? The principles of a written constitution are more fixed and certain, and more apparent to the apprehension of the people, than principles which depend on tradition and the vague comprehension of the individuals who compose the nation, and who cannot all be expected to receive the same impressions or entertain the same notions on any given subject. But there is no magic or inherent power in parchment and ink, to command respect and protect principles from violation. . . .

For these reasons, I am of opinion that it rests with the people, in whom full and absolute sovereign power resides to correct abuses in legislation, by instructing their representatives to repeal the obnoxious act. What is wanting to plenary power in the government, is reserved by the people for their own immediate use; and to redress an infringement of their rights in this respect, would seem to be an accessory of the power thus reserved. It might, perhaps, have been better to vest the power in the judiciary; as it might be expected that its habits of deliberation, and the aid derived from the arguments of counsel, would more frequently lead to accurate conclusions. On the other hand, the judiciary is not infallible; and an error by it would admit of no remedy but a more distinct expression of the public will, through the extraordinary medium of a convention; whereas, an error by the legislature admits of a remedy by an exertion of the same will, in the ordinary exercise of the right of suffrage,—a mode better calculated to attain the end, without popular excitement. It may be said, the people would probably not notice an error of their representatives. But they would as probably do so, as notice an error of the judiciary; and, beside, it is a postulate in the theory of our government, and the very basis of the superstructure, that the people are wise, virtuous, and competent to manage their own affairs: and if they are not so, in fact, still every question of this sort must be determined according to the principles of the constitution, as it came from the hands of its framers, and the existence of a defect which was not foreseen, would not justify those who administer the government, in applying a corrective in practice, which can be provided only by a convention.

Part I
Theories of
Judicial Behavior

2

The Attitudinal Model

WHEN JUSTICE ANTONIN Scalia died unexpectedly in early 2016, many people expected that President Barack Obama would appoint his successor. Article II of the Constitution gives presidents the power to make appointments to the Supreme Court "by and with the Advice and Consent of the Senate," and there was almost a year left in the president's term. But within hours of Scalia's death, the Republicans who controlled the Senate made it clear that there would be no confirmation hearings until after the next presidential election in November. According to Senate Majority Leader Mitch McConnell (R-KY), the reason for the delay was to give the American people an opportunity to weigh in on such an important issue, but other Senators were more transparent about their political motivations. "President Obama and I strongly disagree about which direction to take our nation," said Senator Richard Shelby (R-AL), "and I believe that we should do everything in our power to block him from further damaging the future of America."[1]

The unspoken assumption was that whoever President Obama appointed to the Supreme Court would share his policy views and vote accordingly. Otherwise, the opposition to his nomination made little sense. Republican Senators expected President Obama to appoint a liberal justice who would move the law in a liberal direction, just as Democrats would have expected a Republican president to appoint justices who favored conservative outcomes. This perception of the Supreme Court, and of judging, is profoundly political because it views judicial decision making as driven by policy considerations instead of the rule of law. It is also controversial, because many people think that one's personal ideology should have no role in judging at all.

You may be surprised, then, to learn that many political scientists share this view of the Supreme Court. The attitudinal model, which posits that the sincere policy preferences of judges influence their behavior, is the dominant theory of judicial decision making. It is the starting premise for political scientists who study judicial behavior, particularly the behavior of Supreme Court justices. Time and again, research has found that the justices' sincere policy preferences are the single best predictors of their behavior, so that if you know a justice's ideology at the time of their appointment, you can accurately predict how they will vote in a large proportion of cases. It is understandable, then, that Senators let policy considerations influence their evaluation of Supreme Court appointments. The social science evidence backs them up. The Supreme Court is a political institution, and the attitudes of the justices can and do shape their behavior.

The fact that judges are political does not necessarily mean that they have prejudged cases or that they are biased against particular litigants. Judges would be expected to withdraw from cases if they harbored these prejudices. Instead, what the attitudinal model suggests is that when judges have discretion about how to resolve cases they do so consistently with their personal beliefs and values. Like all of us, judges have strong opinions about many issues based on their personalities, professional backgrounds, and other life experiences. These attitudes influence how judges see the world, how they interpret facts, and how they resolve the legal disputes before them. If the law is uncertain, or if judges can legitimately choose from among a number of legal options, then it is only natural that they would fall back on their policy preferences.

At the same time, judicial behavior is more complicated than any single theory can explain. The attitudinal model might be a strong predictor of judicial behavior, but it is not the only one. Far from it. Beyond the U.S. Supreme Court, the model explains the behavior of other judges less successfully. Lower-court judges, who are much more numerous, frequently have less discretion about how to resolve cases because they must follow the rules and precedents set by their superiors. These judges have fewer opportunities to act on their values. Even on the U.S. Supreme Court, the attitudinal model does not explain all types of judicial behavior equally well. The model is better at predicting how judges vote in cases than at how they write their opinions, select their dockets, or make opinion assignments.

This first part of the textbook examines the leading theories of judicial behavior, starting with the attitudinal model. The pages that follow explain how the attitudinal came to become the dominant theory of judicial behavior, assess the evidence for it, and discuss some of the major critiques of the theory. Then the next two chapters examine the major alternative theories, the legal model and the strategic model. All three theories are animated by the same basic research question: "What influences judicial behavior?" (See Methodological Note 2.1.) Are judges fundamentally political, as Senators and other politicians seem to assume? Or are judges motivated by legal principles? And how would we know which view of judging is correct?

OVERVIEW OF THE ATTITUDINAL MODEL

The attitudinal model is a theory of judging that holds that the sincere policy preferences of judges influence their behavior. (See Figure 2.1.) As a theory, it has a number of observable implications, or hypotheses, that can be subjected to rigorous quantitative and qualitative

METHODOLOGICAL NOTE 2.1	Formulating a Research Question

All of the theories of judicial behavior that we examine in Part I of the textbook seek to answer the same basic research question: "What influences judicial behavior?"

Formally, the question can be expressed this way:

$$? \quad \rightarrow \quad \text{judicial behavior}$$
$$\text{(or)}$$
$$? \quad \rightarrow \quad (Y)$$

The letter Y represents the dependent variable, "judicial behavior," which is the political phenomenon that we are trying to explain with our theories. Yet, as written, the research question needs refinement because the phrase "judicial behavior" is expansive, encompassing many different types of courts and forms of behavior. Our assessment of the theories may depend on what we mean by this phrase, so it is important to define it carefully.

As you study judicial behavior, think about alternative ways of defining "judicial behavior" and how these choices might matter. Are we most concerned about the U.S. Supreme Court, trial courts, or some other tribunal? Which behaviors are we trying to explain? Is it how judges vote on the merits of cases? Is it how they write opinions? Or is it some other form of behavior?

Figure 2.1   The Attitudinal Model

---

sincere policy preferences   →   judicial behavior

(X)   (Y)

analysis. Some of these hypotheses are explained in Methodological Note 2.2. Most social scientists who study the Supreme Court are primarily concerned with just one form of judicial behavior: the final vote on the merits (H_1). This vote is the most consequential because it determines who wins and who loses, and by how much. Will the justices side with the **petitioner,** who brought the case to the justices? Or will they vote for the **respondent?** Will the justices decide the case unanimously, by a 9–0 vote, or will they divide 5–4? The attitudinal model holds that the justices' sincere policy preferences determine these choices. If you know whether justices are liberal or conservative at the time of their appointment, then you will be able to predict their voting behavior.

The final vote on the merits is just one stage in the Supreme Court's process of decision making. The attitudinal model predicts that the justices' sincere policy preferences influence their behavior at other stages of the process as well. For example, before casting their final votes, the justices circulate opinion drafts among themselves (H_2), providing them with opportunities to decide on what the rules, or rationales, will be that justify the outcomes. These rationales are very important because they establish legal precedents that will guide lower courts, as well as litigants, in future cases. Do the justices choose to write precedents broadly, with implications for many subsequent cases, or do they write narrower precedents with less reach? The attitudinal model would hold that the justices' policy preferences determine these choices.

Going back a step further is the decision about who gets to write the majority opinion (H_3). The practice on the U.S. Supreme Court is for the Chief Justice to make the opinion assignment if he or she is in the majority. Otherwise, the assignment is made by the justice in the majority coalition who has the most seniority. The justices decide for themselves whether to write separate concurrences or dissents, but sometimes one justice speaks for the minority as well. What factors guide these choices? Here, too, the attitudinal model would theorize that the policy preferences of the justices are determinative. Justices assign cases to the justices who are the closest to them ideologically.

METHODOLOGICAL NOTE 2.2 | Deriving Hypotheses

A theory is a broad statement about the world that has many observable implications. To test a theory, it is necessary to **operationalize** it, deriving hypotheses that social scientists can evaluate systematically by observing human behavior. For example, social scientists testing the attitudinal model must decide which forms of "judicial behavior" to study.

Listed below are several hypotheses derived from the attitudinal model. They all follow the same basic format: variation in the independent variable (X) explains variation in the dependent variable (Y). But the dependent variable has been operationalized in several different ways. What do you think? What other forms of judicial behavior should social scientists be studying?

Theory (T): The Attitudinal Model

T: sincere policy preferences   →   judicial behavior
        (X)   (Y)

Hypotheses (H):

H_1:   sincere policy preferences   →   final vote on the merits
              (X_1) (Y_1)

H_2:   sincere policy preferences   →   opinion drafting
              (X_1) (Y_2)

H_3:   sincere policy preferences   →   opinion assignment
              (X_1) (Y_3)

H_4:   sincere policy preferences   →   initial conference vote
              (X_1) (Y_4)

H_5:   sincere policy preferences   →   case selection
              (X_1) (Y_5)

There are even earlier stages in the process. Shortly after the oral arguments, the justices meet privately behind closed doors to cast tentative votes on the merits to structure the opinion writing process that follows (H_4). Sometimes justices change their minds between the initial conference vote and the final vote on the merits. Prior to that point, the justices make choices about which cases to review in the first place (H_5). Petitioners ask the justices for a **writ of certiorari**, an order empowering the justices to review the proceedings of the lower court. The justices have almost complete discretion to choose which petitions to grant out of the thousands of cases that they could decide in a particular term. By convention, it takes four votes to grant a petition. But how do the justices decide which cases to review? The attitudinal model maintains that Supreme Court justices select cases that best advance their policy goals.

There are many venues in which attitudes can influence judging. The examples above are just a few examples. The attitudinal model predicts that whenever judges, at any level, have discretion, they act on the basis of their policy preferences. Yet, just because a theory seems plausible does not mean that it is correct—it also needs to be backed by strong logic and observable evidence. As it turns out, the attitudinal model meets both of these criteria well, which explains why it has so much support among political scientists. However, the theory does not meet these criteria perfectly, or apply in all contexts. As you read about the theoretical justifications for the attitudinal model, and the evidence for it, think critically about them. Is it reasonable to think that judges will act on their policy preferences whenever they can? Does the evidence really show that they do? Use your own judgment and conduct your own analysis.

Origins of the Attitudinal Model

The attitudinal model developed primarily in response to a now-outdated view of judging called **legal formalism**. This perspective, which was dominant in the nineteenth century, viewed the act of judging as a mechanical process. It assumed that there were "right" and "wrong" answers to legal questions, and that the role of the judge was not to make law, but to find it, discovering the objective principles that would enable judges to resolve legal disputes. As one noted federal judge and legal scholar Richard A. Posner has characterized it, "Formalism enables a commentator to pronounce the outcome of the case as being correct or incorrect, in approximately the same way that a solution to a mathematical problem can be pronounced correct or incorrect."[2]

A famous exponent of legal formalism was Christopher Columbus Langdell, the dean of the faculty of Harvard University from 1870 to 1895, and considered by many to be the father of the modern American law school. Langdell developed the **case method** of legal instruction, still in use today, whereby students would use inductive reasoning to discover the logical principles that were said to determine case outcomes. "Law, considered as a science, consists of certain principles or doctrines," Langdell wrote. "To have such a mastery of these as to be able to apply them with constant facility and certainty to the ever-tangled skein of human affairs, is what constitutes a true lawyer; and hence to acquire that mastery should be the business of every earnest student of law."[3]

To find answers to legal questions, legal formalists consulted sources of **positive law**, or man-made rules, such as statutes, legal precedents, and constitutional texts. They also drew upon **natural law** principles that were supposedly inherent in nature, or reason, or the divine. For example, in *Fletcher v. Peck* (1810), Chief Justice John Marshall ruled that a Georgia law revoking a land contract was unconstitutional because it violated "general principles which are common to our free institutions." Writing separately, Justice William Johnson went even further, announcing that his decision was based on "a principle which will impose laws even on the deity." Today, reliance on natural law is considered particularly controversial because it is hard to know how a judge could engage in such an inquiry objectively. Surely, critics maintain, a judge's own values shape their perspectives on what is "natural" or what is "just."

The shortcomings of legal formalism as a theory of judging have been known for some time, but the attitudinal model in its contemporary form is of relatively recent origin. The starting point for most contemporary political scientists is the work of Jeffrey A. Segal and Harold J. Spaeth, whose pathbreaking book *The Supreme Court and the Attitudinal Model* (1993), redefined the field of judicial politics. Segal and Spaeth's work combined two intellectual trends from earlier in the twentieth century, legal realism and behavioralism, into a single unified theory of judging, which they termed the attitudinal model. Segal and Spaeth then subjected their theory to rigorous quantitative analysis using the Supreme Court Database, an original database that has since become the central resource for scholars conducting work in the field of judicial politics.

Both of the intellectual precursors to the attitudinal model are important to understanding the theory. The **legal realism** movement emerged at the turn of the twentieth century from within the legal profession itself, with its leading proponents judges such as Oliver Wendell Holmes and law professors such as Karl Llewellyn and Jerome Frank. In "The Path of the Law" (1897) (excerpted at the end of the chapter), Holmes challenged the central tenets of legal formalism, denying that law was grounded in logic or morality, or that one could find the correct answers to legal problems through careful study.[4] "When we study law," Holmes wrote, "we are not studying a mystery but a well-known profession." For the legal realists, the law was not a "mystery" to be solved but a profession in which judges crafted law themselves. Legal realists believed that legal formalism did not fully recognize the role of judges in making law, or how a judge's values shaped their interpretations of legal authorities. "Behind the logical form," Holmes wrote, "lies a judgment as to the relative worth and importance of competing legislative grounds, often an inarticulate and unconscious judgment, it is true, and yet the very root and nerve of the whole proceeding. You can give any conclusion a logical form. You always can imply a condition in a contract."

Legal realists did not necessarily assume that judges were being *deliberately* attitudinal. As Holmes stated above, a judge could be guided by an "inarticulate" or "unconscious" judgment. Contemporary research on **motivated reasoning** confirms the role of unconscious motivations in decision making, finding that personal values shape one's interpretation of facts and evaluation of competing claims. Psychologists have identified a **confirmation bias** in the selection and use of evidence, whereby "people tend to overweight positive confirmatory evidence or underweight negative disconfirmatory evidence."[5] Or, as another psychologist put it, "People are more likely to arrive at those conclusions that they want to arrive at."[6] Judges therefore may not be fully aware of the extent to which their own values shape their behavior.

Regardless of whether judges are driven by conscious or unconscious motivations, legal realists like Holmes believed that at the root of judicial decision making is a value choice. "It is because of some belief as to the practice of the community," he wrote, "or of a class, or because of some opinion as to policy, or, in short, because of some attitude of yours upon a matter not capable of exact quantitative measurement, and therefore not capable of founding exact logical conclusions." According to Holmes, the reason to study law was not to discover legal truths but to make predictions about how judges might decide future cases by observing what other judges have done in the past. "The object of our study, then, is prediction," Holmes wrote, "the prediction of the incidence of the public force through the instrumentality of the courts."

In this respect, the writings of Holmes and the other legal realists anticipated the **behavioralism** movement that would develop in the field of political science in the middle of the twentieth century. Behavioralists, then and now, maintain that our ability to understand and predict political events can be improved through systematic

observation and analysis of human behavior. Behavioralists have intro-
duced sophisticated quantitative sampling and analysis techniques to
the profession, bringing a methodological perspective that is animated
by the spirit of scientific investigation rather than moral inquiry. The
goal of the behavioralist is to describe human behavior as it truly is
instead of how the observer might want it to be.

The attitudinal model represents a fusion of these two perspectives, drawing upon the theoretical insights of legal realism but investigating these insights systematically using contemporary behavioralist
techniques. The theory also reflects a century of knowledge from
related fields such as psychology and economics. Like the legal realists, the attitudinal model assumes that judges have discretion about
how to decide cases and that judges make choices that are consistent
with their own values. Like the behavioralists, the attitudinal model
makes falsifiable empirical claims that can be subjected to rigorous
scientific investigation.

Theoretical Justifications for the Attitudinal Model

The legal realism movement laid much of the theoretical groundwork
for the attitudinal model, establishing the indeterminacy of law and
the potential for a judge's attitudes to influence decision making.
Legal realists such as Oliver Wendell Holmes assumed that their theory applied to all courts because every judge must contend with legal
uncertainty to some degree. Yet, it is also true that some judges have
more discretion about how to decide cases than others. When Segal
and Spaeth first developed the attitudinal model, they had one specific court in mind: the U.S. Supreme Court. For a number of reasons,
discussed below, Supreme Court justices are much freer than other
judges to act on the basis of their sincere policy preferences.[7]

To begin with, Supreme Court justices have almost complete
control over their **docket**, which leaves them free to select cases that
permit attitudinal voting. During the twentieth century, Congress
reduced the number of **mandatory appeals** that the justices had to
decide, beginning with the Judges' Bill of 1925 and culminating in the
passage of the Case Selections Act of 1988. (See Judicial Process Box
2.1.) Today, virtually all of the Court's docket is discretionary. Cases
come to the Supreme Court in the form of **certiorari petitions**, which
the justices may grant or deny as they choose. With so much control
over case selection, the justices avoid granting certiorari when the law
is settled or when the sources of law are clear. These more routine disputes are left for lower courts to decide. The justices believe that their

JUDICIAL PROCESS BOX 2.1 | The Supreme Court's Docket

When a person has a legal problem, they often say that they will take the issue all the way up to the Supreme Court. But the truth is that the Supreme Court decides very few cases each year, and the justices choose for themselves which cases to decide.

A court's docket is the calendar of cases that they decide in a year. The Supreme Court's docket is composed of mandatory appeals, which they must decide, and certiorari petitions, which are discretionary. Congress determines, through ordinary legislation, how much of the Court's docket is discretionary.

Over time, Congress has given the Supreme Court almost complete control over its docket, culminating in the passage of the Case Selections Act of 1988, which eliminated mandatory appeals in all but a few highly specialized areas, such as voting rights cases. In consequence, the Supreme Court hears about half the number of cases that it did a few decades ago.

The justices say that they do not need to decide so many cases because litigants have already had one appeal in the courts below. The justices think that their judgment is needed primarily in important cases, or when the law is unsettled. What do you think? Should the justices decide more cases each year? Should they get to choose for themselves which cases to review?

Figure 2.2 The Supreme Court's Docket

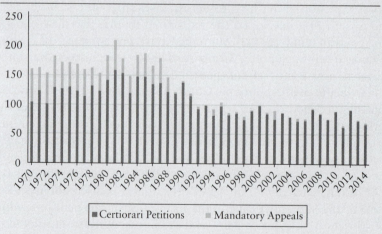

Source: Data are from the *Journal of the Supreme Court of the United States.*

intervention is most needed when lower courts disagree about how to answer legal questions. Such occasions are prime conditions for attitudinal voting because the justices can legitimately choose from among a number of legal policy alternatives. Increased docket control therefore increases attitudinal voting by reducing the need for the justices to decide routine disputes when the law is settled. The justices instead take the harder cases, in which they have more flexibility about what to do.

A second feature that distinguishes Supreme Court justices from other judges is their lack of accountability to other courts. No higher court reviews Supreme Court decisions to correct their interpretations of federal law, which means that if the justices decide to resolve legal controversies solely on the basis of their policy preferences, no other tribunal will tell them to do otherwise. The Supreme Court's judgments are final and authoritative. The justices can reverse their own precedents, invalidate state and federal laws, or base decisions on novel theories of law, with no threat of correction by a higher court. Without the constraints of direct supervision, Supreme Court justices are freer to make choices that reflect their own personal beliefs and values.

Supreme Court justices also have relatively low levels of accountability to the other branches of government and to the public. The Constitution guarantees life tenure to federal judges as long as they maintain "good behaviour," which means that Supreme Court justices do not require the support of the public, or politicians, to keep their jobs. The justices will not be removed from office for voting their policy preferences, although in extraordinary circumstances they could be impeached. This is not to say that Congress and the president lack any resources to curb judicial power. As we will discuss in chapter 4, the independence of Supreme Court justices is not absolute. Yet, compared to other judges, Supreme Court justices are relatively free from political and electoral accountability for their actions. Most state judges have less independence because they do not have life tenure and must win reelection or face reappointing authorities to retain office.

Finally, Supreme Court justices generally have no further career ambitions, so there is no need to mask their policy preferences to be competitive for other jobs. The justices are already at the top of the legal profession. Only a few times in the twentieth century have justices resigned to pursue other opportunities. In 1916, Charles Evans Hughes left the Court to run for president, and in 1965 Arthur Goldberg became the U.S. ambassador to the United Nations.[8] However, in the twenty-first century there have been no examples of justices leaving the Court to pursue other offices. It is possible that some associate justices have ambitions to become chief justice, yet the opportunities for promotion are infrequent, and it is unclear that ideological voting would be disqualifying. Justice Rehnquist's conservative voting record as an associate justice did not prevent his confirmation as chief justice in 1986.

For all of these reasons, U.S. Supreme Court justices are in a unique position to act on their sincere policy preferences. The freedom to select the cases on their docket, the relative absence of supervision and electoral accountability, and the lack of further career ambitions give justices exceptional freedom to make choices that reflect their values. In other courts, where the same conditions do not obtain, the model applies less well. For example, lower federal court judges have less control over their dockets and hear many cases in which the law is settled. If these judges simply ignored higher court precedents that they disliked, they would probably get reversed. In states that elect judges, ideological voting might cost a judge an election, particularly when voters have different views about legal issues.

All theories of judging are based on certain assumptions that may not be appropriate in each context. Before examining the evidence for the attitudinal model, or any theory, it is important to evaluate these assumptions and determine what our theoretical expectations should be in each case. When do we think attitudinal voting is more likely to occur? Do we expect judges to make choices based on their policy preferences in every circumstance, or just sometimes? Do we expect attitudes to be equally influential in all courts? Our answers to these questions will influence the type of evidence we look for, and how we analyze it.

Evidence for the Attitudinal Model

Political scientists have found evidence for the attitudinal model at all levels of the federal and state judiciaries, but to do so they have had to overcome the same fundamental challenge: How do you measure a judge's policy preferences? It is not as easy as you might think. We can readily observe when a judge chooses a liberal or conservative outcome, but how do we know if their policy preferences are causing this behavior? The decision could reflect a judge's principled view of the law, or political or electoral pressures. Even a consistent pattern of voting is not necessarily evidence of attitudinal motivations. To be persuaded that policy preferences influence judging, we need measures of judicial attitudes that are independent of judges' votes.

Unfortunately, we cannot look into a judge's head to see what their values are, and we cannot just ask them. People are not always fully aware of what influences their behavior, even when they are willing to talk about it. For research on the U.S. Supreme Court, the breakthrough came in 1989 with the development of the **Segal-Cover scores**, named for the researchers who created them, Jeffrey Segal and Albert Cover.[9] Segal and Cover's insight was that there was one source of information that was available about every Supreme Court justice that was independent of their voting behavior: newspaper coverage. Every time a justice is appointed, editorial writers comment on the nomination, drawing upon all available sources of information to determine a justice's policy views. Segal and Cover realized that if you classified the contents of these editorials, then you could create a snapshot of a justice's ideology at the time of nomination.

Segal and Cover created their scores by collecting editorials that were written about every Supreme Court justice between the time of their nomination by the president and their confirmation by the Senate. They selected two newspapers with conservative editorial pages (*Chicago Tribune*, *Los Angeles Times*), and two with liberal pages (*New York Times*, *Washington Post*), examining each paragraph to see whether the author made statements predicting that the judge would be liberal, moderate, or conservative. The information was then used to develop composite ideology scores. (See Table 2.1.) The Segal-Cover scores range from values of 0 to 1, with a score of 0 indicating a strongly conservative justice (e.g., Scalia) and a score of 1 indicating a strongly liberal justice (e.g., Marshall, Brennan). Most of the justices fall somewhere in between.

For other courts, the technique developed by Segal and Cover is unavailable because there is no consistent newspaper coverage at the time of a judge's selection. Editorials might appear in exceptional cases, but not frequently enough to serve as the foundation of a measurement. Instead, for lower federal courts, the leading measures are the **GHP scores**, named for the scholars who developed them, Michael Giles, Virginia Hettinger, and Todd Peppers.[10] These scholars reasoned that, because the president appoints federal judges, then a good proxy for a judge's ideology is the ideology of the appointing president. The exception occurs when a vacancy opens up in a state where one or both of the senators are from the president's party. In these cases, the president consults with home state senators before selecting nominees because, under norms of **senatorial courtesy**, the Senate will not approve a nomination when these Senators object

METHODOLOGICAL NOTE 2.3 | Measurement

After specifying a hypothesis, it is necessary to measure the independent (X) and dependent (Y) variables before we can analyze the relationship between them. Consider, for example, the challenges posed with measuring the variables in the following hypothesis:

H_1: sincere policy preferences → final vote on the merits
(X_1) (Y_1)

The hypothesis is not in a form that we can measure easily. What do we mean by "sincere policy preferences"? What, precisely, do we want to know about the "final vote on the merits"? Before we can measure these concepts, we need to operationalize them further:

H_1:   judicial ideology   →   ideological direction of
at time of appointment   votes after appointment
(X_1) (Y_1)

Now the hypothesis has much better specificity, but we still need to make choices about how to measure the independent and dependent variables. In their classic study, *The Supreme Court and the Attitudinal Model* (1993), Jeffrey Segal and Harold Spaeth measured the justices' sincere policy preferences by looking at the judgments of newspaper editorial writers in the period between a candidate's nomination and confirmation. The more statements there were that predicted liberal voting behavior, the more liberal Segal and Spaeth expected the justices to be.

Segal and Spaeth measured the dependent variable by classifying the justices' votes after they arrived on the bench, looking primarily at civil liberties cases. A liberal vote was a case outcome that favored criminal defendants, the poor, civil rights groups, Native Americans, and antigovernment groups in cases involving due process and privacy issues. Conservative votes took the opposite point of view.

What do you think? Are these good measurements? Social scientists say that the best measures meet the standards of **validity** and **reliability**. A valid measurement accurately represents the concept we are studying, whereas a reliable measurement produces consistent results each time we use it. So if we are interested in knowing the influence of "judicial ideology at time of appointment," then a

METHODOLOGICAL NOTE 2.3 | **Continued**

valid measurement will actually measure ideology and not something else. A reliable measure will produce the same ideology score when different coders employ it.

Do these measurements meet the standards? Or would you select different measures? When studying judicial behavior, it is important to recognize that you always need to make choices about how to measure the concepts that interest you. The decisions you make can affect your ability to analyze your hypotheses and evaluate the underlying theories.

to the appointment. A federal judge's ideology is therefore a better reflection of the ideologies of the home state senators from the president's party when senatorial courtesy is invoked.

For state judges, ideology scores take into account the fact that judges in most states are elected. The standard measures for state supreme court justices are the **party-adjusted ideology (PAJID) scores,** which factor in a judge's party affiliation as well as the preferences of the appointers.[11] For judges who are appointed by governors or legislators, elite ideology is included in the score; for elected judges, the ideology of citizens is used. Alternative measures are the **campaign finance (CF) scores,** which reflect the ideologies of the contributors to judicial election campaigns.[12] For appointed judges, the scores are based on the candidates to whom the judges themselves have contributed or the campaign activity of their appointing presidents or legislators. Much like the Segal-Cover scores, these measures of ideology are independent of judges' votes, which facilitates a comparison with their behavior on the bench.

How well does ideology predict judicial behavior? You can analyze some of the data yourself using Table 2.1, which replicates and updates Segal and Spaeth's analysis of the values and votes of Supreme Court justices.[13] The independent variable (X_1) is the justices' ideologies at the time of their appointment to the Supreme Court, as measured by their Segal-Cover scores. Remember that higher scores are associated with more liberal justices.[14] The dependent variables measure the percentage of the time that justices actually voted in a liberal direction in civil liberties cases (Y_1) and economics cases (Y_2). Liberal civil rights cases include cases favoring criminal defendants, the poor,

Table 2.1   **Predicted Ideologies and Votes of Supreme Court Justices, 1946–2014**

Justice	Appointing President	Segal-Cover Score (Ideology)	% Liberal in Civil Liberties	% Liberal in Economics
Black	Roosevelt (D)	0.875	73.60	81.30
Reed	Roosevelt (D)	0.725	34.70	55.80
Frankfurter	Roosevelt (D)	0.665	53.90	40.20
Douglas	Roosevelt (D)	0.73	88.30	77.70
Murphy	Roosevelt (D)	1	77.80	81.60
Jackson	Roosevelt (D)	1	40.30	38.10
Rutledge	Roosevelt (D)	1	74.80	81.40
Burton	Truman (D)	0.28	38.20	50.70
Vinson	Truman (D)	0.75	36.00	54.00
Clark	Truman (D)	0.5	43.90	69.80
Minton	Truman (D)	0.72	35.70	60.10
Warren	Eisenhower (R)	0.75	78.90	77.90
Harlan	Eisenhower (R)	0.875	43.30	41.70
Brennan	Eisenhower (R)	1	79.40	69.70
Whittaker	Eisenhower (R)	0.5	43.80	35.50
Stewart	Eisenhower (R)	0.75	51.10	48.70
White	Kennedy (D)	0.5	42.80	58.60
Goldberg	Kennedy (D)	0.75	88.70	65.70
Fortas	Johnson (D)	1	80.90	68.70
Marshall	Johnson (D)	1	81.40	65.00
Burger	Nixon (R)	0.115	29.40	44.20
Blackmun	Nixon (R)	0.115	52.20	57.40
Powell	Nixon (R)	0.165	37.20	46.10
Rehnquist	Nixon (R)	0.045	22.20	44.60
Stevens	Ford (R)	0.25	65.40	58.60
O'Connor	Reagan (R)	0.415	36.20	44.60
Scalia	Reagan (R)	0	29.50	44.30
Kennedy	Reagan (R)	0.365	38.10	44.60
Souter	Bush I (R)	0.325	63.00	54.80
Thomas	Bush I (R)	0.16	24.30	44.60
Ginsburg	Clinton (D)	0.68	65.70	59.80
Breyer	Clinton (D)	0.475	60.30	54.20
Roberts	Bush II (R)	0.12	35.40	45.40
Alito	Bush II (R)	0.1	26.70	43.00
Sotomayor	Obama (D)	0.78	67.10	56.10
Kagan	Obama (D)	0.73	65.70	57.10

civil rights groups, and antigovernment groups in cases involving due process and privacy issues. Liberal economics cases are generally pro-union and pro-consumer. If the attitudinal model is well-supported, then you should expect to see higher proportions of liberal voting from justices with Segal-Cover scores at or near 1. Justices with Segal-Cover scores closer to 0 should have lower percentages of liberal voting. Is that what you actually observe?

Here is another way of looking at the same data. Figure 2.3 graphs the relationship between the Segal-Cover scores (X_1) and the votes of judges in civil liberties cases (Y_1).[15] The gray guideline represents how frequently judges are *expected* to vote in a liberal direction, and the dots represent their *actual* liberal voting percentages. When a justice's dot is above the line, it means that they ended up being *more liberal* than expected; when dots are below the line, the justices were *less liberal* than expected. For example, Justice Stevens's dot is relatively far above the line. His Segal-Cover score is 0.250, which means that he was expected to be a moderately conservative justice, but his actual voting record in civil liberties cases was much higher, at 65.4 percent liberal. In contrast, Justice Kennedy's dot is almost exactly on the line, so his moderately conservative voting record, of 38.1 percent liberal, is very consistent with what his Segal-Cover score of 0.365 would predict.

What do you think? To what extent are the data consistent with the hypothesis that a justice's sincere policy preferences influence judging? To what extent are the data inconsistent with the hypothesis? Take some time to analyze the data and see what conclusions of your own you can draw, recognizing that no one variable is likely to explain everything. Segal and Spaeth described attitudes as the single best predictor of judicial behavior because no other variable has comparable explanatory power. But the model is not a perfect fit. Although liberal judges do tend to vote in a liberal direction much of the time, and conservatives tend to vote in a conservative direction, there are many deviations from the line. What do you think might account for this variation? Were our predictions about how the justices would vote inaccurate? Or could it be that, for some justices, other factors besides ideology affect their behavior?

Limitations of the Attitudinal Model

The primary strength of the attitudinal model is its predictive power. No other single factor does as good of a job at predicting the voting behavior of Supreme Court justices. However, there are limitations

Figure 2.3 Predicted Ideologies and Votes in Civil Liberties Cases, 1946–2014

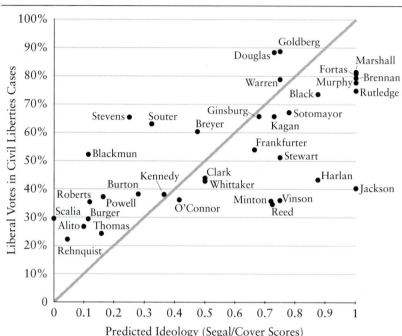

to the model as well. To begin with, it is less successful at explaining other forms of judicial behavior besides the justices' votes, such as the selection of their docket, opinion assignment, and opinion drafting. Attitudes still play a key role in these behaviors but account for less of the variation, as the next few chapters will discuss. Even when it comes to the final votes on the merits, there is a weaker correlation between the justices' attitudes and their decisions in issue areas beyond civil liberties cases. For example, Figure 2.4 graphs the relationship between the justices' Segal-Cover scores and their votes in economics cases, and as you can see there is much more deviation from the line. (See Figure 2.4.) Justices such as Roberts, Rehnquist, Alito, and Thomas are much more liberal than predicted in economics cases, while justices such as Brennan, Marshall, Fortas, and Jackson are more conservative than expected.

The observed trends in Figure 2.4 might partly be attributable to how we have measured judicial policy preferences. The Segal-Cover scores best describe the attitudes of the justices in civil liberties cases

Figure 2.4 Predicted Ideologies and Votes in Economics Cases, 1946–2014

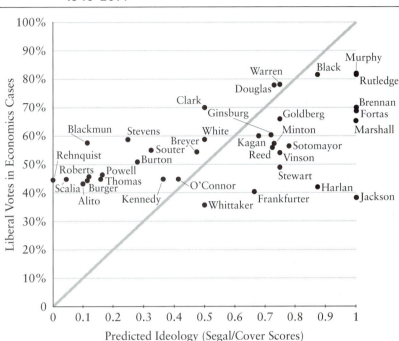

because newspaper editorial writers are most likely to have these particular issue areas in mind when they are making predictions about a nominee's ideology.[16] Researchers might make better predictions with different measures. Yet, there are also theoretical reasons for thinking that judicial policy preferences will have less influence in other areas. Civil liberties cases frequently involve highly visible **morality policies** such as abortion, affirmative action, and religious freedom. Like the rest of us, Supreme Court justices are likely to have strong opinions about these issues. The weakness of the attitudinal model outside of civil liberties cases might be attributable to the fact that other issue areas are less likely to encourage preferential voting.

Another limitation of the attitudinal model is that it does not adequately account for drift in the voting preferences of Supreme Court justices over time. Segal and Spaeth's original test of the theory assumed that a justice's votes would be stable, reflecting what their attitudes were when they first arrived on the bench. However, the reality is that the voting behavior of the justices can change over time, sometimes dramatically. Figure 2.5 illustrates this behavior for recent justices using the **Martin-Quinn scores**, which are dynamic yearly estimates of a justice's policy preferences, based on their voting behavior.[17] The data reveal dramatic shifts in judicial choice. For example, Justices John Paul Stevens and Harry Blackmun both became more liberal during their years of service on the Court. Justice Blackmun acknowledged as much, stating in a death penalty case toward the end of his career that his views on the subject had changed: "From this day forward, I no longer shall tinker with the machinery of death."[18] Other justices have exhibited similar tendencies, with the general trend being that justices have become increasingly liberal over time. Because Segal-Cover scores are measured before justices arrive on the bench, it is unclear whether the observed drift in their voting behavior is attributable to ideological changes or something else.

A third limitation of the attitudinal model is that it tends to be less successful at explaining the behavior of judges on other courts besides the Supreme Court. As discussed above, the attitudinal model is premised on certain assumptions about how courts are organized and what constraints judges face. The U.S. Supreme Court is relatively free of constraints, but lower federal courts are more encumbered, bound by the precedents of their superiors. They also have less docket control and therefore less freedom to avoid controversies in which the law is settled. Still, there is evidence of attitudinal voting on these courts. The developers of the GHP scores found that U.S. courts of appeals judges appointed by Democratic presidents were 41.8 percent more likely than Republican appointees to support liberal outcomes, assuming that senatorial courtesy was not in play.[19] Anecdotally, there have also been occasions when lower federal court judges have accused one another of preferential voting. For example, in one Second Amendment case, *Silveira v. Lockyer* (9th Cir., 2003), Judge Alex Kozinski said that the majority was using its "power as federal judges to constitutionalize our personal preferences."[20]

On many state courts, judicial elections impose further constraints on attitudinal behavior because judges are directly accountable to the voting public. Judges who stray too far from the preferences of their constituents can find themselves voted out of office. Nevertheless, research on state courts has found evidence of attitudinal behavior. For example, work on gay rights litigation has shown that

Figure 2.5 Ideological Drift of Supreme Court Justices, 1967–2014

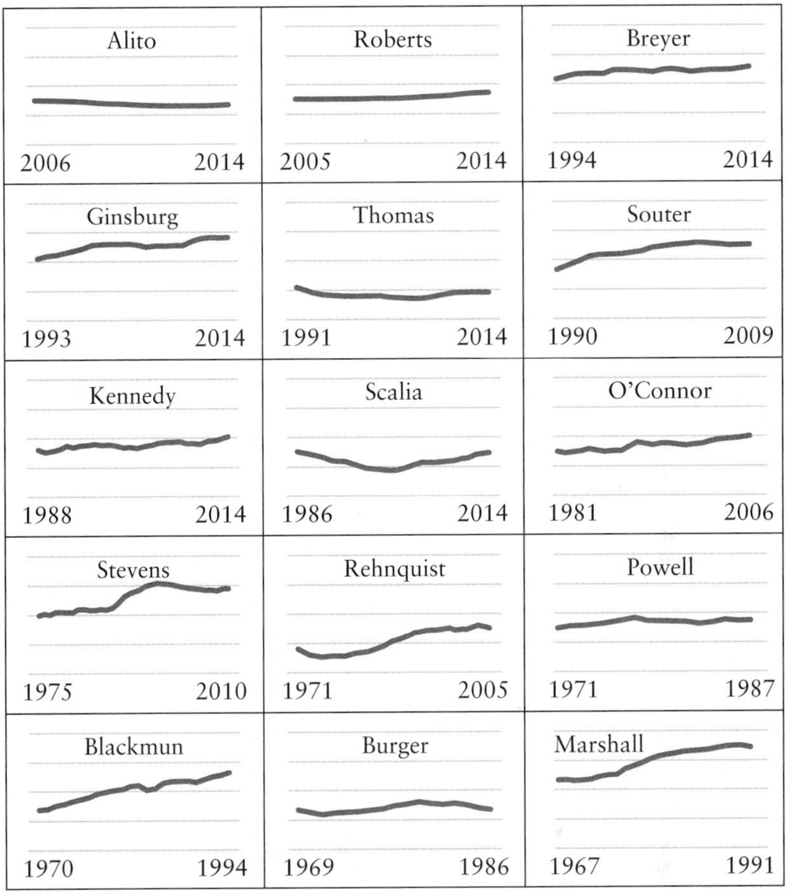

Alito	Roberts	Breyer
2006 — 2014	2005 — 2014	1994 — 2014
Ginsburg	Thomas	Souter
1993 — 2014	1991 — 2014	1990 — 2009
Kennedy	Scalia	O'Connor
1988 — 2014	1986 — 2014	1981 — 2006
Stevens	Rehnquist	Powell
1975 — 2010	1971 — 2005	1971 — 1987
Blackmun	Burger	Marshall
1970 — 1994	1969 — 1986	1967 — 1991

Note: Higher values are associated with more liberal judicial ideology scores. Data are based on the Martin-Quinn scores.

Source: See Andrew D. Martin and Kevin M. Quinn, "Dynamic Ideal Point Estimation via Markov Chain Monte Carlo for the U.S. Supreme Court, 1953–1999," *Political Analysis* 10 (2002):134–53.

the attitudes of judges in state appellate courts have shaped their behavior in cases concerning sexual orientation discrimination, particularly family issues such as child custody, adoption, and same-sex marriage.[21] The first state supreme court justices to issue judgments favoring marriage equality, in Hawaii, Vermont, and Massachusetts, were among the most liberal judges in the country, based on their PAJID scores.[22]

SOCIAL BACKGROUND THEORY

A final limitation of the attitudinal model is that it does not tell us much about the wealth of perspectives that judges bring to the bench aside from being liberal or conservative. The attitudinal model describes a judge's general ideological leanings, but many of us want to know how particular life experiences shape judging. For example, Justice Sonia Sotomayor famously said, before she was nominated to the Supreme Court, "I would hope that a wise Latina woman with the richness of her experiences would more often than not reach a better conclusion than a white male who hasn't lived that life."[23] Research on social background theory introduces these additional perspectives, showing how a judge's life experiences shape judging.

One of the challenges for social background theory has been to show that background characteristics are a truly independent influence on judging. What do these characteristics teach us that simply knowing a judge's ideology does not? Critics of social background theory maintain that it is not really a distinct theory of judging but merely an account of how judges come to form their attitudes. Judges might become liberal or conservative for a variety of reasons, but once we know their policy preferences, their life experiences recede into the background and have no further explanatory power. In contrast, supporters of social background theory maintain that certain experiences do bring perspectives to judging that are separate from knowing how liberal or conservative people are, and that these perspectives are important and worth understanding.

Another challenge for social background theory has been to avoid making stereotyped generalizations about people. It can be perilous to make assumptions about how a judge will act based on their religious backgrounds, their sex or race, or the region of the country where they are from. The theory has had to be careful to identify common group experiences that are actually relevant to judging. For example, early research on social background theory found that judges who previously worked as criminal prosecutors are more likely to cast conservative votes in civil liberties cases because former prosecutors tend to be tough on crime.[24] More recently, researchers have found that Supreme Court justices favor judgments from lower courts where they have worked in the past. Justice Ruth Bader Ginsburg voted 58 percent of the time to affirm cases from the D.C. Circuit, where she was a judge from 1980 to 1993. Ordinarily she affirms circuit court decisions about 40 percent of the time.[25] Other justices with prior judicial experience exhibit similar tendencies.

Of special interest to social background theorists is whether a judge's race or sex influences judging. Justice Sotomayor's comments above indicate that she thinks her own life experiences have been influential, specifically her experiences as a Latina woman, and her behavior on the Supreme Court seems to be consistent with this statement. For example, Justice Sotomayor's dissent from *Schuette v. Coalition to Defend Affirmative Action* (2014) (excerpted at the end of the chapter) appears to reflect her direct knowledge of how "democratically approved legislation can oppress minority groups."[26] But if Justice Sotomayor's life experiences have shaped her behavior, how have they done so? And how common is it for these types of experiences to influence judging?

Research that has looked at the influence of race and sex on judging has developed alternative theories about when and how social background characteristics might matter. **Difference theory** suggests that judges who share certain traits or experiences think about legal problems differently from other judges. Work by Carol Gilligan, for example, suggests that women tend to emphasize the rights of the community, whereas men focus more on hierarchies and rules.[27] In contrast, **representational theories** suggest that people from different backgrounds do not necessarily think differently about the law, but they identify with other individuals who have similar traits or experiences.[28] For example, judges might be more sympathetic to litigants who have experienced discrimination or other hardships that they have encountered themselves.

Overall, evidence has found more support for representational accounts than difference theory. There is little evidence that judges think about the law in fundamentally different ways depending on their background experiences. Most likely, the training that judges receive in law school establishes a common manner of thinking about the law that transcends the influence of other socializing experiences. However, consistent with representational accounts, researchers have found evidence that judges favor litigants with whom they can relate. These trends are most apparent in employment discrimination cases. Susan Haire and Laura Moyer found that African American judges on the U.S. courts of appeals side with plaintiffs in race discriminations cases 47 percent of the time, compared to 27 percent for white judges, and 31 percent for Latino judges. (See Table 2.2.) Similarly, women judges side with female plaintiffs in 42 percent of cases, compared to 35 percent for male judges.

Some political scientists have theorized that social background characteristics are less influential on judicial behavior because a

Table 2.2 Voting in Employment Discrimination Cases, U.S. Courts of Appeals, 1995–2008

Percent favoring the plaintiff in race discrimination cases:

White Judge	Latino Judge	African American Judge
27.0	31.0	47.0

Percent favoring the plaintiff in sex discrimination cases:

Male Judge	Female Judge
35.0	42.0

Sources: Data are based on a sample of 1,589 U.S. courts of appeals decisions concerning race discrimination and 1,694 concerning sex discrimination. Predicted probabilities were generated by Susan B. Haire and Laura P. Moyer, *Diversity Matters: Judicial Policymaking in the U.S. Courts of Appeals* (Charlottesville: University of Virginia Press, 2015), using data from Lee Epstein, William M. Landes, and Richard Posner, *The Behavior of Federal Judges: A Theoretical and Empirical Study of Rational Choice* (Cambridge, MA: Harvard University Press, 2013).

critical mass is needed before group characteristics gain expression. The logic behind **critical mass theory** is that until minority representation in a profession goses beyond token status, members of a minority will exhibit characteristics of the dominant group. There is evidence to support critical mass theory at the trial court level. Paul Collins, Kenneth Manning, and Robert Carp discovered that female federal district court judges are more likely to vote in a liberal direction in cases concerning criminal justice and civil rights and liberties when there are other female district court judges in their home cities.[29] When Haire and Moyer looked at the U.S. courts of appeals, they found no evidence that a critical mass of female or African American judges had an impact on employment discrimination cases, but they did find that the presence of a nontraditional chief judge could be significant. Specifically, judges have a greater tendency to vote for plaintiffs in discrimination cases when their chief judges are not white males. "This is true for female chief judges in sex discrimination cases and for minority chief judges in Title VII racial discrimination cases."[30]

Most of the leading studies of social background theory focus on the role of race and sex in judging, but representational theories point to other background characteristics that might also matter. For example, one might expect LGBT judges to identify with litigants who have faced sexual orientation discrimination or for disabled people to be more attuned to ableism. As you think about judicial behavior, reflect on your own experiences and consider how they have shaped who you are and how they might affect the decisions you make. Which experiences have been the most important and why are they important? How might these experiences influence judging?

DISCUSSION QUESTIONS

1. Much of the political science literature on courts focuses on explaining case outcomes. How would you define "judicial behavior"? What other forms of judicial behavior do you think are important to study besides case outcomes?
2. What does it mean to say that "sincere policy preferences" influence judging? Is there more to a judge's attitudes than just whether they are liberal or conservative? How would you go about measuring a judge's policy preferences?
3. What life experiences do you think are the most likely to influence judging? Is it a person's race? their sex? their sexual orientation? What about their religion or the region of the country where they are from? How might these experiences influence judicial behavior?
4. To what extent do you think Justice Sonia Sotomayor's own life experiences influenced her dissent in *Schuette v. Coalition to Defend Affirmative Action* (2014)? How do you think her status as a "wise Latina woman" shaped her judgment in this case?

KEY TERMS

petitioner
respondent
operationalize
writ of certiorari
legal formalism
case method
positive law
natural law
legal realism
motivated reasoning
confirmation bias
behavioralism
docket
mandatory appeals

certiorari petitions
Segal-Cover scores
GHP scores
senatorial courtesy
validity
reliability
party-adjusted ideology
    (PAJID) scores
campaign finance (CF) scores
morality policies
Martin-Quinn scores
difference theory
representational theories
critical mass theory

FURTHER READING

Segal, Jeffrey A., and Harold J. Spaeth. 2002. *The Supreme Court and the Attitudinal Model Revisited.* New York: Cambridge University Press.

Kimball, Bruce A. 2009. *The Inception of Modern Professional Education: C.C. Langdell, 1826–1909.* Chapel Hill: The University of North Carolina Press.

Haire, Susan B., and Laura P. Moyer. 2015. *Diversity Matters: Judicial Policymaking in the U.S. Courts of Appeals.* Charlottesville: University of Virginia Press.

NOTES

1. "Shelby: The American People Deserve a Voice in SCOTUS Nomination," *Shelby.Senate.Gov* (March 16, 2016), http://www.shelby.senate.gov/public/index .cfm/2016/3/shelby-the-american-people-deserve-a-voice-in-scotus-nomination.

2. Richard A. Posner, "Legal Formalism, Legal Realism, and the Interpretation of Statutes and the Constitution," *Case Western Law Review* 37 no. 2 (1986): 181.

3. C. C. Langdell, *A Selection of Cases on the Law of Contracts: With References and Citations* (Boston: Little, Brown & Co., 1871), vi.

4. Oliver Wendell Holmes, "The Path of Law," *Harvard Law Review* 457 (1897): 10.

5. Raymond S. Nickerson, "Confirmation Bias: A Ubiquitous Phenomenon in Many Guises," *Review of General Psychology* 2, no. 2 (1998): 175–220; *see also* Frank B. Cross, *The Failed Promise of Originalism*, Stanford University Press (2013), at 166.

6. Ziva Kunda, "The Case for Motivated Reasoning," *Psychological Bulletin* 108 (1990): 495.

7. For a fuller elaboration of these points, see Jeffrey A. Segal and Harold J. Spaeth, *The Supreme Court and the Attitudinal Model Revisited* (Cambridge: Cambridge University Press, 2002), 92–96.

8. *See* Lawrence Baum, *The Puzzle of Judicial Behavior* (Ann Arbor: University of Michigan Press, 1997), 43.

9. Jeffrey A. Segal and Albert Cover, "Ideological Values and Votes of U.S. Supreme Court Justices," *American Political Science Review* 83, no. 2 (1989): 557–65.

10. Michael W. Giles, Virginia A. Hettinger, and Todd Peppers, "Picking Federal Judges: A Note on Policy and Partisan Selection Agendas," *Political Research Quarterly* 54, no. 3 (2001): 623–41.

11. Paul Brace, Laura Langer, and Melinda Gann Hall, "Measuring the Preferences of State Supreme Court Judges," *Journal of Politics* 62, no. 2 (2000): 387–413.

12. Adam Bonica and Michael J. Woodruff, "A Common-Space Measure of State Supreme Court Ideology," *Journal of Law, Economics, and Organization* 31, no. 3 (2015): 472–98.

13. For the original table, *see* Segal and Spaeth, *The Supreme Court and the Attitudinal Model Revisited*, 322.

14. The most recent appointment to the Supreme Court, Justice Neil Gorsuch, is not included in the table, but for reference, his Segal-Cover score is 0.110.

15. A similar analysis appears in Lee Epstein and Jeffrey A. Segal, *Advice and Consent: The Politics of Judicial Appointments* (Oxford: Oxford University Press, 2005), 125.

16. Lee Epstein and Carol Mershon, "Measuring Political Preferences," *American Journal of Political Science* 40, no. 1 (1996): 261–94.

17. The directions of the Martin-Quinn scores were changed to match previous figures. *See* Andrew D. Martin and Kevin M. Quinn, "Dynamic Ideal Point Estimation via Markov Chain Monte Carlo for the U.S. Supreme Court, 1953–1999," *Political Analysis* 10 (2002):134–53.

18. Callins v. Collins, 510 U.S. 1141 (1994).

19. Giles et al., Picking Federal Judges," 635.

20. Silveira v. Lockyer, 328 F.3d 567 (9th Cir., 2003) (Kozinski, J., dissenting from denial of rehearing en banc).

21. Daniel R. Pinello, *Gay Rights and American Law* (New York: Cambridge University Press, 2003), 84.

22. *See* Robert J. Hume, *Courthouse Democracy and Minority Rights: Same-Sex Marriage in the States* (Oxford: Oxford University Press, 2013).

23. Sonia Sotomayor, "Judge Mario G. Olmos Memorial Lecture: Latina Judge's Voice," *La Raza Law Journal* 13 (2002): 92.

24. Neal Tate, "Personal Attribute Models of the Voting Behavior of U.S. Supreme Court Justices: Liberalism in Civil Liberties and Economics Decisions, 1946–1978," *American Political Science Review* 75, no. 2 (1981): 355–67; but see Rob Robinson, "Does Prosecutorial Experience 'Balance Out' a Judge's Liberal Tendencies?" *Justice System Journal* 32, no. 2 (2011): 143–68 (finding no influence of prosecutorial experience based on a forty-year sample of criminal cases from the Supreme Court and the courts of appeals).

25. Andrew D. Martin, Kevin M. Quinn, and Jeffrey A. Segal, "Circuit Effects: How the Norm of Federal Judicial Experience Biases the Supreme Court," *University of Pennsylvania Law Review* 157 (2008): 874–75.

26. Schuette v. Coalition to Defend Affirmative Action, 572 U.S. ___ (2014) (Sotomayor, J., dissenting).

27. Carol Gilligan, *In a Different Voice: Psychological Theory and Women's Development* (Cambridge, MA: Harvard University Press, 1982); *see also* Sue Davis, Susan Haire, and Donald R. Songer, "Voting Behavior and Gender on the U.S. Courts of Appeals," *Judicature* 77 (1993): 129–33.

28. Christina L. Boyd, Lee Epstein, and Andrew D. Martin (2010), "Untangling the Causal Effects of Sex on Judging," *American Journal of Political Science* 54, no. 2 (2010): 389–411.

29. Paul M. Collins Jr., Kenneth L. Manning, and Robert A. Carp, "Gender, Critical Mass, and Judicial Decision Making," *Law & Policy* 32 (2010): 260–81.

30. Susan B. Haire and Laura P. Moyer, *Diversity Matters: Judicial Policymaking in the U.S. Courts of Appeals* (Charlottesville: University of Virginia Press, 2015), 121.

In Their Own Words:
Justice Oliver Wendell Holmes Jr., U.S. Supreme Court

Prior to becoming a U.S. Supreme Court justice, Oliver Wendell Holmes Jr. wrote an influential essay in which he stated that the personal values of judges shaped the development of the law. What do you think? Does Justice Holmes offer a persuasive account of judging? Or is his perspective too cynical?

The Path of the Law (1897)
Oliver Wendell Holmes Jr.

When we study law we are not studying a mystery but a well-known profession. We are studying what we shall want in order to appear before judges, or to advise people in such a way as to keep them out of court. The reason why it is a profession, why people will pay lawyers to argue for them or to advise them, is that in societies like ours the command of the public force is intrusted to the judges in certain cases, and the whole power of the state will be put forth, if necessary, to carry out their judgments and decrees. People want to know under what circumstances and how far they will run the risk of coming against what is so much stronger than themselves, and hence it becomes a business to find out when this danger is to be feared. The object of our study, then, is prediction, the prediction of the incidence of the public force through the instrumentality of the courts.

The means of the study are a body of reports, of treatises, and of statutes, in this country and in England, extending back for six hundred years, and now increasing annually by hundreds. In these sibylline leaves are gathered the scattered prophecies of the past upon the cases in which the axe will fall. These are what properly have been called the oracles of the law. Far the most important and pretty nearly the whole meaning of every new effort of legal thought is to make these prophecies more precise, and to generalize them into a thoroughly connected system. The process is one, from a lawyer's statement of a case, eliminating as it does all the dramatic elements with which his client's story has clothed it, and retaining only the facts of legal import, up to the final analyses and abstract universals of theoretic jurisprudence. The reason why a lawyer does not mention that his client wore a white hat when he made a contract, while Mrs. Quickly would be sure to dwell upon it along with the parcel gilt goblet and the sea-coal fire, is that he foresees that the public force will act in the same way whatever his client had upon his head. It is to make the prophecies easier to be remembered and to be understood that the teachings of the decisions of the past are put into general propositions and gathered into textbooks, or that statutes are passed in a general form. The primary rights and duties with which jurisprudence busies itself again are nothing but prophecies. . . .

I wish, if I can, to lay down some first principles for the study of this body of dogma or systematized prediction which we call the law, for men who want to use it as the instrument of their business to enable them to prophesy in their turn, and, as bearing upon the study, I wish to point out an ideal which as yet our law has not attained.

The first thing for a businesslike understanding of the matter is to understand its limits, and therefore I think it desirable at once to point out and dispel a confusion between morality and law, which sometimes rises to the height of conscious theory, and more often and indeed constantly is making trouble in detail without reaching the point of consciousness. You can see very plainly that a bad man has as much reason as a good one for wishing to avoid an encounter with the public force, and therefore you can see the practical importance of the distinction between morality and law. A man who cares nothing for an ethical rule which is believed and practised by his neighbors is likely nevertheless to care a good deal to avoid being made to pay money, and will want to keep out of jail if he can. . . .

I do not say that there is not a wider point of view from which the distinction between law and morals becomes of secondary or no importance, as all mathematical distinctions vanish in presence of the infinite. But I do say that that distinction is of the first importance for the object which we are here to consider—a right study and mastery of the law as a business with well understood limits, a body of dogma enclosed within definite lines. I have just shown the practical reason for saying so. If you want to know the law and nothing else, you must look at it as a bad man, who cares only for the material consequences which such knowledge enables him to predict, not as a good one, who finds his reasons for conduct, whether inside the law or outside of it, in the vaguer sanctions of conscience. The theoretical importance of the distinction is no less, if you would reason on your subject aright. The law is full of phraseology drawn from morals, and by the mere force of language continually invites us to pass from one domain to the other without perceiving it, as we are sure to do unless we have the boundary constantly before our minds. The law talks about rights, and duties, and malice, and intent, and negligence, and so forth, and nothing is easier, or, I may say, more common in legal reasoning, than to take these words in their moral sense, at some state of the argument, and so to drop into fallacy. For instance, when we speak of the rights of man in a moral sense, we mean to mark the limits of interference with individual freedom which we think are prescribed by conscience, or by our ideal, however reached. Yet it is certain that many laws have been enforced in the past, and it is likely that some are enforced now, which are condemned by the most enlightened opinion of the time, or which at all events pass the limit of interference, as many consciences would draw it. . . .

So much for the limits of the law. The next thing which I wish to consider is what are the forces which determine its content and its growth. You may assume, with Hobbes and Bentham and Austin, that all law emanates from the sovereign, even when the first human beings to enunciate it are the judges, or you may think that law is the voice of the Zeitgeist, or what you like. It is all one to my present purpose. Even if every decision required the sanction of an emperor with despotic power and a whimsical turn of mind, we should be interested none the less, still with a view to prediction, in discovering some order, some rational explanation, and some principle of growth for the rules which he laid down. In every system there are such explanations and principles to be found. It is with regard to them that a second fallacy comes in, which I think it important to expose.

The fallacy to which I refer is the notion that the only force at work in the development of the law is logic. In the broadest sense, indeed, that notion would be true. The postulate on which we think about the universe is that there is a fixed quantitative relation between every phenomenon and its antecedents and consequents. If there is such a thing as a phenomenon without these fixed quantitative relations, it is a miracle. It is outside the law of cause and effect, and as such transcends our power of thought, or at least is something to or from which we cannot reason. The condition of our thinking about the universe is that it is capable of being thought about rationally, or, in other words, that every part of it is effect and cause in the same sense in which those parts are with which we are most familiar. So in the broadest sense it is true that the law is a logical development, like everything else. The danger of which I speak is not the admission that the principles governing other phenomena also govern the law, but the notion that a given system, ours, for instance, can be worked out like mathematics from some general axioms of conduct. This is the natural error of the schools, but it is not confined to them. I once heard a very eminent judge say that he never let a decision go until he was absolutely sure that it was right. So judicial dissent often is blamed, as if it meant simply that one side or the other were not doing their sums right, and if they would take more trouble, agreement inevitably would come.

This mode of thinking is entirely natural. The training of lawyers is a training in logic. The processes of analogy, discrimination, and deduction are those in which they are most at home. The language of judicial decision is mainly the language of logic. And the logical method and form flatter that longing for certainty and for repose which is in every human mind. But certainty generally is illusion, and repose is not the destiny of man. Behind the logical form lies a judgment as to the relative worth and importance of competing legislative grounds, often an inarticulate and unconscious judgment, it is true, and yet the very root and nerve of the whole proceeding. You can give any conclusion a logical form. You always can imply a condition in a contract. But why do you imply it? It is because of some belief as to the practice of the community or of a class, or because of some opinion as to policy, or, in short, because of some attitude of yours upon a matter not capable of exact quantitative measurement, and therefore not capable of founding exact logical conclusions. Such matters really are battle grounds where the means do not exist for the determinations that shall be good for all time, and where the decision can do no more than embody the preference of a given body in a given time and place. We do not realize how large a part of our law is open to reconsideration upon a slight change in the habit of the public mind. . . .

So much for the fallacy of logical form. Now let us consider the present condition of the law as a subject for study, and the ideal toward which it tends. . . . The development of our law has gone on for nearly a thousand years, like the development of a plant, each generation taking the inevitable next step, mind, like matter, simply obeying a law of spontaneous growth. It is perfectly natural and right that it should have been so. . . . Most of the things we do, we do for no better reason than that our fathers have done them or that our neighbors do them, and the same is true of a larger part than we suspect of what we think. The reason is a good one, because our short life gives us no time for a better, but it is not the best. . . . It is revolting to have no better reason for a rule of law than that so it was laid down in the time of Henry IV. It is still more revolting if the grounds upon which it was laid down have vanished long since, and the rule simply persists from blind imitation of the past. . . .

I trust that no one will understand me to be speaking with disrespect of the law, because I criticise it so freely. I venerate the law, and especially our system of law, as one of the vastest products of the human mind. No one knows better than I do the countless number of great intellects that have spent themselves in making some addition or improvement, the greatest of which is trifling when compared with the mighty whole. . . . But one may criticise even what one reveres. Law is the business to which my life is devoted, and I should show less than devotion if I did not do what in me lies to improve it, and, when I perceive what seems to me the ideal of its future, if I hesitated to point it out and to press toward it with all my heart. . . .

Originally published as Oliver Wendell Holmes Jr., "The Path of the Law," *Harvard Law Review* 10 (1897): 457.

CASE ANALYSIS

Schuette v. Coalition to Defend Affirmative Action, 572 U.S. ___ (2014)

Before she was nominated to the U.S. Supreme Court, Justice Sonia Sotomayor famously stated, "I would hope that a wise Latina woman with the richness of her experiences would more often than not reach a better conclusion than a white male who hasn't lived that life." Compare Justice Kennedy's plurality opinion in Schuette v. Coalition to Defend Affirmative Action *(2014), which concerned an affirmative action policy in Michigan, with Justice Sotomayor's dissent. In your view, how might Justice Sotomayor's personal life experiences have influenced her opinion? Is it appropriate for justices to take their own personal experiences into account when they are deciding cases? Or should these considerations be irrelevant to judging?*

JUSTICE KENNEDY announced the judgment of the Court
The Court in this case must determine whether an amendment to the Constitution of the State of Michigan, approved and enacted by its voters, is invalid under the Equal Protection Clause of the Fourteenth Amendment to the Constitution of the United States.

In 2003 the Court reviewed the constitutionality of two admissions systems at the University of Michigan, one for its undergraduate class and one for its law school. The undergraduate admissions plan was addressed in *Gratz v. Bollinger*, 539 U.S. 244. The law school admission plan was addressed in *Grutter v. Bollinger*, 539 U.S. 306. Each admissions process permitted the explicit consideration of an applicant's race. In *Gratz*, the Court invalidated the undergraduate plan as a violation of the Equal Protection Clause. In *Grutter*, the Court found no constitutional flaw in the law school admission plan's more limited use of race-based preferences. In response to the Court's decision in *Gratz*, the university revised its undergraduate admissions process, but the revision still allowed limited use of race-based preferences. After a statewide debate on the question of racial preferences in the context of governmental decisionmaking, the voters, in 2006, adopted an amendment to the State Constitution prohibiting state and other governmental entities in Michigan from granting certain preferences, including race-based preferences, in a wide range of actions and decisions. Under the terms of the amendment, race-based preferences cannot be part of the admissions process for state universities. That particular prohibition is central to the instant case.

The ballot proposal was called Proposal 2 and, after it passed by a margin of 58 percent to 42 percent, the resulting enactment became Article I, §26, of the Michigan Constitution. As noted, the amendment is in broad terms. Section 26 states, in relevant part, as follows:

> "(1) The University of Michigan, Michigan State University, Wayne State University, and any other public college or university, community college, or school district shall not discriminate against, or grant preferential treatment to, any individual or group on the basis of race, sex, color, ethnicity, or national origin in the operation of public employment, public education, or public contracting.
>
> "(2) The state shall not discriminate against, or grant preferential treatment to, any individual or group on the basis of race, sex, color, ethnicity, or national origin in the operation of public employment, public education, or public contracting.
>
> "(3) For the purposes of this section 'state' includes, but is not necessarily limited to, the state itself, any city, county, any public college, university, or community college, school district, or other political subdivision or governmental instrumentality of or within the State of Michigan not included in sub-section 1.". . .

Before the Court addresses the question presented, it is important to note what this case is not about. It is not about the constitutionality, or the merits, of race-conscious admissions policies in higher education. The consideration of race in admissions presents complex questions, in part addressed last Term in *Fisher v. University of Texas at Austin*, 570 U.S. ___ (2013). In *Fisher*, the Court did not disturb the principle that the consideration of race in admissions is permissible, provided that certain conditions are met. In this case, as in *Fisher*, that principle is not challenged. The question here concerns not the permissibility of race-conscious admissions policies under the Constitution but whether, and in what manner, voters in the States may choose to prohibit the consideration of racial preferences in governmental decisions, in particular with respect to school admissions. . . .

By approving Proposal 2 and thereby adding §26 to their State Constitution, the Michigan voters exercised their privilege to enact laws as a basic exercise of their democratic power. In the federal system States "respond, through the enactment of positive law, to the initiative of those who seek a voice in shaping the destiny of their own times." *Bond*, 564 U.S., at ___ (slip op., at 9). Michigan voters used the initiative system to bypass public officials who were deemed not responsive to the concerns of a majority of the voters with respect to a policy of granting race-based preferences that raises difficult and delicate issues.

The freedom secured by the Constitution consists, in one of its essential dimensions, of the right of the individual not to be injured by the unlawful exercise of governmental power. The mandate for segregated schools, *Brown v. Board of Education*, 347 U.S. 483 (1954); a wrongful invasion of the home, *Silverman v. United States*, 365 U.S. 505 (1961); or punishing a protester whose views offend others, *Texas v. Johnson*, 491 U.S. 397 (1989); and scores of other examples teach that individual liberty has constitutional protection, and that liberty's full extent and meaning may remain yet to be discovered and affirmed. Yet freedom does not stop with individual rights. Our constitutional system embraces, too, the right of citizens to debate so they can learn and decide and then, through the political process, act in concert to try to shape the course of their own times and the course of a nation that must strive always to make freedom ever greater and more secure. Here Michigan voters acted in concert and statewide to seek consensus and adopt a policy on a difficult subject against a historical background of race in America that has been a source of tragedy and persisting injustice. That history demands that we continue to learn, to listen, and to remain open to new approaches if we are to aspire always to a constitutional order in which all persons are treated with fairness and equal dignity. Were the Court to rule that the question addressed by Michigan voters is too sensitive or complex to be within the grasp of the electorate; or that the policies at issue remain too delicate to be resolved save by university officials or faculties, acting at some remove from immediate public scrutiny and control; or that these matters are so arcane that the electorate's power must be limited because the people cannot prudently exercise that power even after a full debate, that holding would be an unprecedented restriction on the exercise of a fundamental right held not just by one person but by all in common. It is the right to speak and debate and learn and then, as a matter of political will, to act through a lawful electoral process. . . .

This case is not about how the debate about racial preferences should be resolved. It is about who may resolve it. There is no authority in the Constitution of the United States or in this Court's precedents for the Judiciary to set aside Michigan laws that commit this policy determination to the voters. Deliberative debate on sensitive issues such as racial preferences all too often may shade into rancor. But that does not justify removing certain court-determined issues from the voters' reach. Democracy does not presume that some subjects are either too divisive or too profound for public debate.

The judgment of the Court of Appeals for the Sixth Circuit is reversed.
It is so ordered.

JUSTICE SOTOMAYOR, dissenting

We are fortunate to live in a democratic society. But without checks, democrat-ically approved legislation can oppress minority groups. For that reason, our Constitution places limits on what a majority of the people may do. This case implicates one such limit: the guarantee of equal protection of the laws. Although that guarantee is traditionally understood to prohibit intentional discrimination under existing laws, equal protection does not end there. Another fundamental strand of our equal protection jurisprudence focuses on process, securing to all citizens the right to participate meaningfully and equally in self-government. That right is the bedrock of our democracy, for it preserves all other rights.

Yet to know the history of our Nation is to understand its long and lam-entable record of stymieing the right of racial minorities to participate in the political process. At first, the majority acted with an open, invidious purpose. Notwithstanding the command of the Fifteenth Amendment, certain States shut racial minorities out of the political process altogether by withholding the right to vote. This Court intervened to preserve that right. The majority tried again, replacing outright bans on voting with literacy tests, good character require-ments, poll taxes, and gerrymandering. The Court was not fooled; it invalidated those measures, too. The majority persisted. This time, although it allowed the minority access to the political process, the majority changed the ground rules of the process so as to make it more difficult for the minority, and the minority alone, to obtain policies designed to foster racial integration. Although these political restructurings may not have been discriminatory in purpose, the Court reaffirmed the right of minority members of our society to participate meaning-fully and equally in the political process.

This case involves this last chapter of discrimination: A majority of the Mich-igan electorate changed the basic rules of the political process in that State in a manner that uniquely disadvantaged racial minorities. Prior to the enactment of the constitutional initiative at issue here, all of the admissions policies of Michigan's public colleges and universities—including race-sensitive admissions policies—were in the hands of each institution's governing board. The members of those boards are nominated by political parties and elected by the citizenry in statewide elections. After over a century of being shut out of Michigan's institutions of higher education, racial minorities in Michigan had succeeded in persuading the elected board representatives to adopt admissions policies that took into account the benefits of racial diversity. And this Court twice blessed such efforts—first in *Regents of Univ. of Cal. v. Bakke*, 438 U.S. 265 (1978), and again in *Grutter v. Bollinger*, 539 U.S. 306 (2003), a case that itself concerned a Michigan admissions policy.

In the wake of *Grutter*, some voters in Michigan set out to eliminate the use of race-sensitive admissions policies. Those voters were of course free to pursue this end in any number of ways. For example, they could have persuaded existing board members to change their minds through individual or grassroots lobbying efforts, or through general public awareness campaigns. Or they could have mobilized efforts to vote uncooperative board members out of office, replacing them with members who would share their desire to abolish race-sensitive admissions policies. When this Court holds that the Constitution permits a particular policy, nothing prevents a majority of a State's voters from choosing not to adopt that policy. Our system of government encourages—and indeed, depends on—that type of democratic action.

But instead, the majority of Michigan voters changed the rules in the middle of the game, reconfiguring the existing political process in Michigan in a manner that burdened racial minorities. They did so in the 2006 election by amending the Michigan Constitution to enact Art. I, §26, which provides in relevant part that Michigan's public universities "shall not discriminate against, or grant preferential treatment to, any individual or group on the basis of race, sex, color, ethnicity, or national origin in the operation of public employment, public education, or public contracting.". . . .

My colleagues are of the view that we should leave race out of the picture entirely and let the voters sort it out. We have seen this reasoning before. It is a sentiment out of touch with reality, one not required by our Constitution, and one that has properly been rejected as "not sufficient" to resolve cases of this nature.

Race matters. Race matters in part because of the long history of racial minorities' being denied access to the political process. And although we have made great strides, "voting discrimination still exists; no one doubts that." *Shelby County*, 570 U.S., at ___ (slip op., at 2). . . . Race also matters because of persistent racial inequality in society—inequality that cannot be ignored and that has produced stark socioeconomic disparities. . . . And race matters for reasons that really are only skin deep, that cannot be discussed any other way, and that cannot be wished away. Race matters to a young man's view of society when he spends his teenage years watching others tense up as he passes, no matter the neighborhood where he grew up. Race matters to a young woman's sense of self when she states her hometown, and then is pressed, "No, where are you really from?", regardless of how many generations her family has been in the country. Race matters to a young person addressed by a stranger in a foreign language, which he does not understand because only English was spoken at home. Race matters because of the slights, the snickers, the silent judgments that reinforce that most crippling of thoughts: "I do not belong here."

In my colleagues' view, examining the racial impact of legislation only perpetuates racial discrimination. This refusal to accept the stark reality that race matters is regrettable. The way to stop discrimination on the basis of race is to speak openly and candidly on the subject of race, and to apply the Constitution with eyes open to the unfortunate effects of centuries of racial discrimination. As members of the judiciary tasked with intervening to carry out the guarantee of equal protection, we ought not sit back and wish away, rather than confront, the racial inequality that exists in our society. It is this view that works harm, by perpetuating the facile notion that what makes race matter is acknowledging the simple truth that race does matter. . . .

Today's decision eviscerates an important strand of our equal protection jurisprudence. For members of historically marginalized groups, which rely on the federal courts to protect their constitutional rights, the decision can hardly bolster hope for a vision of democracy that preserves for all the right to participate meaningfully and equally in self-government.

I respectfully dissent.

3

The Legal Model

THE ATTITUDINAL MODEL may do a good job of explaining how Supreme Court justices decide cases, but it does not tell the whole story. The Supreme Court is just one tribunal, and many of the factors that make Supreme Court justices especially likely to engage in attitudinal voting behavior do not apply to judges on other courts. Most judges do not have as much discretion as the justices because they are bound by the precedents of their superiors. Nor are they as free from oversight, or from political and electoral accountability. For judges on these other tribunals—which is to say, on most courts—it is reasonable to think that legal principles influence judicial behavior.

There are also certain puzzles that the attitudinal model cannot adequately explain. Take, for example, Justice Clarence Thomas's dissent in *Lawrence v. Texas* (2003), concerning a Texas law prohibiting gay sexual intimacy. (See Box 3.1.) Describing the law as "uncommonly silly," Thomas stated that, "If I were a member of the Texas Legislature, I would vote to repeal it." However, Justice Thomas believed that the Fourteenth Amendment, properly interpreted, prohibited him from reaching this conclusion. "I recognize that as a member of this Court I am not empowered to help petitioners and others similarly situated," he wrote. "I can find neither in the Bill of Rights nor any other part of the Constitution a general right of privacy."

What do you think Justice Thomas was trying to accomplish with this dissent? Did *legal principles* really explain his vote? Some of you might have doubts, saying that Justice Thomas is protesting too much. Maybe he was just trying to disguise his attitudes or make

TEXTBOX 3.1 | **Justice Thomas's Dissent in** *Lawrence v. Texas* **(2003)**

John Geddes Lawrence and Tyron Garner, Petitioners v. Texas, on Writ of Certiorari to the Court of Appeals of Texas, Fourteenth District [June 26, 2003]

JUSTICE THOMAS, dissenting.

I join Justice Scalia's **dissenting opinion**. I write separately to note that the law before the Court today "is . . . uncommonly silly." *Griswold v. Connecticut*, 381 U.S. 479, 527 (1965) (Stewart, J., dissenting). If I were a member of the Texas Legislature, I would vote to repeal it. Punishing someone for expressing his sexual preference through noncommercial consensual conduct with another adult does not appear to be a worthy way to expend valuable law enforcement resources.

Notwithstanding this, I recognize that as a member of this Court I am not empowered to help petitioners and others similarly situated. My duty, rather, is to "decide cases 'agreeably to the Constitution and laws of the United States.'" Id., at 530. And, just like Justice Stewart, I "can find [neither in the Bill of Rights nor any other part of the Constitution a] general right of privacy," ibid., or as the Court terms it today, the "liberty of the person both in its spatial and more transcendent dimensions," ante, at 1.

his sincere policy preferences seem less unkind to gay people. But then why did he bother writing separately at all? He could have just as easily joined Justice Scalia's dissent, which already outlined problems with the majority's analysis. The only thing that Justice Thomas achieved in his short opinion was to suggest that the law, not attitudes, was guiding his behavior.

Justice Thomas's dissent in *Lawrence v. Texas* is a reminder that we should not make assumptions about a justice's ideology, or their intentions, from their voting behavior alone. The fact that a justice such as Clarence Thomas frequently reaches conservative outcomes does not necessarily mean that conservative policy preferences are responsible. The consistent application of legal doctrine could also produce the same behavior. Justice Thomas would say that his principled commitment to originalism explains why he frequently gives conservative answers to constitutional questions. Justice Thomas does not believe it is appropriate for courts to keep the Constitution up to date with the times, but instead to defer to the original meaning of the text.

Critics of the attitudinal model would also question why one would assume that judges *want* to decide cases based on their policy preferences. The legal model begins with a different premise, that judges are professionals who care about producing principled outcomes. When judges have discretion, they draw upon legal goals and principles, not their attitudes. If judges like Clarence Thomas settle into a consistent pattern of behavior while on the bench, it is because legal principles got them there. As exemplars of the legal community, judges share the values of that community, internalize its norms, and promote them through their decision making.

This chapter discusses the theoretical justifications for the legal model and evaluates the evidence for it. As you will see, the biggest challenge for this model has been to identify ways of measuring legal principles. What does it mean to say that a case outcome is "principled"? How would we know if judges were acting on the basis of legal goals, as opposed to their policy preferences? These questions have been difficult for researchers because the answers are not as intuitive as they are for the attitudinal model. It is easier to know what a "liberal" or "conservative" outcome looks like than a "principled" one. Yet, from the standpoint of theory, the legal model is on solid footing. In fact, there are very compelling reasons for supposing that judges care about the law and want to produce principled judgments.

THEORETICAL JUSTIFICATIONS
FOR THE LEGAL MODEL

The legal model is a theory of judging that suggests that legal principles influence judicial behavior. (See Figure 3.1.) Like the attitudinal model, it supposes that judicial decision making is sincere. When confronted with legal questions, judges make choices that reflect their true goals and values. However, the two theories disagree about what these goals and values are. The attitudinal model assumes that judges want their sincere policy preferences to be reflected in the law, but the legal model holds that judges seek to advance legal principles and

Figure 3.1   The Legal Model

---

legal principles   →   judicial behavior

(X)   (Y)

norms. Judges care about producing clear law, they respect precedent, and they respond to persuasive legal arguments.

The contemporary legal model differs from older, more mechanical theories of jurisprudence like legal formalism, which the attitudinal model has done much to discredit. As discussed in the previous chapter, legal formalists assumed that there were objectively "correct" answers to legal questions that could be "found" through careful study of the sources of law. For the legal formalists, the law functioned primarily as a constraint, binding the hands of judges and limiting their discretion. The attitudinal model, much like the legal realism movement before it, demonstrated that judges are often not so constrained. Quite frequently the sources of law are unclear, or else new legal questions arise that lawmakers had not considered.

The contemporary legal model accepts some of the premises of legal realism. It concedes that judges have discretion and that the law does not always force them to reach particular conclusions. However, the legal model holds that it is still possible for judges to make principled decisions, and moreover that judges want to do so. Judges are professionals, and like other professionals they take pride in their work. "Judges have to look in the mirror at least once a day, just like everyone else; they have to like what they see," said Judge Alex Kozinski of the U.S. Court of Appeals for the Ninth Circuit. "Heaven knows we don't do it for the money."[1] For legal professionals, making principled decisions is part of what it means to do a good job and to be a good judge. (See the reading in this chapter, "What I Ate for Breakfast and Other Mysteries of Judicial Decision Making.")

Judges care about legal principles because of their training. Beginning with law school, judges become familiar with the norms and values of the legal community. They are taught to "think like a lawyer," learning how to reason through sound logic and careful analogy.[2] Subsequent professional experiences reinforce these values, and over time lawyers come to internalize them, so by the time judges reach the bench, their own goals and values might be indistinguishable from those of the larger professional community. It is only natural that these norms and values would also be reflected in their behavior. As Judge Richard A. Posner of the Seventh Circuit puts it, "judges for the most part are people who want to be—judges."[3]

Once on the bench, legal values and norms are reinforced by a judge's colleagues. "You are surrounded by eager young law clerks far too smart to be fooled by nonsense," said Judge Kozinski. "I know of no judge who will tell his clerks: 'I want to reach this result, write me an opinion to get me there.' You have to give them reasons, and those reasons better be pretty good."[4] On collegial courts, judges use the language of the law to attract the votes of other judges, while on trial courts, judges seek to maintain credibility within their courtrooms. Judge Posner observes that "a district judge presides more or less continuously at trials and other proceedings in open court in which he is required to make rulings and talk to lawyers and jurors. If he isn't on the ball this soon becomes known and he gets a bad reputation in the legal community."[5] A judge's continued professional standing and reputation might depend on a commitment to legal principles. A bad reputation, or a poorly reasoned opinion, could lead to reversal by a higher court. Judges might also consider a good reputation to be an end in itself.[6] Judges might want to be known among their colleagues for writing persuasive opinions, for following precedent, and for exercising self-restraint.

In all of these ways, professionalization makes judges committed to legal principles. This is not to say that judges only seek to advance legal goals and norms. Research on the attitudinal model has demonstrated too convincingly that policy considerations influence judging. And, to be sure, not every judge is a model jurist. Judge Posner writes, "A federal judge can be lazy, lack judicial temperament, mistreat his staff, berate without reason the lawyers who appear before him."[7] Even judges like Kozinski who are dismissive of legal realism and the attitudinal model acknowledge that "just about any judge can get away with cutting a corner here or there."[8] Yet, neither is legal reasoning simply "window dressing," as the attitudinal model suggests. Judges tell us time and again that that law matters to them and that it systematically influences their behavior. The challenge for social scientists has been to determine precisely when and how it matters.

IDENTIFYING LEGAL PRINCIPLES

Although there are good theoretical reasons for thinking that the law affects judging, measuring the influence of legal principles has been more difficult. Unlike the attitudinal model, it is unclear exactly what social scientists are supposed to be looking for. What do we mean by legal goals and norms? How would we measure these goals once we have identified them? Evaluating the legal model is also complicated by the fact that no single legal consideration is likely to have the same explanatory power as attitudes. A decision can be principled for many reasons, and not every legal goal or norm is relevant in each case.

While acknowledging these challenges, social scientists have focused on three legal principles that judges commonly emphasize.

Stare Decisis

The first legal principle is **stare decisis,** or adherence to precedent. Literally translated as "to stand by things decided," stare decisis is valued by judges and other lawyers because it promotes consistency in the interpretation of state and federal law. Litigants count on judges to reach the same conclusions in similar types of cases because it helps people to know what to expect from the legal system and to arrange their affairs accordingly. The legal model therefore predicts that principled judges will behave in ways that promote legal stability.

The Supreme Court outlined its criteria for evaluating precedent in the landmark abortion case *Planned Parenthood v. Casey* (1992).[9] (See Judicial Process Box 3.1.) In *Casey*, the Court was asked to overturn *Roe v. Wade* (1973), but the justices declined to do so. In an opinion jointly written by Justices O'Connor, Kennedy, and Souter, the Court announced that principles of stare decisis persuaded them not to reconsider *Roe*. The justices also provided guidance about when they might overturn precedent. (See case excerpt at the end of the chapter.)

To begin with, the justices asked whether the *Roe* precedent was *workable.* Did it provide a coherent framework to help judges to decide abortion cases? The Court ruled that it did. The justices next asked whether there was *reliance* on the precedent. Had people come to depend on *Roe* since its enactment? The Court determined that people had. The justices believed that overturning *Roe* would create hardships for women who had come to count on the availability of abortion services.

Then, the joint opinion asked whether any changes had occurred since *Roe* that might lead the Court to reevaluate the precedent. Had the *law's growth* in subsequent years made *Roe* obsolete? Or had the *factual premises* of *Roe* changed? For neither reason did the Court believe that overturning *Roe* was justified. In fact, the joint opinion stated that *Roe* was on even more solid footing than it had been in 1973 because the Court had repeatedly reaffirmed the decision in the years since then. "While it has engendered disapproval," the Court concluded, "it has not been unworkable. An entire generation has come of age free to assume *Roe's* concept of liberty in defining the capacity of women to act in society, and to make reproductive decisions. . . . Within the bounds of normal stare decisis analysis, then,

JUDICIAL PROCESS BOX 3.1 | **Stare Decisis**

One legal principle that judges say is important to them is to decide cases consistently with prior judicial holdings. Respect for precedent is embodied in the principle of stare decisis, or "to stand by things decided," and it is meant to promote stability in the legal system.

Lower-court judges may not overrule precedents set by higher courts, but judges can reconsider their own precedents. The U.S. Supreme Court developed criteria for evaluating precedents in the landmark abortion case *Planned Parenthood v. Casey* (1992):

1. Has the central rule been found to be unworkable?
2. Can the rule be removed without serious inequity to those who have relied upon it, or significant damage to the stability of the society governed by it?
3. Has the law's growth in the intervening years left the central rule a doctrinal anachronism discounted by society?
4. Have the premises of fact so far changed as to render the central holding somehow irrelevant or unjustifiable in dealing with the issue it addressed?

What do you think? When is it reasonable for judges to overturn their own precedents? Is it ever okay, or should judges prioritize having consistency and stability in the law?

and subject to the considerations in which it customarily turns, the stronger argument is for affirming *Roe*'s central holding, with whatever degree of personal reluctance any of us might have, not for overruling it."[10]

Despite the justices' assurances, social scientists have been wary of taking the justices at their word that *stare decisis* explains their behavior in *Casey* or in any other case. The two political scientists who are the most closely associated with the attitudinal model, Jeffrey Segal and Harold Spaeth, have observed that the three authors of the joint opinion were moderate justices who probably already favored abortion rights, at least to some degree.[11] It is difficult to know whether principles of stare decisis actually explain their behavior because the justices' sincere policy preferences might have produced the same outcome. Moreover, Segal and Spaeth point out that every time the authors of the joint opinion found an element of *Roe* that they disliked, they changed it, replacing the original trimester framework with an "undue burden" test.[12]

Segal and Spaeth suggest that a better way to test for the influence of stare decisis is to see how frequently judges who *disagree* with precedents later come to support them. For example, how did the justices who dissented in *Roe v. Wade* subsequently behave? Did they come to accept the view that abortion rights are protected by the Fourteenth Amendment? Or did they adhere to their original positions? Judges who change their voting behavior to conform to precedents are said to engage in **precedential voting**. Segal and Spaeth cite the example of *Georgia v. McCollum* (1992), in which Chief Justice Rehnquist announced his willingness to go along with a precedent that he had previously opposed. In a brief **concurring opinion**, Rehnquist wrote, "I was in dissent in *Edmonson v. Leesville Concrete Co.* (1991), and continue to believe that case to have been wrongly decided. But so long as it remains the law, I believe that it controls the disposition of this case. I therefore join the opinion of the Court."[13] This behavior is consistent with the legal model because Chief Justice Rehnquist was voting against his revealed position on the issue.

Justices engage in **preferential voting** when they refuse to accept precedents and continue to criticize them. For example, in *Fisher v. University of Texas* (2016), Justice Clarence Thomas made it clear that he still opposed the Supreme Court's precedents in affirmative action cases. Characterizing the use of race in college admissions as a "faddish theory," Thomas wrote, "The Court was wrong to hold otherwise in *Grutter v. Bollinger* (2003). I would overrule *Grutter* and reverse the Fifth Circuit's judgment."[14] This behavior is inconsistent with principles of stare decisis because Justice Thomas continued to adhere to his views in *Grutter*.

Segal and Spaeth tested for the influence of stare decisis by seeing how frequently judges engaged in precedential voting and how often they voted preferentially. Figure 3.2 documents the amount of precedential voting behavior that has occurred on the Supreme Court over time, organized by chief justice. It shows the percentage of the time that justices who originally disagreed with precedents later came to support them in progeny cases. What do you think about the trends that you see? To what extent are the data consistent with the hypothesis that stare decisis influences judicial behavior? To what extent are the data inconsistent?

Figure 3.2 Percentage of Voting Behavior That Is Precedential, Organized by Chief Justice

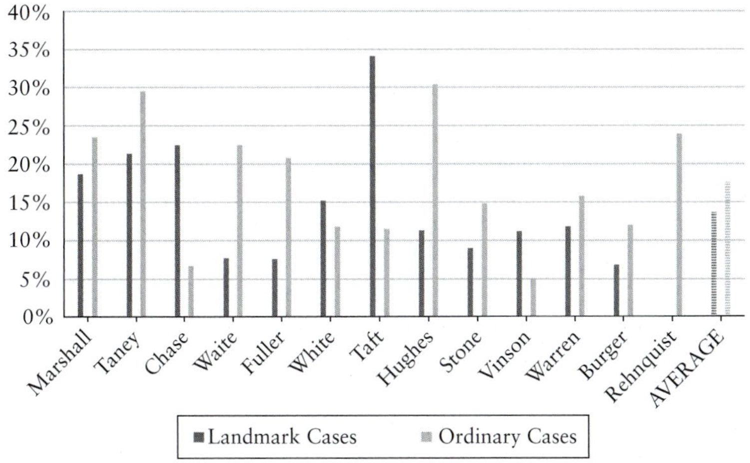

Source: Harold J. Spaeth and Jeffrey A. Segal, *Majority Rule or Minority Will* (New York: Cambridge University Press, 1999).

In general, it would seem that support for the legal model is low. Historically, the justices have tended to behave more like Justice Thomas in *Fisher* than Chief Justice Rehnquist in *Georgia v. McCollum*. There have been just a few periods in which precedential voting has been relatively frequent. During the Taft Court years (1921–1930), for example, precedential voting in landmark cases was at 34.1 percent. Otherwise, justices who originally disapproved of precedents have later changed their policy positions in only about 13.6 percent of landmark cases.[15]

Of course, not every case presents an opportunity for the Supreme Court to evaluate its precedents, and individual justices might give stare decisis different weight. In more recent work, Michael Bailey and Forrest Maltzman examined the influence of stare decisis on the justices in cases in which precedent was a prominent issue.[16] These were cases in which justices or litigants specifically endorsed striking down precedents and the justices became divided over the question. Their results are in Figure 3.3, which estimates changes in the probability that justices cast conservative votes when precedent is implicated, after controlling for the justices' ideology. Justices with the highest probability scores have been the most supportive of precedent.

Figure 3.3 Relative Support of U.S. Supreme Court Justices for Challenged Precedents

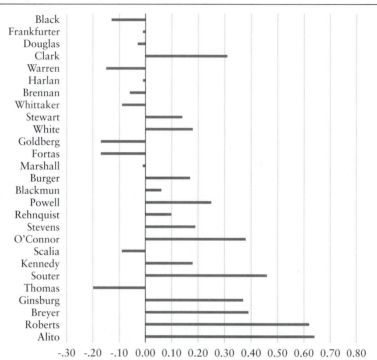

Source: Michael A. Bailey and Forrest Maltzman, *The Constrained Court: Law, Politics, and the Decisions Justices Make* (Princeton, NJ: Princeton University Press, 2011).

What do you think? Does looking at the behavior of individual justices make you more or less persuaded that legal principles influence their behavior? The trends in Figure 3.3 reveal substantial variation in the justices' valuation of precedent. Some justices, such as Samuel Alito and John Roberts, have been strongly pro-precedent, while other justices have not been. In recent years, the justices who have valued precedent the least have been Clarence Thomas and Antonin Scalia. However, over the past few decades, the principle of stare decisis does seem to have influenced many of the justices, at least to some degree. Moreover, the justices on the Court today appear to value precedent more than justices have in the past.

Other studies of the influence of precedent have looked at the legal rules announced in **majority opinions** to see if judges apply them consistently. Mark Richards and Herbert Kritzer suggested that certain landmark precedents create **jurisprudential regimes** that establish criteria for judges to apply in future cases.[17] For example, *Roe v. Wade* (1973) established a trimester framework for evaluating abortion cases, which was then replaced in *Planned Parenthood v. Casey* (1992) with the undue burden test. Richards and Kritzer observed that even when judges reach different policy results, they can still be faithful to precedents if they apply the specified rules. Not every regulation poses an undue burden to abortion rights, for example. It could be entirely compatible with principles of stare decisis for judges to uphold abortion regulations after *Casey*, even though the original precedent supported abortion rights. It is the judges' acceptance of the undue burden test, and their consistent application of it, that matters.

One jurisprudential regime that Richards and Kritzer found to be particularly influential is the Lemon Test.[18] Established in *Lemon v. Kurtzman* (1971), the Lemon Test outlined criteria for determining whether a law violated the Establishment Clause of the First Amendment.[19] According to the Court, a law would be struck down if any of three conditions were met: the law lacked a secular purpose; its primary effect either advanced or inhibited religion; or the law created excessive governmental entanglement with religion. Richards and Kritzer looked at Establishment Clause cases in the years before and after *Lemon* and found that the standards the justices used to evaluate government laws changed in response to the precedent. Before *Lemon*, the justices were not more likely to strike down a law because it had a secular purpose, but after *Lemon* they were. Before *Lemon*, the neutrality of a law had no impact on the outcome of Establishment Clause cases, but after *Lemon* it did have an effect. The Court applied the Lemon Test consistently, even though the justices did not always use it to achieve the exact same policy result that they did in *Lemon*.

Some people might say that the Supreme Court should be more responsive to stare decisis, but it is important to remember that the justices are technically not obligated to follow their own precedents. The Court can change its rules if it wants to, and there might be principled reasons for them to do so, as they indicated in *Planned Parenthood v. Casey*. The Supreme Court's control over case selection also means that the justices can screen out cases in which their precedents clearly determine the results, dismissing such "easy" cases summarily. More commonly, the justices are interpreting precedents or deciding whether and how to extend them. It might therefore be unreasonable to expect the justices to engage in precedential voting more frequently than they do.

Lower courts are bound to follow the precedents of higher courts and have less control over case selection. Not surprisingly, judges on these courts are more likely to engage in precedential voting behavior, as I discuss later in the chapter. When considering the influence of precedent on judging, it is important to think about what your theoretical expectations are and how they might vary depending on the context. How responsive to precedent do we expect judges to be? Do we expect all judges to react the same way? Are there occasions when other legal principles might matter more and lead to different outcomes? After all, stare decisis is just one legal principle that judges might take into account, and it is not necessarily the most important one.

Legal Persuasiveness

A second legal goal is for judges to endorse legally persuasive arguments. The legal model predicts that judges will be more likely to side with litigants who have better defended, more well-reasoned interpretations of the law. "I firmly believe in the fidelity to the law," said Justice Sonia Sotomayor at her confirmation hearings. "In every case I approach, I start from that working proposition and apply the law to the facts before us."[20] Judges who favor persuasive legal arguments enhance the overall quality of law by producing coherent and principled legal doctrine. "That is how I seek to strengthen both the rule of law and faith in the impartiality of the justice system," said Sotomayor.

The difficulty for researchers, and for judges too, is that there is no consensus about what a persuasive legal argument looks like. Judges can be persuaded by many things. Some judges are interested in the plain meaning of legal texts, while others might be more interested in knowing what the drafters of a law had in mind when they wrote it. Still other judges might focus on the contemporary understanding of a legal text or the societal implications of their prospective judgments, looking to law review articles and even international law for guidance.

Not surprisingly, then, social scientists who have focused on particular types of legal arguments have found that they do not have a consistent influence on judging. Take originalism, for example, which is the idea that judges should interpret legal texts consistently with their original meanings. Researchers have found that originalist sources only occasionally lead justices to reach conclusions that are different from their policy preferences.[21] Frank Cross examined the percentage of the time that justices voted liberally when they cited originalist sources, expecting that if originalist sources had a persuasive influence on judicial behavior, then the justices would moderate their policy views when they were citing these materials.[22] His results are in Figure 3.4.

What do you think? To what extent are the data consistent with the view that originalist sources influence judicial behavior? To what extent are they inconsistent? It is striking that two of the justices who are the most closely associated with originalist sources, Scalia and Thomas, show almost no differences in their voting behavior when they cite these sources, although Justice Thomas does become slightly more liberal than expected when he cites originalist materials. A few other justices exhibit stronger effects, with Justices Black, Marshall,

Figure 3.4 The Influence of Originalist Sources on Supreme Court Voting Behavior

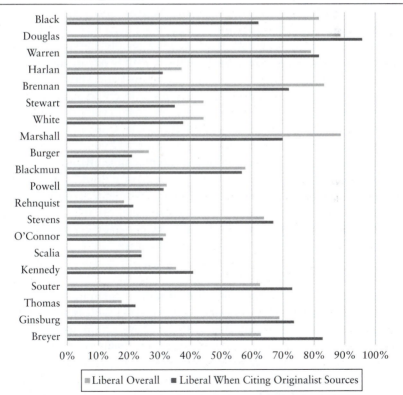

Source: Frank Cross, *The Failed Promise of Originalism* (Stanford, CA: Stanford University Press, 2013).

and Brennan all voting more conservatively when they cite originalist materials. But a few other justices cite originalist sources in ways that reinforce their policy views. Justices Breyer and Souter, for example, become *more* liberal than usual when they cite these sources.

At most, then, one can conclude that judges disagree about which legal arguments are persuasive. By looking at only particular forms of evidence, such as originalism, one is unlikely to find strong support for the legal model. Some political scientists have gotten around this problem by constructing composite measures of legally persuasive arguments. For example, Pamela Corley, Amy Steigerwalt, and Artemus Ward combined several legal considerations together into a "legal certainty" index.[23] They defined a "certain" outcome as one in which the law is not complex, when there is consensus among the lower courts about the result, and when there is less interest group participation, among other factors. They hypothesized that judges will be more likely to favor legal arguments that share these features, and in fact they did find that Supreme Court justices are less likely to vote based on their policy preferences when legal certainty is high.

Other political scientists have defined legally persuasive arguments with reference to how well supported they are in the broader legal community. Research by Stefanie Lindquist and David Klein has shown that Supreme Court justices are more likely to select answers to legal questions that have widespread support in the lower courts.[24] Lindquist and Klein also found that the justices are more likely to support legal arguments that have been endorsed by judges with prestigious reputations.[25] "We can think of no plausible attitudinal explanation for this finding," they write.[26] What do you think? How would you go about measuring a persuasive legal argument? Are there some sources of law that judges should give more weight than others? What would convince you that judges are actually persuaded by the law and are not just using it to disguise attitudinal voting?

Judicial Self-Restraint

A third legal principle is **judicial self-restraint,** or deference to the rules of other policymakers. A restrained judge is one who is reluctant to strike down legislation or interfere with executive action, instead deferring to the choices of the people's elected representatives. The arguments in favor of judicial self-restraint are perhaps the strongest on tribunals such as the U.S. Supreme Court and other federal courts, which are unelected and lack direct accountability to the voting public. But even in state judiciaries, where many judges are elected, principled judges might resist second-guessing legislatures and overturn statutes only when there is no alternative.

Perhaps the most prominent recent advocate of judicial self-restraint is Chief Justice John Roberts, who during his confirmation hearings characterized himself as a "modest" judge. (See Box 3.2.) "I don't think the courts should have a dominant role in society and stressing society's problems," Roberts said. "It is their job to say what the law is."[27] It is open to question just how committed Chief Justice Roberts has actually been to principles of judicial self-restraint. On the one hand, he did vote twice to uphold the Affordable Care Act, otherwise known as Obamacare, even though he probably disagreed with the law as a matter of policy.[28] But, on the other hand, the chief justice's decision to strike down campaign finance legislation in *Citizens United v. Federal Election Commission* (2010) was not particularly restrained, nor was his decision in *Shelby County v. Holder* (2013) to invalidate portions of the Voting Rights Act.[29]

Social scientists who have studied the subject of judicial self-restraint have found that Supreme Court justices have varying levels of commitment to this principle. Michael Bailey and Forrest Maltzman studied cases in which the constitutionality of congressional legislation was at issue to see how deferential individual justices are to Congress. Their findings are in Figure 3.5. It estimates changes in the probability that justices would cast conservative votes when deference to Congress was implicated, after controlling for the justices' ideology. What do you think? Do Supreme Court justices adhere to principles of judicial self-restraint? In recent years, the answer would seem to be no, although it is worth noting that Chief Justice John Roberts was not included in the analysis. Otherwise, not since the Burger Court have there regularly been justices who were even moderately deferential to Congress. Many of the most restrained justices, such as Reed, Burton, Minton, and Frankfurter, retired from the bench in the middle of the twentieth century.

Of course, not all justices claim to be committed to principles of judicial self-restraint. Justice Kennedy puts more of an emphasis on liberty, which in recent terms has led him to strike down state regulations of abortion and same-sex marriage,[30] while Justice Thomas focuses more on enforcing the original meaning of constitutional words and phrases, so it is not surprising that Bailey and Maltzman found these two justices to be among the least deferential to Congress. Even Chief Justice Roberts said during his confirmation hearings that it is "emphatically the obligation of the courts" to strike

TEXTBOX 3.2 | Modest Judging

During his confirmation hearings to be chief justice of the United States, John Roberts called himself a "modest" judge. What do you think he meant by this? Read the excerpt below and see if you agree with Chief Justice Roberts's conception of the judicial role. Should judges be modest, as he suggests, or play a more active role in society?

Confirmation Hearings of Chief Justice John Roberts
Day Two, September 13, 2005

Like most people, I resist the labels. I have told people, when pressed, that I prefer to be known as a modest judge. . . . It means an appreciation that the role of the judge is limited; the judge is to decide the cases before them; they're not to legislate; they're not to execute the laws. Another part of that humility has to do with respect for precedent that forms part of the rule of law that the judge is obligated to apply under principles of stare decisis. Part of that modesty has to do with being open to the considered views of your colleagues on the bench. I would say that's one of the things I've learned the most in the past two years on the court of appeals: how valuable it is to function in a collegial way with your colleagues on the bench; other judges being open to your views; you being open to theirs. They, after all, are in the same position you're in. They've read the same briefs. They've heard the same arguments. They've looked at the same cases. If they're seeing things in a very different way, you need to be open to that and try to take another look at your view and make sure that you're on solid ground.

Now, I think that general approach results in a modest approach to judging, which is good for the legal system as a whole. I don't think the courts should have a dominant role in society and stressing society's problems. It is their job to say what the law is. That's what Chief Justice Marshall said, of course, in *Marbury v. Madison*. And, yes, there will be times when either the executive branch or the legislative branch exceeds the limits of their powers under the Constitution or transgresses one of the provisions of the Bill of Rights. Then it is emphatically the obligation of the courts to step up and say what the Constitution provides, and to strike down either unconstitutional legislation or unconstitutional executive action. But the court has to appreciate that the reason they have that authority is because they are interpreting the law. They are not making policy. And to the extent they go beyond their confined limits and make policy or execute the law, they lose their legitimacy. And I think that calls into question the authority they will need when it's necessary to act in the face of unconstitutional action.

Figure 3.5 Relative Deference of U.S. Supreme Court Justices to Congress

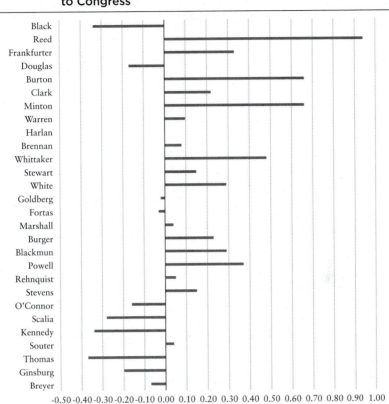

Source: Michael A. Bailey and Forrest Maltzman, *The Constrained Court: Law, Politics, and the Decisions Justices Make* (Princeton, NJ: Princeton University Press, 2011).

down a government policy "when either the executive branch or the legislative branch exceeds the limits of their powers under the Constitution."[31] Once again, then, it would seem that judges can disagree about what it means to be principled.

EVIDENCE FOR THE LEGAL MODEL ON THE SUPREME COURT

What is the extent of the law's influence on judging? Answering this question is complicated by the variety of considerations that might impact on particular legal questions, as the sections above described. Judges might put different weight on principles of stare decisis or judicial self-restraint, or find other legal arguments to be more persuasive.

The influence of legal goals might also vary across courts. On the U.S. Supreme Court, the justices have more flexibility than other judges to act on their sincere policy preferences, for reasons discussed in the previous chapter. Evidence for the legal model might therefore be stronger on lower courts. But even on the Supreme Court, there are at least three behaviors that are probably best explained by the legal model.

First is the fact that many Supreme Court decisions are unanimous. With all of the talk in the news media about how divided the justices are in landmark cases, and how polarized the Court has become, one might expect to find that the justices were dividing 5–4 all of the time. But Figure 3.6 shows that, on the Roberts Court, the most common outcome has been for the Supreme Court to be unanimous, which occurs in about 45.4 percent of cases. When decisions in which the justices have divided 8–1 and 7–2 are added to the total, the percentage rises to about 60.0 percent, which is further evidence that most Supreme Court decision making is strongly consensual.

How is it that justices routinely work together when they are as ideologically distant as Justices Sotomayor and Thomas? The attitudinal model might dismiss these as "easy" cases in which the law is the clearest, in which no self-respecting judge would reach a different

Figure 3.6 Vote Split in U.S. Supreme Court Merits Cases

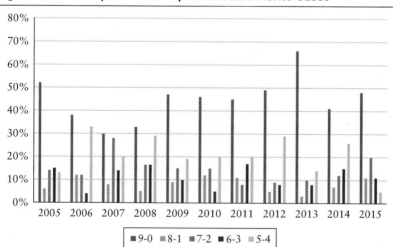

Source: "Stat Pack Archive," *ScotusBlog,* http://www.scotusblog.com/reference/stat-pack.

outcome. But the legal model would say that is exactly the point. On some matters, the outcomes might be so certain that it is difficult for judges to make other choices with legitimacy.[32] Legal persuasiveness outweighs ideological considerations in these cases. It is only when the law is unclear, or when legal questions are politically charged, that the justices divide along ideological lines.

Second, legal considerations do appear to influence the justices' case selection process. Rule 10 of the Supreme Court's rules states that the justices are more likely to accept cases for review when the courts below have given conflicting answers to the same legal questions. The justices are also more likely to review important cases. (See Judicial Process Box 3.2.) Research has found that, for the most part, the justices adhere to these criteria.[33] "We see it as a job of the Court to resolve federal conflicts," said a Supreme Court justice who was interviewed by H. W. Perry for his classic study of Supreme Court agenda-setting. "It is intolerable to have a certain law of the people in the Second Circuit and something else for people in the Eighth."[34]

The justices delay granting certiorari when a question is not yet ripe for review, even when they plan to address it eventually. For example, in the fall of 2014, the justices originally declined to consider whether same-sex marriage was protected by the Constitution because every federal court that had reviewed the question had agreed that state laws prohibiting same-sex marriage were unconstitutional. There was not yet a conflict in the circuits. As Justice Ginsburg said in remarks about the case at the University of Minnesota, "when all the courts of appeals are in agreement there is no need for us to rush to step in."[35] It was only when the Sixth Circuit created a conflict by upholding a marriage ban that the justices intervened, leading to the landmark holding in *Obergefell v. Hodges* (2015).[36]

A third form of behavior that is consistent with the legal model is the responsiveness of justices to specific legal arguments raised in the proceedings of a case. Using plagiarism software, researchers have found substantial similarities between Supreme Court opinions and the language used in lower court opinions and parties' briefs.[37] Paul Collins also found that justices consider legal arguments raised in **amicus briefs**, or "friend of the court" briefs.[38] Collins concluded that "a justice carefully reviews all of the available evidence and argumentation for the purpose of reaching a sound legal decision."[39] What do you think? Does this type of evidence persuade you that Supreme Court justices care about advancing legal goals? How else might we know whether the justices are committed to the rule of law?

JUDICIAL PROCESS BOX 3.2 | **Criteria for Granting Certiorari**

Most of the Supreme Court's docket is discretionary, which means that cases come to the justices in the form of petitions for a writ of certiorari, asking the justices to review the record of the lower-court proceedings. By convention, the justices grant certiorari when at least four of them agree that review is meritorious. This practice is known as the **Rule of Four**.

The justices have published rules outlining when they are more likely to grant review:

Rule 10. Considerations Governing Review on Writ of Certiorari

Review on a writ of certiorari is not a matter of right, but of judicial discretion. A petition for a writ of certiorari will be granted only for compelling reasons. The following, although neither controlling nor fully measuring the Court's discretion, indicate the character of the reasons the Court considers:

- (a) a United States court of appeals has entered a decision in conflict with the decision of another United States court of appeals on the same important matter; has decided an important federal question in a way that conflicts with a decision by a state court of last resort; or has so far departed from the accepted and usual course of judicial proceedings, or sanctioned such a departure by a lower court, as to call for an exercise of this Court's supervisory power;
- (b) a state court of last resort has decided an important federal question in a way that conflicts with the decision of another state court of last resort or of a United States court of appeals;
- (c) a state court or a United States court of appeals has decided an important question of federal law that has not been, but should be, settled by this Court, or has decided an important federal question in a way that conflicts with relevant decisions of this Court.

A petition for a writ of certiorari is rarely granted when the asserted error consists of erroneous factual findings or the misapplication of a properly stated rule of law.

EVIDENCE FOR THE LEGAL MODEL ON OTHER COURTS

Social scientists have also found evidence for the legal model on lower courts. Much like on the U.S. Supreme Court, most decisions on the U.S. courts of appeals are unanimous, although the rate of dissent has increased over the past century. Whereas in the 1920s dissents occurred in less than 5 percent of cases, by the 1990s the dissent rate was frequently over 10 percent.[40] Still, decision making on these tribunals remains strongly consensual. Lower-court judges are also more likely to follow precedent, particularly the rules set by higher courts, although it is unclear whether this behavior is intrinsically motivated or imposed by external constraints.

When asked to explain the high levels of consensual decision making, judges on the U.S. courts of appeals will say that many cases are easy ones in which the law is settled.[41] "We're hemmed in," said one judge interviewed by David Klein in his study of the federal circuits. "Within certain bounds, we can move around a bit. But there are some cases where we're very hemmed in."[42] Before he was a Supreme Court justice, Harry Blackmun served as a judge on the U.S. Court of Appeals for the Eighth Circuit. In *Ashe v. Swenson* (1968), Blackmun was asked to provide relief to a prisoner who had been denied his Fifth Amendment protection against **double jeopardy**. Although he suspected that the Supreme Court would be sympathetic to the prisoner's claims, Blackmun felt obligated to rule differently because the Supreme Court's precedents at the time pointed to a different result. "It usually is difficult for a lower federal court to forecast with assurance a Supreme Court decision as to the continuing validity of a holding of a decade ago," he wrote. "We feel, however, that our task is not to forecast but to follow those dictates."[43] As it turned out, Blackmun was correct that the justices would be open to a change of policy. The Supreme Court reversed Blackmun's judgment on appeal, and set a new precedent.[44]

Other evidence for the legal model includes the adherence of lower-court judges to the norm of **affirmance deference**, the principle that appellate judges are supposed to defer to a trial court judge's findings of fact. If appellate judges follow this principle, then they should have a greater tendency to affirm the cases they review, and in fact Frank Cross found strong evidence of this behavior on the U.S. courts of appeals. Moreover, Cross found that the rate of affirmance was higher when it was warranted as a matter of law. Trial judgments, which are entitled to the most deference, were affirmed at a rate of 68.0 percent, compared to a rate of 55.0 percent in other cases.[45] "These results are generally consistent with what the legal model would dictate," Cross concluded. "The highest affirmance rates are associated with the trial judgment context in which the greatest deference is due the lower court ruling."[46] Political scientists have also found that when lower federal court judges adopt new rules, they are guided by legal principles. Research by David Klein has shown that judges on the U.S. courts of appeals are more likely to adopt rules that have been developed by prestigious judges, or that have already been endorsed by judges in other circuits.[47]

The legal model does not deny that ideology influences judging. The evidence in favor of the attitudinal model is simply too persuasive to be ignored. In addition to legal influences, both Cross and Klein found that lower-court judges' sincere policy preferences affect their behavior. Instead of rejecting the influence of attitudes, the contemporary legal model would say that judges pursue legal goals in tandem with policy goals. Judges who seek to advance policy goals *also* care about maintaining consistency and stability in the law, authoring legally persuasive opinions, and deferring to the other branches of government. When you are thinking about judicial behavior, you should keep in mind that judges are capable of having multiple goals at once. How much would we expect any one of them to influence judicial behavior?

DISCUSSION QUESTIONS

1. Why do you think Justice Clarence Thomas dissented in *Lawrence v. Texas* (2003)? Do you take him at his word that legal principles explain his vote, or do you favor an attitudinal explanation? How would you know which view is correct?

2. Is it ever okay for judges to disregard precedent? When might it be acceptable for them to do so? Did the Supreme Court offer helpful guidelines for evaluating precedent in *Planned Parenthood v. Casey* (1992)? Why or why not?

3. What are the components of a persuasive legal argument? Would you be able to recognize a persuasive legal argument if you saw one? Would a judge? If you were a social scientist, how would you try to measure legal persuasiveness?

4. Judge Alex Kozinski denounces legal realism and other attitudinal theories of judging as "horse manure." Do you agree with Kozinski, or does he overstate his argument? Can judges be committed to both law and policy?

KEY TERMS

dissenting opinion

stare decisis

precedential voting

concurring opinion

preferential voting

majority opinion

jurisprudential regimes

judicial self-restraint

amicus briefs

Rule of Four

double jeopardy

affirmance deference

FURTHER READING

Baum, Lawrence. 1997. *The Puzzle of Judicial Behavior*. Ann Arbor, MI: University of Michigan Press.

Spaeth, Harold J., and Jeffrey A. Segal. 1999. *Majority Rule or Minority Will: Adherence to Precedent on the U.S. Supreme Court*. New York: Cambridge University Press.

Klein, David E. 2002. *Making Law in the United States Courts of Appeals*. New York: Cambridge University Press.

Cross, Frank. 2008. *Decision Making on the U.S. Courts of Appeals*. Stanford, CA: Stanford University Press.

Bailey, Michael A., and Forrest Maltzman. 2011. *The Constrained Court: Law, Politics, and the Decisions Justices Make*. Princeton, NJ: Princeton University Press.

Corley, Pamela C., Amy Steigerwalt, and Artemus Ward. 2013. *The Puzzle of Unanimity: Consensus on the United States Supreme Court*. Stanford, CA: Stanford University Press.

NOTES

1. Alex Kozinski, "What I Ate for Breakfast and Other Mysteries of Judicial Decision Making," *Loyola of Los Angeles Law Review* 26 (1993): 993.

2. *See* Mark C. Miller, *The High Priests of American Politics: The Role of Lawyers in American Political Institutions* (Knoxville: University of Tennessee Press, 1995), 21. "Learning how to think like a lawyer requires enormous and sometimes wrenching changes in how an individual sees and understands the world around them. Inherent in the teaching of a professional ideology is the view that law school must mold and reshape the mushy minds of law students." *See also* Lawrence Baum, *The Puzzle of Judicial Behavior* (Ann Arbor: University of Michigan Press, 1997); Arthur L. Stinchcombe, "Reason and Rationality," in *The Limits of Rationality*, ed. Karen Schweers Cook and Margaret Levi (University of Chicago Press, 1990), 285–317; J. Woodford Howard Jr., *Courts of Appeals in the Federal Judicial System: A Study of the Second, Fifth, and District of Columbia Circuits* (Princeton, NJ: Princeton University Press, 1981).

3. Richard A. Posner, "What Do Judges and Justices Maximize? (The Same Thing Everybody Else Does)," *Supreme Court Economic Review* 3 (1993): 28.

4. Kozinski, "What I Ate for Breakfast," 994.

5. Posner, "What Do Judges and Justices Maximize?," 7.

6. Id., 13. "Federal appellate judges, although they are in no way dependent upon the goodwill of the bar (unlike their counterparts in elected state judiciaries), are sensitive to their popularity with members of the bar, especially if, as is common, many of their friends are drawn from the bar. People like to be liked."

7. Id., 5. Judge Posner goes on to say that judges can be "reprimanded for ethical lapses, verge on or even slide into senility, be continually reversed for elementary legal mistakes, hold under advisement for years cases that could be decided perfectly well in days or weeks, leak confidential information to the press, pursue a nakedly political agenda, and misbehave in other ways that might get even a tenured civil servant or university professor fired."

8. Kozinski, "What I Ate for Breakfast," 995.

9. Planned Parenthood v. Casey, 505 U.S. 833 (1992).

10. Id., at 860–61.

11. Harold J. Spaeth and Jeffrey A. Segal, *Majority Rule or Minority Will: Adherence to Precedent on the U.S. Supreme Court* (New York: Cambridge University Press, 1999), 4.

12. Id., 3–4.

13. Georgia v. McCollum, 505 U.S. 42, at 52 (1992).

14. Fisher v. University of Texas, 579 U.S. ___ (2016).

15. *But see* Donald R. Songer and Stefanie A. Lindquist, "Not the Whole Story: The Impact of Justices' Values on Supreme Court Decisionmaking," *American Journal of Political Science* 40 (1996): 1049–63 (arguing that precedential voting increases when summary judgments are included in the sample of progeny cases); *see also* Saul Brenner and Marc Stier, "Retesting Segal and Spaeth's Stare Decisis Model," *American Journal of Political Science* 40 (1996): 1036–48.

16. Michael A. Bailey and Forrest Maltzman, *The Constrained Court: Law, Politics, and the Decisions Justices Make* (Princeton, NJ: Princeton University Press, 2011).

17. Mark J. Richards and Herbert M. Kritzer, "Jurisprudential Regimes in Supreme Court Decision Making," *American Political Science Review* 96 (2002): 305–20; *but see* Jeffrey R. Lax and Kelly T. Rader, "Legal Constraints on Supreme Court Decision Making: Do Jurisprudential Regimes Exist?," *Journal of Politics* 72 (2010): 282 (finding "only weak evidence that major Supreme Court precedents affect the way the justices themselves vote in subsequent cases"). *See also* Brandon L. Bartels, "The Constraining Capacity of Legal Doctrine on the U.S. Supreme Court," *American Political Science Review* 103 (2009): 474–95 (finding that strict scrutiny constrains judicial policy preferences); *and* Thomas G. Hansford and James F. Spriggs II, *The Politics of Precedent on the Supreme Court* (Princeton, NJ: Princeton University Press, 2006) (finding that precedent both constrains justices and provides them with opportunities to shape the law).

18. Herbert M. Kritzer and Mark J. Richards, "Jurisprudential Regimes and Supreme Court Decisionmaking: The Lemon Regime and Establishment Clause Cases," *Law & Society Review* 37 (2003): 827–40.

19. Lemon v. Kurtzman, 403 U.S. 602 (1971).

20. "Sotomayor Confirmation Hearings, Day Two," *New York Times*, July 14, 2009, http://www.nytimes.com/2009/07/14/us/politics/14confirm-text.html?_r=0.

21. Robert M. Howard and Jeffrey A. Segal, "An Original Look at Originalism," *Law & Society Review* 36: 113–38.

22. Frank B. Cross, *The Failed Promise of Originalism* (Stanford, CA: Stanford University Press, 2013). Cross defines originalist materials as "the leading originalist sources employed by the Court (*The Federalist, Elliot's Debates,* and *Farrand*), as well as leading roughly contemporary dictionaries and the Declaration of Independence" (72).

23. Pamela C. Corley, Amy Steigerwalt, and Artemus Ward, *The Puzzle of Unanimity: Consensus on the United States Supreme Court* (Stanford, CA: Stanford University Press, 2013).

24. Stefanie Lindquist and David E. Klein, "The Influence of Jurisprudential Considerations on Supreme Court Decisionmaking: A Study of Conflict Cases," *Law & Society Review* 40 (2006): 135–62.

25. Lindquist and Klein define a prestigious judge as one who has been cited frequently by name by judges in other jurisdictions. *See also* David Klein and Darby Morrisroe, "The Prestige and Influence of Individual Judges on the U.S. Courts of Appeals," *Journal of Legal Studies* 28 (1999): 371–91.

26. Lindquist and Klein, "The Influence of Jurisprudential Considerations," 154.

27. "Day Two of the Roberts Confirmation Hearings," *Washington Post*, September 13, 2005, http://www.washingtonpost.com/wp-dyn/content/article/2005/09/13/AR2005091300876.html.

28. National Federation of Independent Business v. Sebelius, 567 U.S. ___ (2012); King v. Burwell, 576 U.S. ___ (2015).

29. Citizens United v. FEC, 558 U.S. 310 (2010); Shelby County v. Holder 570 U.S. ___ (2013).

30. Whole Woman's Health v. Hellerstedt, 579 U.S. ___ (2016); Obergefell v. Hodges, 576 U.S. ___ (2015).

31. "Day Two of the Roberts Confirmation Hearings."

32. *See* Corley et al., *The Puzzle of Unanimity.*

33. *See, for example,* Joseph Tanenhaus, Marvin Schick, Matthew Muraskin, and Daniel Rosen, "The Supreme Court's Certiorari Jurisdiction: Cue Theory," in *Judicial Decision Making,* ed. Glendon Schubert (Glencoe, IL: The Free Press, 1963), 111–32; S. Sidney Ulmer, "The Supreme Court's Certiorari Decisions: Conflict as a Predictive Variable," *American Political Science Review* 78 (1984): 901–11; Ryan C. Black and Ryan J. Owens, "Agenda Setting in the Supreme Court: The Collision of Policy and Jurisprudence," *Journal of Politics* 71 (2009): 1062–75.

34. H. W. Perry Jr., *Deciding to Decide: Agenda Setting in the United States Supreme Court* (Cambridge, MA: Harvard University Press, 1991), 247.

35. "Justice Ruth Bader Ginsburg in Conversation at the Law School," University of Minnesota Law School, available at https://youtu.be/ByFnOE0f1Z8.

36. Obergefell v. Hodges, 576 U.S. ___ (2015).

37. Pamela C. Corley, Paul M. Collins Jr., and Bryan Calvin, "Lower Court Influence on U.S. Supreme Court Opinion Content," *Journal of Politics* 73

(2011): 31–44; Pamela C. Corley, "The Supreme Court and Opinion Content: The Influence of Parties' Briefs," *Political Research Quarterly* 61 (2008): 468–78.

38. Paul M. Collins Jr., *Friends of the Supreme Court: Interest Groups and Judicial Decision Making* (New York: Oxford University Press, 2008).

39. Id., 175.

40. Donald R. Songer, Reginald S. Sheehan, and Susan B. Haire, *Continuity and Change on the United States Courts of Appeals*, Ann Arbor, MI: University of Michigan Press (2000), 104–7.

41. J. Woodford Howard Jr., *Courts of Appeals in the Federal Judicial System: A Study of the Second, Fifth, and District of Columbia Circuits* (Princeton, NJ: Princeton University Press, 1981), 187.

42. David E. Klein, *Making Law in the United States Courts of Appeals* (New York: Cambridge University Press, 2002), 23.

43. Ashe v. Swenson, 399 F.2d 40 (8th Cir., 1968).

44. Ashe v. Swenson, 397 U.S. 436 (1970).

45. Frank B. Cross, *Decision Making on the U.S. Courts of Appeals* (Stanford, CA: Stanford University Press, 2007), 49–53.

46. Id., 51.

47. Klein, *Making Law in the United States Courts of Appeals*, 75–81.

In Their Own Words:
Judge Alex Kozinski, Ninth Circuit Court of Appeals

Judge Alex Kozinski delivered these remarks on March 19, 1993, at the Symposium on the California Judiciary at Loyola Law School, Los Angeles. In them, he makes a strong defense of the influence of the law on judging. What do you think? Do you agree with Judge Kozinski that legal realism and, by implication, the attitudinal model, are inaccurate accounts of judicial behavior?

What I Ate for Breakfast and Other Mysteries of Judicial Decision Making
Alex Kozinski

It is popular in some circles to suppose that judicial decision making can be explained largely by frivolous factors, perhaps for example the relationship between what judges eat and what they decide. Answering questions about such relationships is quite simple—it is like being asked to write a scholarly essay on the snakes of Ireland: There are none.

But as far back as I can remember in law school, the notion was advanced with some vigor that judicial decision making is a farce. Under this theory, what judges do is glance at a case and decide who should win—and they do this on the basis of their digestion (or how they slept the night before or some other variety of personal factors). If the judge has a good breakfast and a good night's sleep, he might feel lenient and jolly, and sympathize with the downtrodden. If he had indigestion or a bad night's sleep, he might be a grouch and take it out on the litigants. Of course, even judges can't make both sides lose; I know, I've tried. So a grouchy mood, the theory went, is likely to cause the

judge to take it out on the litigant he least identifies with, usually the guy who got run over by the railroad or is being foreclosed on by the bank. This theory immodestly called itself Legal Realism.

Just to prove that even the silliest idea can be pursued to its illogical conclusion, Legal Realism spawned Critical Legal Studies. As I understand this so-called theory, the notion is that because legal rules don't mean much anyway, and judges can reach any result they wish by invoking the right incantation, they should engraft their own political philosophy onto the decision-making process and use their power to change the way our society works. So, if you accept that what a judge has for breakfast affects his decisions that day, judges should be encouraged to have a consistent diet so their decisions will consistently favor one set of litigants over the other.

I am here to tell you that this is all horse manure. And, like all horse manure, it contains little seeds of truth from which tiny birds can take intellectual nourishment. The little truths are these: Under our law judges do in fact have considerable discretion in certain of their decisions: making findings of fact, interpreting language in the Constitution, statutes and regulations; determining whether officials of the executive branch have abused their discretion; and, fashioning remedies for violations of the law, including fairly sweeping powers to grant injunctive relief. The larger reality, however, is that judges exercise their powers subject to very significant constraints. They simply can't do anything they well please.

These constraints come in many forms, some subtle, some quite obvious. I want to focus here only on three that I believe are among the most important. The first, and to my mind the most significant, is internal: the judge's own self-respect. Cynics and academics (a redundancy) tend to belittle this if they consider it at all. Don't make that mistake. Judges have to look in the mirror at least once a day, just like everyone else; they have to like what they see. Heaven knows, we don't do it for the money; if you can't have your self-respect, you might as well make megabucks doing leveraged buyouts.

More concretely, the job is just too big to be done by one person alone. You are surrounded by eager young law clerks far too smart to be fooled by nonsense. I know of no judge who will tell his law clerks: "I want to reach this result, write me an opinion to get me there." You have to give them reasons, and those reasons better be pretty good—any law clerk worth his salt will argue with you if the reasons you give are unconvincing. Should you choose to abandon principle to reach a result, you will not be able to fool yourself into believing you're just following the law. It will have to be a deliberate choice, and it's a choice that, by and large, judges tend not to make. As Senator Thurmond said at my investiture as Chief Judge of the Claims Court in 1982, "You are in a different world when you put a robe on. It is something that just makes you feel that you have got to do what is right, whether you want to or not. I think the moment you put on that robe, you enter this ultraworld." A little corny, perhaps, but true.

The second important constraint comes from your colleagues. If you're a district judge, your decisions are subject to review by three judges of the court of appeals. If you are a circuit judge, you have to persuade at least one other colleague, preferably two, to join your opinion. Even then, litigants petition for rehearing and en banc review with annoying regularity. Your shortcuts, errors and oversights are mercilessly paraded before the entire court and, often enough, someone will call for an en banc vote.

If you survive that, judges who strongly disagree with your approach will file a dissent from the denial of en banc rehearing. If powerful enough, or if joined by enough judges, it will make your opinion subject to close scrutiny by the Supreme Court, vastly increasing the chances that certiorari will be granted. Even Supreme Court Justices are subject to the constraints of colleagues and the judgments of a later Court.

Now, don't get me wrong, just about any judge can get away with cutting a corner here or there. There are too many cases and too little time to catch all the errors, deliberate or unintentional. But what you absolutely cannot get away with is abandoning legal principles in favor of results on a consistent basis. Any judge who tries to do this cuts deeply into his credibility and becomes suspect among his colleagues. There are, from time to time, district judges whose decisions come to the court of appeals with a presumption of reversibility. I have heard lawyers say, with good reason, that they dread winning before those judges because it becomes very difficult to defend their judgments on appeal. Circuit judges who break the rules too often become especially vulnerable to en banc calls and ultimately to reversal by the Supreme Court. . . .

The third important constraint on judicial excesses lies in the political system, a constraint often overlooked but awesome nonetheless. By its nature, the political process seldom reacts to specific cases, although it does so from time to time. The passage of the Civil Rights Act of 1991 was exclusively a response to five Supreme Court decisions from the recent terms; Congress believed the Court had misread civil rights legislation and moved swiftly and decisively to overrule the decisions by statute. But the political process occasionally operates in even blunter ways. Examples of these from the past are FDR's plan to pack the Supreme Court and proposals to clip the federal courts' jurisdiction over sensitive matters. . . .

Now, there is an unspoken premise to what I have said, namely that there are more or less objective principles by which the law operates, principles that dictate the reasoning and often the result in most cases. I know you are taught to doubt this in law school, as I was; it is nevertheless true. Now, these principles are not followed by every judge in every case, and even when followed, there is frequently some room for the exercise of personal judgment.

But none of this means principles don't exist or that judges can use them interchangeably or ignore them altogether. Let me give you an example of one principle I think is extremely important: Language has meaning. This doesn't mean every word is as precisely defined as every other word, or that words always have a single, immutable meaning. What it does mean is that language used in statutes, regulations, contracts and the Constitution place an objective constraint on our conduct. The precise line may be debatable at times, but at the very least the language used sets an outer boundary that those interpreting and applying the law must respect. When the language is narrowly drawn, the constraints are fairly strict;

when it is drawn loosely they're more generous, but in either case they do exist. Let me illustrate.

An example of a Constitutional provision that is very strict is contained in Article II, Section 1, Clause 5: "No person except a natural born Citizen, or a Citizen of the United States, at the time of the Adoption of this Constitution, shall be eligible to the Office of the President. . . ." This language allows little or no room for interpretation. While there could possibly be some debate as to whether someone born of American parents abroad would be considered a natural born citizen, there is absolutely no room to argue that someone like me, who was born outside the United States to foreign parents, is eligible to be President. Language here, indeed, provides a firm and meaningful constraint on conduct.

Obviously not all clauses of the Constitution are as narrowly drawn as this provision. For example, the Fourth Amendment prohibits unreasonable searches and seizures. What is unreasonable is subject to judgment. But it is not a judgment made in a vacuum. It must be made in light of almost two centuries of interpretation and our shared notions of individual privacy and personal autonomy. I submit that, regardless of what any particular judge may subjectively think, a warrantless nighttime search of every house on a particular block would not be reasonable. Again, marginal cases may present difficult line-drawing problems, but this doesn't negate the fact that the language of the Constitution does provide a meaningful constraint for the large majority of cases.

Another very important principle is that judges must deal squarely with precedent. They may not ignore it or distinguish it on an insubstantial or trivial basis. Few of us write on a truly clean slate and what has gone before provides an important constraint on what we can do in cases now before us. Precedent, like language, frequently leaves room for judgment. But there is a difference between judgment and dishonesty, between distinguishing precedent and burying it. Judges get incensed when lawyers fail to cite controlling authority or when they misstate the holdings of cases they cannot distinguish in a principled fashion. When judges do this, it is doubly shameful, because the results are far more damaging. I've heard lawyers complain, with good reason, that within the same circuit there will be two lines of authority on the very same subject. The two lines go off in different directions without acknowledging each other's existence, like ships passing in the night. In such circumstances lawyers have much difficulty in advising clients how to conduct their affairs, the rule of law depending on who the judges in their case happen to be.

Let me give you a final principle that's not frequently recognized as such, but is, in my view, extremely important. We all view reality from our own peculiar perspective; we all have biases, interests, leanings, instincts. These are important. Frequently, something will bother you about a case that you can't quite put into words, will cause you to doubt the apparently obvious result. It is important to follow those instincts, because they can lead to a crucial issue that turns out to make a difference. But it is even more important to doubt your own leanings, to be skeptical of your instincts. It is frequently very difficult to tell the difference between how you think a case should be decided and how you hope it will come out. It is very easy to take sides in a case and subtly shade the decision-making process in favor of the party you favor, much like the Legal Realists predict. My prescription is not, however, to yield to these impulses with abandon, but to fight them. If you, as a judge, find yourself too happy with the result in a case, stop and think. Is that result justified by the law, fairly and honestly applied to the facts? Or is it merely a bit of self-indulgence?

Judging is a job where self-indulgence is a serious occupational hazard. One must struggle against it constantly if one is to do the job right. I guess what I ultimately object to in the teachings of the Legal Realists and their modern day disciples is that they play on judges' already inflated egos by telling them that they can follow their leanings with abandon and everything will be all right. Everything will not be all right. There are awesome forces in our society that extract a heavy price for judicial self-indulgence. Judges have traditionally held a special place in the public's mind as arbiters of our disputes and protectors of our individual freedoms. But judges can only do that job if they are trusted. . . . Woe be us when that trust in the judiciary is lost. If the public should become convinced—as many academicians apparently are—that judges are reaching results not based on principle but to serve a political agenda, unpopular decisions will become not merely points of dissatisfaction but the impetus for far-reaching changes that will affect our way of life for years to come, perhaps permanently. . . .

Originally published as Alex Kozinski, "What I Ate for Breakfast and Other Mysteries of Judicial Decision Making," *Loyola of Los Angeles Law Review* 26 (1993): 993.

CASE ANALYSIS

Planned Parenthood v. Casey, 505 U.S. 833 (1992)

In the landmark abortion case Planned Parenthood v. Casey *(1992), the Supreme Court announced the criteria that it would use for evaluating, and perhaps overturning, its own precedents. Applying these criteria, the justices declined to overturn* Roe v. Wade *(1973), although they did replace* Roe's *original trimester framework with an "undue burden" test. In your view, how useful are the Court's criteria for overturning precedents? Would you change the criteria in any way? What would you say to critics such as Justice Scalia, in dissent, who maintain that the justices are not really applying these criteria at all but are voting their policy preferences?*

JUSTICES O'CONNOR, KENNEDY, and SOUTER delivered the opinion of the Court
The obligation to follow precedent begins with necessity, and a contrary necessity marks its outer limit. With Cardozo, we recognize that no judicial system could do society's work if it eyed each issue afresh in every case that raised it. See B. Cardozo, *The Nature of the Judicial Process* 149 (1921). Indeed, the very concept of the rule of law underlying our own Constitution requires such continuity over time that a respect for precedent is, by definition, indispensable. At the other extreme, a different necessity would make itself felt if a prior judicial ruling should come to be seen so clearly as error that its enforcement was for that very reason doomed.

Even when the decision to overrule a prior case is not, as in the rare, latter instance, virtually foreordained, it is common wisdom that the rule of *stare decisis* is not an "inexorable command," and certainly it is not such in every constitutional case. Rather, when this Court reexamines a prior holding, its judgment is customarily informed by a series of prudential and pragmatic considerations designed to test the consistency of overruling a prior decision with the ideal of the rule of law, and to gauge the respective costs of reaffirming and overruling a prior case. Thus, for example, we may ask whether the rule has proven to be intolerable simply in defying practical workability; whether the rule is subject to a kind of reliance that would lend a special hardship to the consequences of overruling and add inequity to the cost of repudiation; whether related principles of law have so far developed as to have left the old rule no more than a remnant of abandoned doctrine; or whether facts have so changed, or come to be seen so differently, as to have robbed the old rule of significant application or justification.

So in this case we may enquire whether *Roe*'s central rule has been found unworkable; whether the rule's limitation on state power could be removed without serious inequity to those who have relied upon it or significant damage to the stability of the society governed by it; whether the law's growth in the intervening years has left *Roe*'s central rule a doctrinal anachronism discounted by society; and whether *Roe*'s premises of fact have so far changed in the ensuing two decades as to render its central holding somehow irrelevant or unjustifiable in dealing with the issue it addressed.

Although *Roe* has engendered opposition, it has in no sense proven "unworkable," representing as it does a simple limitation beyond which a state law is unenforceable. While *Roe* has, of course, required judicial assessment of state laws affecting the exercise of the choice guaranteed against government infringement, and although the need for such review will remain as a consequence of today's decision, the required determinations fall within judicial competence.

The inquiry into reliance counts the cost of a rule's repudiation as it would fall on those who have relied reasonably on the rule's continued application. Since the classic case for weighing reliance heavily in favor of following the earlier rule occurs in the commercial context, where advance planning of great precision is most obviously a necessity, it is no cause for surprise that some would find no reliance worthy of consideration in support of *Roe*.

While neither respondents nor their amici in so many words deny that the abortion right invites some reliance prior to its actual exercise, one can readily imagine an argument stressing the dissimilarity of this case to one involving property or contract. Abortion is customarily chosen as an unplanned response to the consequence of unplanned activity or to the failure of conventional birth control, and except on the assumption that no intercourse would have occurred but for *Roe*'s holding, such behavior may appear to justify no reliance claim. Even if reliance could be claimed on that unrealistic assumption, the argument might run, any reliance interest would be *de minimis*. This argument would be premised on the hypothesis that reproductive planning could take virtually immediate account of any sudden restoration of state authority to ban abortions.

To eliminate the issue of reliance that easily, however, one would need to limit cognizable reliance to specific instances of sexual activity. But to do this would be simply to refuse to face the fact that for two decades of economic and social developments, people have organized intimate relationships and made choices that define their views of themselves and their places in society, in reliance on the availability of abortion in the event that contraception should fail. The ability of women to participate equally in the economic and social life of the nation has been facilitated by their ability to control their reproductive lives. The Constitution serves human values, and while the effect of reliance on *Roe* cannot be exactly measured, neither can the certain cost of overruling *Roe* for people who have ordered their thinking and living around that case be dismissed.

No evolution of legal principle has left *Roe*'s doctrinal footings weaker than they were in 1973. No development of constitutional law since the case was decided has implicitly or explicitly left *Roe* behind as a mere survivor of obsolete constitutional thinking.

It will be recognized, of course, that *Roe* stands at an intersection of two lines of decisions, but in whichever doctrinal category one reads the case, the result for present purposes will be the same. The *Roe* Court itself placed its holding in the succession of cases most prominently exemplified by *Griswold v. Connecticut*, 381 U.S. 479 (1965). When it is so seen, *Roe* is clearly in no jeopardy, since subsequent constitutional developments have neither disturbed, nor do they threaten to diminish, the scope of recognized protection accorded to the liberty relating to intimate relationships, the family, and decisions about whether or not to beget or bear a child.

Roe, however, may be seen not only as an exemplar of *Griswold* liberty but as a rule (whether or not mistaken) of personal autonomy and bodily integrity, with doctrinal affinity to cases recognizing limits on governmental power to mandate medical treatment or to bar its rejection. If so, our cases since *Roe* accord with *Roe*'s view that a State's interest in the protection of life falls short of justifying any plenary override of individual liberty claims.

Finally, one could classify *Roe* as *sui generis*. If the case is so viewed, then there clearly has been no erosion of its central determination. The original holding resting on the concurrence of seven Members of the Court in 1973 was expressly affirmed by a majority of six in 1983, see *Akron v. Akron Center for Reproductive Health, Inc.*, 462 U.S. 416, and by a majority of five in 1986, see *Thornburgh v. American College of Obstetricians and Gynecologists*, 476 U.S. 747, expressing adherence to the constitutional ruling despite legislative efforts in some States to test its limits. More recently, in *Webster v. Reproductive Health Services*, 492 U.S. 490 (1989), although two of the present authors questioned the trimester framework in a way consistent with our judgment today, a majority of the Court either decided to reaffirm or declined to address the constitutional validity of the central holding of *Roe*. . . .

The soundness of this prong of the *Roe* analysis is apparent from a consideration of the alternative. If indeed the woman's interest in deciding whether to bear and beget a child had not been recognized as in *Roe*, the State might as readily restrict a woman's right to choose to carry a pregnancy to term as to terminate it, to further asserted state interests in population control, or eugenics, for example. Yet *Roe* has been sensibly relied upon to counter any such suggestions. In any event, because *Roe*'s scope is confined by the fact of its concern with postconception potential life, a concern otherwise likely to be implicated only by some forms of contraception protected independently under *Griswold* and later cases, any error in *Roe* is unlikely to have serious ramifications in future cases.

We have seen how time has overtaken some of *Roe*'s factual assumptions: advances in maternal health care allow for abortions safe to the mother later in pregnancy than was true in 1973, and advances in neonatal care have advanced viability to a point somewhat earlier. But these facts go only to the scheme of time limits on the realization of competing interests, and the divergences from the factual premises of 1973 have no bearing on the validity of *Roe*'s central holding, that viability marks the earliest point at which the State's interest in fetal life is constitutionally adequate to justify a legislative ban on nontherapeutic abortions. The soundness or unsoundness of that constitutional judgment in no sense turns on whether viability occurs at approximately 28 weeks, as was usual at the time of *Roe*, at 23 to 24 weeks, as it sometimes does today, or at some moment even slightly earlier in pregnancy, as it may if fetal respiratory capacity can somehow be enhanced in the future. Whenever it may occur, the attainment of viability may continue to serve as the critical fact, just as it has done since *Roe* was decided; which is to say that no change in *Roe*'s factual underpinning has left its central holding obsolete, and none supports an argument for overruling it.

The sum of the precedential enquiry to this point shows *Roe*'s underpinnings unweakened in any way affecting its central holding. While it has engendered disapproval, it has not been unworkable. An entire generation has come of age free to assume *Roe*'s concept of liberty in defining the capacity of women to act in society, and to make reproductive decisions; no erosion of principle going to liberty or personal autonomy has left *Roe*'s central holding a doctrinal remnant; *Roe* portends no developments at odds with other precedent for the analysis of personal liberty; and no changes of fact have rendered viability more or less appropriate as the point at which the balance of interests tips. Within the bounds of normal stare decisis analysis, then, and subject to the considerations on which it customarily turns, the stronger argument is for affirming *Roe*'s central holding, with whatever degree of personal reluctance any of us may have, not for overruling it.

JUSTICE SCALIA, dissenting

The authors of the joint opinion . . . do not squarely contend that *Roe v. Wade* was a correct application of "reasoned judgment"; merely that it must be followed, because of *stare decisis*. But in their exhaustive discussion of all the factors that go into the determination of when *stare decisis* should be observed and when disregarded, they never mention "how wrong was the decision on its face?" Surely, if "the Court's power lies . . . in its legitimacy, a product of substance and perception," the "substance" part of the equation demands that plain error be acknowledged and eliminated. *Roe* was plainly wrong—even on the Court's methodology of "reasoned judgment," and even more so (of course) if the proper criteria of text and tradition are applied. . . .

The Court's reliance upon *stare decisis* can best be described as contrived. It insists upon the necessity of adhering not to all of *Roe*, but only to what it calls the "central holding." It seems to me that *stare decisis* ought to be applied even to the doctrine of *stare decisis*, and I confess never to have heard of this new, keep-what-you-want-and-throw-away-the-rest version. . . .

I must confess, however, that I have always thought, and I think a lot of other people have always thought, that the arbitrary trimester framework, which the Court today discards, was quite as central to *Roe* as the arbitrary viability test, which the Court today retains. It seems particularly ungrateful to carve the trimester framework out of the core of *Roe*, since its very rigidity . . . is probably the only reason the Court is able to say, in urging *stare decisis*, that *Roe* "has in no sense proven 'unworkable.'" I suppose the Court is entitled to call a "central holding" whatever it wants to call a "central holding"—which is, come to think of it, perhaps one of the difficulties with this modified version of *stare decisis*.

4

The Strategic Model

THE THEORIES OF judicial behavior that you have studied so far have assumed that judges make choices based primarily on their own goals and preferences. But judging is a collaborative process, and the views of other actors might also influence their decision making. Consider, for example, the behavior of the justices on the Vermont Supreme Court when they were deciding whether to legalize same-sex marriage in *Baker v. Vermont* (1999).[1] At the time, all states prohibited same-sex marriage, and it would be years before the U.S. Supreme Court finally settled the question in *Obergefell v. Hodges* (2015).[2] Writing for the majority in *Baker*, Chief Justice Jeffrey L. Amestoy ruled that the Common Benefits Clause of Vermont's constitution required same-sex couples to receive the same benefits and protections as opposite-sex couples. (See case excerpt at the end of the chapter.)

However, the Court stopped short of requiring full marriage equality, ruling that the state legislature could create civil unions or domestic partnerships as a compromise. "We do not purport to infringe upon the prerogatives of the Legislature to craft an appropriate means of addressing this constitutional mandate," Chief Justice Amestoy wrote.[3] Why didn't the Court go further? Of course, it is possible that the justices got exactly the outcome they wanted. Maybe Chief Justice Amestoy was a moderate on gay rights issues or he believed in exercising restraint. But let us assume for a moment that Amestoy really did want to extend full marriage equality to gay people. What do you think could have happened? What kept Amestoy from achieving his goals?

The strategic model of judicial behavior would suggest that other actors influenced the chief justice's decision. A few years after *Baker*, Amestoy delivered a speech at Rutgers Law School in which he stated that his decision to settle for civil unions had been a strategic one, in response to external pressures that his court was facing at the time. (See the reading in this chapter, "Pragmatic Constitutionalism.") "Considerations of strategy have long been held suspect by constitutional scholars," Amestoy said. "But I cannot agree that the same skepticism ought to attach to the examination of strategic considerations in state constitutionalism." Amestoy explained that the Vermont Supreme Court's ruling had to be "persuasive to those with 'extra-judicial authority' to change the result (i.e., the Legislature and citizens of Vermont)."[4]

Chief Justice Amestoy knew that if the court had ordered the state legislature to do more than it was prepared to accept, then there could have been a backlash. The year before, the people of Hawaii had passed a state constitutional amendment to overturn another court decision that had tried to legalize same-sex marriage in that state, and it was easy to imagine a similar reaction occurring in Vermont.[5] What Amestoy did not say in his speech, but he must have known, was that the justices also could have lost their jobs if they had issued a decision that strayed too far from what the legislature wanted. Justices on the Vermont Supreme Court serve for six-year terms, after which they are reappointed by the state legislature. Legislators could have denied the justices reappointment if they thought the court was moving too far too fast.

Chief Justice Amestoy recognized that other actors had power to influence same-sex marriage policy, and that he needed to accommodate their preferences if his decision in *Baker* was going to endure. The strategic model maintains that these types of compromises are a routine feature of judging. Judges regularly consider the views of other actors, both on and off the court, and factor their goals and preferences into their decision making. These actors might include fellow judges, the legislative and executive branches, bureaucrats, and even the public. Strategic judges believe that by making compromises, they can be more effective decision makers in the long run, even if they end up having to sacrifice some of their immediate legal or policy goals.

OVERVIEW OF THE STRATEGIC MODEL

The strategic model is a theory of judging that holds that other actors influence judicial behavior. (See Figure 4.1.) Judges are embedded in

Figure 4.1   The Strategic Model

---

other actors   →   judicial behavior

(X)   (Y)

---

institutions with other people who have power to influence their decision making and require them to make compromises. The strategic model differs from the other two leading theories of judicial behavior that we have studied, the attitudinal and legal models, because it maintains that judicial behavior is not necessarily sincere. Judges cannot always get what they want, regardless of whether they are trying to achieve legal or policy goals, because their views are not the only ones that matter. Judging is an interactive process that requires judges to work with other people who have goals and preferences of their own.

The strategic model traces back to the work of Walter F. Murphy, whose *Elements of Judicial Strategy* (1964) described judging as a sophisticated process in which judges rationally seek to achieve their goals.[6] Years later, the theory received its fullest elaboration by Lee Epstein and Jack Knight in their landmark book, *The Choices Justices Make* (1998). Focusing primarily on the U.S. Supreme Court, Epstein and Knight described the justices as "strategic actors who realize that their ability to achieve their goals depends on a consideration of the preferences of other actors, the choices they expect others to make, and the institutional context in which they act."[7] Judges can use strategies to advance either legal or policy goals, but most research to date has assumed that judges are trying to advance their policy preferences.[8]

Judges employ numerous strategies in pursuit of their goals. **Policy-choice strategies** occur when judges make substantive changes to their favored policy choices to accommodate other actors. Chief Justice Amestoy's behavior in *Baker v. Vermont* is one example of a policy-choice strategy. Another is Justice William Brennan's opinion in the U.S. Supreme Court case *Craig v. Boren* (1976), discussed below. In both cases, judges could not get enough support for the policies they wanted, so they settled for policy alternatives that were less ambitious. The difference was that Chief Justice Amestoy was reacting to pressures from external actors whereas Justice Brennan was responding to colleagues inside the Court.

The question in *Craig v. Boren* was how the U.S. Supreme Court should evaluate claims of sex discrimination under the Fourteenth

Amendment's Equal Protection Clause. Justice Brennan was a strong proponent of women's rights, as revealed by his behavior three years earlier in *Frontiero v. Richardson* (1973). That case had involved a military policy that set different rules for the distribution of employment benefits based on sex. The wives of male employees automatically received benefits, but female employees had to prove that their husbands were really dependent on them. Justice Brennan believed that the military's policy was discriminatory and that it should be subjected to the most demanding standard of review. Applying **strict scrutiny**, Justice Brennan maintained that sex-based classifications needed to be justified by *compelling interests*, and that legislation had to be *narrowly tailored* to achieving those interests.

However, Justice Brennan could not get a majority of the Court to agree to use strict scrutiny. Only three other justices supported that analysis, so when the issue of sex discrimination came back to the Court a few years later, Justice Brennan decided to make a compromise. *Craig v. Boren* involved an Oklahoma law that let women purchase low-alcohol beer at a younger age than men. Once again, Justice Brennan believed that the law was discriminatory, but this time instead of applying strict scrutiny, Brennan used **intermediate scrutiny**. Under this test, legislation had to be justified by *important interests* and be *substantially related* to attaining those interests. By making this compromise, Brennan was able to attract one more vote. To this day, intermediate scrutiny is the standard the Supreme Court uses for sex discrimination cases.

Another way that judges can be strategic is with **instrument-choice strategies**. Judges who use these strategies do not change their favored policies but instead focus on how to defend them. Some of the earliest work on instrument-choice strategies was by Emerson H. Tiller and Pablo T. Spiller, who observed that "actors make choices not only about policy outcomes, but also the means (instruments) to achieve those policy outcomes."[9] Strategic judges will avoid selecting rationales for their decisions that make it more likely that higher courts will overturn them. In administrative law cases, for example, basing a decision on the substantive interpretation of a statute is more likely to attract the attention of higher courts than other legal grounds.[10]

Judges who use instrument-choice strategies are also more attentive to the sources that they cite in their opinions. For example, judges will cite a greater number of precedents when they expect their decisions to be controversial, such as when they are adopting new or far-reaching legal doctrines.[11] On the U.S. Supreme Court, justices are more likely to cite persuasive authorities, such as the Federalist Papers, when they are overturning acts of Congress or reconsidering their own precedents.[12] By including a greater number of citations, judges can make their choices seem better supported, and therefore more legitimate. "There is no better way to provide protective 'cover' for policy preferences than to assert the authority of a text widely considered the definitive assertion of the meaning and intent of the Constitution," wrote the authors of the study of the Federalist Papers. "The use of the Federalist Papers protects institutional legitimacy."[13]

Some people might say that judges should never engage in these strategies because they should be deciding cases based on their own independent judgments, not what others think. But the strategic model would suggest that judges must be forward thinking if they are going to be effective at their jobs. Judges who refuse to take the views of other actors into account might have trouble finding consensus with other judges, or they might end up making decisions that are out of touch with society or the rest of the political system. When you are thinking about judicial behavior, take some time to consider how interactive you think judging ought to be. When should judges be responsive to other actors? When would it be less appropriate?

STRATEGIC DECISION-MAKING CONTEXTS

Strategic judges respond to the preferences of many different actors. Most political science research on the strategic model focuses on the interactions that judges have with fellow judges and the other branches of government. But strategic judges might also think about a host of other actors, including the public, interest groups, the media, or the bureaucrats and other implementing groups who are responsible for putting court decisions into effect. The next two sections describe some of the internal and external actors who have the potential to influence judicial behavior, but you should think about whether there are any other actors who might be missing from the list. Whose preferences would you expect a strategic judge to take into account?

Internal Actors
The first set of actors with whom judges engage are the other judges on their court. Most appellate courts are collegial institutions, with multiple judges presiding over each case. Supreme Court justices decide cases as a tribunal of nine, while judges on the U.S. courts of

appeals usually sit on three-judge panels. State supreme courts vary in size, with seven justices the most common but some states having as many as nine justices or as few as five. With multiple decision makers at work, some coordination is needed for these institutions to function. As Walter Murphy explained in his study of strategic behavior on the U.S. Supreme Court, "Since he shares decision-making authority with eight other judges, the first problem that a policy-oriented Justice would confront is that of obtaining at least four, and hopefully eight, additional votes for the results he wants."[14]

One context in which strategic behavior occurs is when judges are deciding who will write the majority opinion. On the U.S. Supreme Court, chief justices make the opinion assignment when they are in the majority; otherwise, the justice with the most seniority does it. On the U.S. courts of appeals, the process is similar, with the choice going to the most senior active judge on the panel.[15] State supreme courts use a variety of practices, with some states permitting the senior justice in the majority coalition to make the assignment, but most use a system of randomization or rotation.[16] When the assignment is not random, a strategic judge might assign the opinion to the "least persuaded" member of the coalition to secure that judge's vote.

For example, after Justice John Paul Stevens retired from the Supreme Court, he admitted to giving assignments to swing justices such as Anthony Kennedy to keep these justices aligned with the majority. "There were cases I think that I may have asked Tony to write," Justice Stevens said, "because I thought if he wrote it out himself he was more sure to stick to his first vote."[17] Justice Stevens acknowledged that some opinion assigners were more strategic than others. He pointed to Chief Justice Burger as an example of a justice who was less strategic than some have thought. "A lot of people assumed he was making strategic assignments and that sort of thing," Justice Stevens said. "I think he was just not as careful a scholar as he should have been, and he didn't do a careful job keeping track of exactly how everyone voted and the reasons why."

Political scientists who have studied opinion assignments have found that chief justices pursue multiple goals when they are deciding who will write the majority opinions.[18] Chief Justice Rehnquist, for example, was concerned about making sure that every justice had an approximately equal workload, a practice that Chief Justice Roberts has repeated.[19] Chief justices also give opinion assignments to their ideological allies, but this tendency becomes weaker when a majority coalition is fragile.[20] If there is a **minimum winning coalition**, with no

JUDICIAL PROCESS BOX 4.1	Opinion Assignment, Drafting, and Circulation

Who decides who will write the majority opinion on a multi-member court? The process varies with the institution. In some states, majority opinion assignments occur randomly or by rotation, while on other courts a particular judge makes the assignment.

On the U.S. Supreme Court, the justices hold a private conference after the oral arguments to share their views of a case and to take an initial conference vote on the merits. When the Chief Justice is in the majority, the Chief decides who will write the majority opinion. Otherwise the assignment is made by the justice in the majority coalition who has the most seniority.

After completing the first draft, the majority opinion writer circulates it to the other justices for comment. Justices might immediately agree to join the opinion, offer suggestions for changes, or threaten to hold their support unless certain accommodations are made. The majority opinion writer might then choose to circulate another draft, or drafts, incorporating the changes. Voting **fluidity** occurs when a justice who was originally in one coalition changes sides.

Social scientists disagree about how much bargaining and accommodation occurs at the opinion writing stage. After reviewing the evidence below, what is your assessment?

room for further dissent, the chief justice assigns cases to ideologically distant colleagues to keep the majority together.[21] In other words, chief justices act strategically. As political scientist Paul Wahlbeck explains, "By assigning this opinion to a more ideologically distant Justice in an effort to maintain a majority for his preferred disposition, the Chief minimizes policy loss."[22]

Some of these trends are illustrated in Table 4.1, which lists the justices who received opinion assignments from Chief Justice Rehnquist from 1986 to 1993. Focusing on the first six justices, who served for the entire period, the figures show that the chief justice did not favor his closest ideological allies, but swing justices at the center of the Court. Although Rehnquist did give the most assignments to himself, the justices he chose next were O'Connor and White, who were less closely aligned with him than other conservative justices whom Rehnquist might have chosen, such as Scalia. Of course, very liberal justices such as Brennan and Marshall also did not get many

Table 4.1   Opinion Assignments by Chief Justice Rehnquist, 1986–1993

Justice	Segal-Cover Score	Ideological Distance from Chief	Percentage of Assignments
William H. Rehnquist	0.045	0.000	15.5
Sandra Day O'Connor	0.415	0.370	13.4
Byron R. White	0.500	0.455	11.5
John Paul Stevens	0.250	0.205	11.3
Antonin Scalia	0.000	0.045	11.3
Harry Blackmun	0.115	0.070	8.6
Anthony M. Kennedy*	0.365	0.320	7.7
Thurgood Marshall*	1.000	0.955	7.3
David H. Souter*	0.325	0.280	4.0
William J. Brennan Jr.*	1.000	0.955	3.3
Clarence Thomas*	0.160	0.115	3.3
Lewis F. Powell*	0.165	0.120	2.3
Ruth Bader Ginsburg*	0.680	0.635	0.5

*These justices did not serve for the entire period under analysis.

Note: Assignment data are from Paul J. Wahlbeck, "Strategy and Constraints on Supreme Court Opinion Assignment," *University of Pennsylvania Law Review* 154 (2006): 1729.

assignments, but these justices were not voting with Rehnquist frequently anyway.

Another context in which strategic behavior occurs is at the opinion-writing stage, in which the judge who has the responsibility to write the opinion for the court must represent the views of the majority. What makes this task challenging is that even when judges agree about who should win and who should lose a case, they might disagree about the rationale. For many judges, the reasoning is just as important as the holding because it establishes what the rule will be that governs future cases. The judge who is writing the majority opinion might receive a number of suggestions from colleagues proposing changes to the opinion, sometimes accompanied by threats to refuse to join the opinion unless the revisions are incorporated. A strategic opinion writer will accommodate these suggestions to hold the majority coalition together, even if it means that the final opinion does not truly reflect the opinion writer's sincere preferences.

One sign that Supreme Court justices engage in this behavior is that, from time to time, justices write concurrences to their own majority opinions explaining how their personal views of cases differ from those of the majority coalition.[23] Political scientists have also found evidence of strategic behavior by looking at the number of drafts that the justices circulate before releasing the final opinions. The leading research is by Forrest Maltzman, James F. Spriggs, and Paul J. Wahlbeck, who in *Crafting Law on the Supreme Court* (2000) studied the justices' private papers to find evidence of bargaining activity.[24] (See Methodological Note 4.1.) They reasoned that if the justices were strategic, then we would observe majority opinion writers circulating a greater number of draft opinions when the need for compromise was most urgent, such as when opinion writers were one vote short of attaining a majority or when the majority coalitions were diverse.

The authors' findings are in Figure 4.2, which reports the average number of drafts that majority opinion writers circulated during the

METHODOLOGICAL NOTE 4.1 | The Justices' Private Papers

How do we know what happens behind the scenes at the U.S. Supreme Court? Among the best resources are the justices' private papers, the documents that justices assemble while they are serving on the Court. It is up to each justice to decide whether and when to release their papers. Some justices set dates long after they have left the bench, such as when all the justices with whom they served have retired. Other justices permit the much faster release of their papers.

Among the best sources of information about the Supreme Court are the papers of Justice Harry Blackmun, whose papers became available in 2004, five years after his death. Justice Blackmun was a meticulous record keeper, with detailed and comprehensive notes on case selection, oral arguments, and opinion assignments. Some of these records are available at the Digital Archive of the Papers of Harry A. Blackmun, which you can access online. Another good record keeper was Justice William Brennan, who, like Blackmun, made his papers readily available to researchers.

Because these records are so complete, it has been possible to conduct systematic quantitative analysis of the data they contain. The research by Maltzman, Spriggs, and Wahlbeck that is discussed below, for example, was based largely on Justice Brennan's circulation records. What obligation do you think justices have to keep their papers in good order? Now that we are in the digital age, should justices make their papers available electronically? Why or why not?

To explore some of these resources yourself, see the Digital Archive of the Papers of Harry A. Blackmun (available at http://epstein.wustl.edu/blackmun.php).

Figure 4.2 Factors Influencing Opinion Draft Circulation on the U.S. Supreme Court

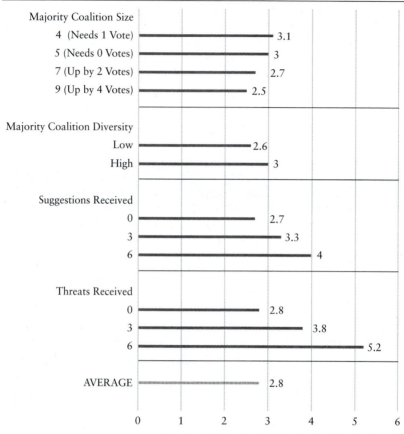

Source: Paul J. Wahlbeck, James F. Spriggs, and Forrest Maltzman, "Marshalling the Court: Bargaining and Accommodation on the United States Supreme Court," *American Journal of Political Science* 42 (1998): 294.

Burger Court years (1969–1985 terms). The data show that opinion writers usually circulated about 2.8 drafts on average, but the number could change depending on the circumstances. Specifically, the authors tested whether circulations varied based on the size of the majority coalition, its ideological diversity, and whether the opinion writer received **bargaining statements** from other members of the majority coalition making suggestions or threatening to withhold support unless the author made changes. What do you think about the trends that you see? To what extent is the evidence consistent with the hypothesis that opinion writers strategically accommodate their colleagues? To what extent are the data inconsistent? Take some time to study the data and form your own conclusions before proceeding.

On the one hand, it does appear that majority opinion writers circulate more drafts when they have incentives to compromise. If they need another vote, or if they have a minimum winning coalition, opinion writers circulate about three drafts, which is slightly more than they do ordinarily. Majority opinion writers also circulate more drafts when the majority coalition is ideologically diverse or when other members of the majority coalition circulate bargaining statements that suggest revisions or threaten to withhold support. These trends are consistent with the hypothesis that a greater amount of bargaining and accommodation occurs behind the scenes when opinion writers are having trouble keeping their coalitions together.

On the other hand, the effects in Figure 4.2 are not large. The most substantial differences occur when colleagues threaten to withhold their support from opinions, which can increase the number of circulations to as many as five drafts. However, the impact of the other variables on bargaining activity is more modest, with an ideologically diverse coalition only increasing circulations by about half a draft. Of course, it is worth remembering that majority opinion writers do not write many drafts to begin with, and it is possible that justices are so efficient that they only need an extra draft or two to accommodate their colleagues. Opinion writers might also engage in **preemptive accommodation**, anticipating the goals and preferences of the other members of the majority coalition before circulating their first drafts. Still, critics would say that the amount of bargaining activity is less than one would expect to observe if Supreme Court justices are truly committed to compromising with their fellow justices.

In fact, a persistent criticism of the strategic model is that the evidence for it is not as widespread as it could be.[25] While Justice Brennan's behavior in *Craig v. Boren* would seem to be a clear example of a judge accommodating colleagues, other times judges choose the opinion language they prefer and do not worry about whether their colleagues will join them. A **plurality opinion** is one that receives the most support from the members of the majority coalition, but not the five votes needed to command a majority of the Court as a whole. When the justices can agree on the result but not a rationale, there is no single opinion to serve as precedent.

For example, in *Hein v. Freedom from Religion Foundation* (2007), the Supreme Court was deciding whether taxpayers could sue President George W. Bush over how he was spending their tax money.[26] President Bush had created an Office of Faith-Based and Community Initiatives to help religious groups become more competitive for federal grants, but some taxpayers objected that the program violated the Establishment Clause. The question in *Hein* was whether taxpayers had **standing** to sue the federal government. (See Judicial Process Box 4.2.) That is to say, did taxpayers suffer an injury that warranted the intervention of courts?

The taxpayers in *Hein* believed that the president had harmed them by spending their money in a way that violated the Constitution, but others said that the amount paid by any one taxpayer was too small to qualify as an injury. In an earlier case, *Flast v. Cohen*

JUDICIAL PROCESS BOX 4.2 | Standing

Not just anyone can bring a case to court. To participate in litigation, the parties must have standing, which establishes them as the appropriate parties to file suit. The requirements for standing vary from state to state, but in general, litigants need to have suffered an injury, such as a physical harm, the loss of a legal right, a contract violation, or damage to reputation.

The jurisdiction of federal courts is described in Article III of the Constitution, which limits federal judges to deciding "cases" and "controversies." When a litigant does not have an injury, there is no controversy for the judges to decide. Judges would be issuing **advisory opinions**, which the Constitution forbids. The U.S. Supreme Court clarified in *Lujan v. Defenders of Wildlife* (1992) that in order to have standing, a litigant must have an "actual or imminent" injury that is "concrete and particularized."

A question that frequently arises is whether taxpayers have enough of a stake in how their money is spent to sue the government. Some people would say that it is reasonable for taxpayers to go to court when the government is violating the Constitution. But others would say that a taxpayer's financial interest in any single policy is too small to qualify as an injury. Instead of using the courts, taxpayers should express their disapproval at the ballot box.

What do you think? Who should be able to use the courts? Is it appropriate for taxpayers to file lawsuits to challenge how the government is spending their money? Or should the use of the courts be more limited?

(1968), the Supreme Court decided that taxpayers did have standing to sue when Congress appropriated taxpayer funds for unconstitutional purposes, but in *Hein* it was the president who had acted.[27] Did the distinction matter? A majority of the Court thought so, ruling that the taxpayers did not have standing. However, the justices could not agree on a rationale. Justice Samuel Alito wrote the plurality opinion, joined by two other justices, stating that *Flast v. Cohen* was still good law but should not be extended. Justice Scalia, joined by Justice Thomas, wrote a **special concurrence** agreeing that the taxpayers lacked standing but arguing that *Flast* should be overturned. Four other justices dissented, maintaining that the taxpayers did have standing, making the final vote lineup 3–2–4.

The justices in *Hein* were not being strategic, because they were not making much of an effort to find agreement with their colleagues. As it turns out, these types of fragmented majority coalitions happen with some regularity. Figure 4.3 shows the percentage of plurality opinions that occurred on each term of the Court from 1971 to 2015, with data from the Supreme Court Database. It shows that on average about 3.3 percent of argued cases result in plurality opinions, but in some years the percentage has been higher. In the 2003 term, for example, 8.1 percent of cases resulted in plurality opinions. Research has also found that plurality opinions are more likely to occur in

Figure 4.3 Percentage of Supreme Court Cases with Plurality Decisions, 1971–2015 Terms

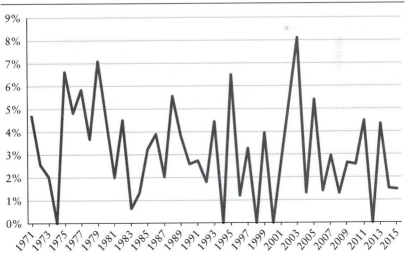

Source: The Supreme Court Database, http://scdb.wustl.edu/

important and divisive cases, in which one might expect the justices to have more difficulty cooperating.[28] It would seem, then, that while Supreme Court justices do frequently make an effort to find consensus, other times they permit themselves to fragment, especially in divisive cases.

A third context in which internal dynamics can influence judges is case selection. The previous chapter described the influence of legal principles on the Supreme Court's decision whether to accept cases for review. We learned that justices are more likely to put cases on the docket when legal questions are important or have divided the lower courts. However, if justices are strategic, they might also be forward thinking with case selection, looking ahead to whether their fellow justices are likely to support the outcomes they prefer. **Aggressive grants** occur when justices grant review to cases that do not otherwise warrant it because they think the cases will be good vehicles for advancing their preferences. **Defensive denials** happen when justices deny review to otherwise worthy cases because they anticipate unfavorable decisions on the merits.[29]

There is some evidence that both of these strategies influence case selection on the Supreme Court, but research indicates that the behavior is not widespread. Justices are more likely to be strategic at the case selection stage when they agree with what the lower court has done and would like to affirm the judgment.[30] In these circumstances, there is some risk to granting review because a majority of the Court could decide to reverse the lower court's decision and select a different policy outcome, leaving the justices who favored the original policy worse off than they were before. However, the strategic payoff is more limited when a justice disapproves of the lower court's judgment and would like to reverse it. An affirmance by the Supreme Court would not change the status quo because the lower court's decision is already on the books. Judges therefore typically always have incentives to grant review for cases that they would like to reverse.

External Actors

Another set of actors whose goals and preferences judges consider are individuals outside of the court. **Separation-of-powers models** study the interactions of courts with the other branches of government. To what extent does the Supreme Court anticipate the preferences of Congress when it is issuing decisions? How much does it think about the president? Politicians frequently criticize court decisions that they dislike, but it does not necessarily follow that judges are, or should be, responsive to them. Many people would say that judging is supposed to be independent of politics. However, the other branches have numerous resources that they can use to keep judicial power in check, and rational judges might take measures to avoid them.

In the federal judicial system, the most powerful sanction is **impeachment**. Federal judges technically hold their offices for life, but only during "good behaviour." The Constitution permits impeachment and removal from office with a vote of at least 50 percent of the House of Representatives and two-thirds of the Senate. In theory, then, it is possible to remove judges from office for their policy views, or for acting contrary to the wishes of Congress and the president, but in practice impeachments are rare. Only one Supreme Court justice has ever been impeached. In 1804, Justice Samuel Chase's opponents in the House accused him of deciding cases based on political motivations, but the Senate acquitted him. Since then, efforts to impeach justices such as Earl Warren and William Douglas for political reasons have gotten little traction. On the lower federal courts, impeachment is more common, but usually because the judge has committed a crime. For example, Judge Thomas Porteus of the U.S. District Court for Eastern Louisiana was removed in 2010 following charges of bribery and perjury. State judges also face impeachment with greater frequency, and sometimes for political reasons. In 2010, the Iowa legislature threatened to impeach four justices on its Supreme Court for legalizing same-sex marriage the year before.[31] In general, however, impeachment is not a routine sanction.

Short of impeachment, the other branches can attempt to overturn, or decline to implement, court decisions that they dislike. Congress can correct a court's interpretation of a federal statute by revising the statute, but reversing a constitutional decision requires passing a constitutional amendment.[32] Congress can also threaten to make institutional changes to the courts. Much of the structure of the federal judiciary is set by statute, which Congress can alter without having to amend the Constitution. For example, Congress can change the size of the Supreme Court. Although Congress cannot remove justices from office without impeaching them, it can increase the number of justices and encourage the president to pack the Court with nominees who share their policy views. President Franklin D. Roosevelt made such a proposal in 1937 when the Supreme Court was striking down much of his New Deal legislation. FDR's court-packing plan would have permitted the president to appoint a new justice to the Supreme Court for every sitting member who was over the age of seventy. The proposal lost support in Congress only when the Supreme Court reversed course and began to uphold FDR's legislative program, a move popularly referred to as the "switch in time that saved nine."

Congress can also prohibit the Supreme Court from hearing certain types of cases. According to Article III of the Constitution, the **original jurisdiction** of the Supreme Court is fixed, but the **appellate jurisdiction** is subject to "such exceptions . . . as the Congress shall make." (See Judicial Process Box 4.3.) In practice, this means that Congress can deny the Court the ability to hear appeals in controversial areas of policy, such as abortion or campaign finance, if justices make decisions that the other branches oppose. Congress has done this a few times before. For example, Congress passed the Military Commissions Act in 2006 to prevent federal courts from hearing appeals from enemy combatants who were detained in Guantanamo Bay, Cuba. In this case, however, the Supreme Court declared the Military Commissions Act unconstitutional.[33]

JUDICIAL PROCESS BOX 4.3	The Jurisdiction of Federal Courts

The jurisdiction of federal courts is described in Article III of the Constitution, which vests the federal judicial power in "one Supreme Court, and in such inferior courts as the Congress may from time to time ordain and establish."

When a court has original jurisdiction over a dispute, it means that a case can originate in that tribunal. Article III establishes the Supreme Court's original jurisdiction over "cases affecting ambassadors, other public ministers and consuls, and those in which a state shall be a party." Congress has also authorized other federal courts to have concurrent jurisdiction over certain matters.

A court's appellate jurisdiction is composed of cases it only hears on appeal. Most cases come before the Supreme Court on its appellate jurisdiction, subject to "such exceptions, and under such regulations as the Congress shall make." Judges have interpreted this provision of Article III to mean that Congress can change the appellate jurisdiction of courts if it chooses.

What do you think? Are there some types of cases that the Supreme Court should not be deciding (e.g., abortion, same-sex marriage, campaign finance, etc.)? Would you be comfortable with Congress telling the courts that it cannot decide cases in these areas?

Even though Congress and the president rarely make use of these checks on judicial power, the possibility of sanctions might be enough to make judges responsive to them. A more potent threat could be the power that Congress has over the Supreme Court's budget. Although the Constitution does not permit Congress to reduce the salaries of federal judges, Congress can deny them pay raises. Congress can also refuse to finance routine administrative needs such as building maintenance and office supplies. Budget cuts might seem minor compared to the other court-curbing measures that Congress employs, but they can affect a judge's quality of life. It is now customary each year for two Supreme Court justices to appear before Congress to justify their proposed budget, and members of Congress use the opportunity to make their views known about various matters, including disagreements that they might have with the justices' policy choices.

How responsive are judges to these constraints on their power? Political scientists who have conducted research on separation-of-powers models have reached no clear consensus about the extent to which other branches influence judicial behavior. Some studies have found evidence of strategic behavior,[34] while others have not.[35] A potential explanation for these inconsistent findings is that judges are selective about when and how they engage the other branches. For example, one study found that Supreme Court justices decline to review cases when they expect Congress to oppose their preferred decisions on the merits.[36] Other research indicates that separation-of-powers strategies occur but lack precision. A study by Jeffrey Segal, Chad Westerland, and Stefanie Lindquist showed that while Supreme Court justices are less likely to invalidate legislation when they are ideologically distant from Congress and the president, the justices do not specifically target key Congressional actors who have the power to overturn their decisions. The researchers conclude that "the Court's strategic calculations regarding a legislative response do not extend to a nuanced evaluation of the likelihood that the sitting Congress and president will overturn the decision."[37]

Individual judges also respond differently to the threat of sanctions. Michael Bailey and Forrest Maltzman examined the behavior of Supreme Court justices in statutory cases and found that among the justices who were the most responsive to the preferences of the other branches were Sandra Day O'Connor, Anthony Kennedy, David Souter, Earl Warren, John Paul Stevens, Antonin Scalia, and Clarence Thomas.[38] Less responsive were Ruth Bader Ginsburg, Stephen

Breyer, William Rehnquist, Lewis Powell, Harry Blackmun, and Warren Burger. The implication of this research is that the responsiveness of the Supreme Court to other actors may depend on which justices are sitting on the Court and who is writing the majority opinion.

Congress and the president are not the only external actors whose preferences judges take into account. Much research has explored the relationship between courts and the public, as well as the relationship of judges with the people who are responsible for interpreting and implementing court decisions. These topics are covered in Part II of the textbook. Still other work has studied the constraining impact of institutional norms and practices on judicial behavior.[39] Uniting this research is the recognition that judicial behavior does not occur in isolation but as part of a broader political, institutional, and cultural environment. It is only natural to expect judges to think about how their decisions will interact with the world around them.

EVIDENCE FOR THE STRATEGIC MODEL

Political scientists have found much evidence to support the strategic model. Some of the most persuasive findings have already been presented to you in the sections above, showing how judges can be responsive to both internal and external actors. In fact, few political scientists doubt that justices are strategic from time to time. The question is whether strategic explanations account for enough judicial behavior to be meaningful. After reviewing the research on the theory, Saul Brenner and Joseph M. Whitmeyer concluded, "Strategic behavior occurs on the Court, but it takes place much less often than the strategic scholars claim."[40] Even Walter Murphy, who originally developed the strategic model, acknowledged that "no Justice who has ever sat on the Court could have taken complete advantage of the strategies and tactics outlined here."[41]

On the U.S. Supreme Court, any strategic account must contend with the fact that most case outcomes are set by the preferences of the justice at the center of the Court. Political scientists describe this theory as the **median voter theorem**. To illustrate the theorem, Figure 4.4 presents an ideological snapshot of the Court shortly after the Senate confirmed Justice Neil Gorsuch in April 2017. The justices are arranged in ideological space, based on their Segal-Cover scores (see chapter 2), with more liberal justices on the left and conservative

Figure 4.4 Ideological Composition of the Roberts Court

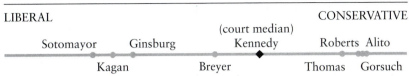

justices on the right. As you can see, the Court median at the time was Kennedy, with four justices more conservative than him and four more liberal. The median voter theorem is a threat to strategic accounts because it denies that the Court's policy fluctuates in response to the preferences of internal and external forces. If judges were consistently responding to other actors, then the Court median would not be such a reliable predictor of judicial behavior. However, research has demonstrated that case outcomes on the U.S. Supreme Court are best explained with reference to the Court median.[42] This means that, for much of the Roberts Court, Justice Kennedy has had a lot of power to decide whether the Court decided cases in a liberal or conservative direction. In the 2015 term, for example, Justice Kennedy was in the majority in 96 percent of divided cases.[43] Another justice who has frequently been in the majority is Stephen Breyer, who is also near the ideological center of the Court.

The major limitation of the strategic model, then, is that it does not consistently explain case outcomes on the U.S. Supreme Court. However, the language of majority opinions is a different matter. Research has found that majority opinions reflect the preferences of the median justice in the majority coalition, which means that the scope of the legal policies that the Court produces, and the precedents it sets, will vary depending on which particular justices are in the majority.[44] These justices work together to find rationales that the other members of the majority coalition can support. As an illustration, consider the behavior of Justice Brennan in *Craig v. Boren* (1976), described earlier in the chapter. If you recall, in *Craig* Justice Brennan made the strategic decision to settle for intermediate scrutiny instead of strict scrutiny for sex discrimination cases.

Figure 4.5 illustrates the dynamics of Justice Brennan's choice, showing the composition of the Supreme Court at the time of *Frontiero* and *Craig*. As you can see, in both cases Justice Brennan was one of the most liberal justices on the Court. If he set policy exactly where he wanted to, at his **ideal point**, then he would have had trouble

Figure 4.5 Ideological Composition of the Supreme Court in Sex Discrimination Cases

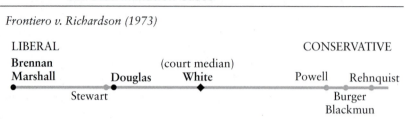

Frontiero v. Richardson (1973)

NOTE: The justices in **bold** supported **strict scrutiny** for sex-based classifications. The symbol ◆ represents the median justice.

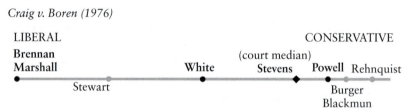

Craig v. Boren (1976)

NOTE: The justices in **bold** supported **intermediate scrutiny** for sex-based classifications. The symbol ◆ represents the median justice.

commanding a majority because most of the other justices were too far away from him in ideological space. In *Frontiero*, Justice Brennan could get Justices Marshall, Douglas, and White to agree to use strict scrutiny, but no one else. By the time of *Craig*, the Court was even more conservative because Justice Douglas was replaced with Justice Stevens, shifting the Court's median to the right. Justice Brennan had little hope of getting a majority of his brethren to apply strict scrutiny, so he modified the policy in a way that would be more acceptable to the conservative justices. By proposing intermediate scrutiny, Justice Brennan won the support of Justices Stevens and Powell and forged a majority.

Even if critics are correct that the strategic model does not describe how Supreme Court justices behave all of the time, it can still be a useful perspective for understanding cases such as *Craig v. Boren*. There is also evidence that strategic behavior systematically influences judicial behavior on other courts. Research on the U.S. courts of appeals, for example, has found evidence of **panel effects**, which means that the way that individual judges vote changes depending on who else is on the panel with them. Remember that judges on the U.S. courts of appeals typically decide cases in groups of three, and that the particular judges on these panels vary from case to case. Frank Cross studied panel behavior and found that group dynamics affect the decisions that circuit judges reach. Contrary to the predictions of the median voter theorem, decisions are not better explained by the preferences of the median judge but by the total ideology of all of the judges on the panel. "The median voter theorem appears entirely inapplicable to circuit court panels," Cross concluded.[45] The presence of a single judge from the opposing political party changes how the other judges on the panel approach a case. Subsequent research has found that the addition of a judge who is female or a racial minority also affects the behavior of the rest of the panel.[46]

Less clear is whether lower court judges strategically anticipate the preferences of higher courts. One might expect judges on the U.S. Courts of Appeals to decide cases with the preferences of U.S. Supreme Court justices in mind to avoid reversal, and in fact some research has shown that lower court judges are responsive to policy changes by the high court.[47] However, research has also found that lower court judges do not fear reversal, most likely because the probability of Supreme Court review is so low.[48] Nor is it clear that lower-court judges act strategically in other ways, such as by sending signals to higher courts to encourage review of decisions they dislike. Dissenting behavior on the U.S. courts of appeals is better explained by judges' sincere disagreements with their colleagues than a desire to encourage higher-court review.[49]

On many state courts, judges have additional incentives to be strategic because they are directly accountable to the public and the other branches of government. As discussed in the beginning of the chapter, Chief Justice Amestoy settled for civil unions instead of marriage equality in *Baker v. Vermont* (1999) because he knew that the state legislature had the power to change the Court's decision. Amestoy also depended on the legislature for his reappointment. When states use elections to retain judges, electoral incentives provide another powerful motivation for judges to be strategic. Research on state supreme courts has shown that elected judges react strategically in response to the preferences of their constituents,[50] particularly in high profile cases, when the public is paying the closest attention.[51] These dynamics, as well as other dimensions of the relationship between courts and the public, are covered in Part II.

DISCUSSION QUESTIONS

1. Is it ever appropriate for judges to consider the views of other actors, or should judges only decide cases based on their own independent judgments? Are there some circumstances in which strategic behavior might be more appropriate than others?
2. How much should Supreme Court justices accommodate the views of other justices when they are writing majority opinions? Is it better for the Court to speak with one voice? Or should justices write opinions that reflect their own views of a case, even if it means that no single opinion commands a majority?
3. Should judges be thinking about the reactions of other branches when they are deciding cases? Is judging supposed to be independent of politics, or are there times when it is appropriate for judges to think about the broader contexts of their decisions?
4. Compare Chief Justice Amestoy's decision in *Baker v. Vermont* (1999) with the speech he delivered at Rutgers Law School, "Pragmatic Constitutionalism." What factors does Amestoy say influenced his decision in *Baker*? Do you think Amestoy made the right decision, or was he worrying too much about what other actors would do?

KEY TERMS

policy-choice strategies
strict scrutiny
intermediate scrutiny
instrument-choice strategies
minimum winning coalition
fluidity
bargaining statements
preemptive accommodation
plurality opinion
standing
advisory opinions

special concurrence
aggressive grants
defensive denials
separation-of-powers models
impeachment
original jurisdiction
appellate jurisdiction
median voter theorem
ideal point
panel effects

FURTHER READING

Murphy, Walter F. 1964. *Elements of Judicial Strategy*. Chicago: The University of Chicago Press.

Epstein, Lee, and Jack Knight. 1998. *The Choices Justices Make*. Washington, DC: CQ Press.

Maltzman, Forrest, James F. Spriggs, and Paul J. Wahlbeck. 2000. *Crafting Law on the Supreme Court: The Collegial Game.* New York: Cambridge University Press.

Brenner, Saul, and Joseph M. Whitmeyer. 2009. *Strategy on the United States Supreme Court.* New York: Cambridge University Press.

NOTES

1. Baker v. Vermont, 744 A.2d 864 (Vt. 1999).
2. Obergefell v. Hodges, 576 U.S. __ (2015).
3. *Baker*, at 886.
4. Jeffrey L. Amestoy, "Pragmatic Constitutionalism: Reflections on State Constitutional Theory and Same-Sex Marriage Claims," *Rutgers Law Journal* 35 (2004): 1249.
5. Baehr v. Miike, No. 91-1394 (Haw. Cir. Ct. 1996); Michael J. Klarman, *From the Closet to the Altar: Courts, Backlash, and the Struggle for Same-Sex Marriage* (Oxford: Oxford University Press, 2012).
6. Walter Murphy, *Elements of Judicial Strategy* (Chicago: University of Chicago Press, 1964).
7. Lee Epstein and Jack Knight, *The Choices Justices Make* (Washington, DC: CQ Press, 1997), 10.
8. *See* Lawrence Baum, *The Puzzle of Judicial Behavior* (Ann Arbor: University of Michigan Press, 1997), 60.
9. Emerson H. Tiller and Pablo T. Spiller, "Strategic Instruments: Legal Structure and Political Games in Administrative Law," *Journal of Law, Economics, and Organization* 15 (1999): 351.
10. Joseph L. Smith and Emerson H. Tiller, "The Strategy of Judging: Evidence from Administrative Law," *Journal of Legal Studies* 31 (2002): 61.
11. David J. Walsh, "On the Meaning and Pattern of Legal Citations: Evidence from State Wrongful Discharge Precedent Cases," *Law & Society Review* 31 (1997): 337.
12. Pamela C. Corley, Robert M. Howard, and David C. Nixon, "The Supreme Court and Opinion Content: The Use of the Federalist Papers," *Political Research Quarterly* 58 (2005): 329; Robert J. Hume, "The Use of Rhetorical Sources by the U.S. Supreme Court," *Law & Society Review* 40 (2006): 817.
13. Corley et al., "The Supreme Court and Opinion Content," 339.
14. Murphy, *Elements of Judicial Strategy*, 37.
15. Sean Farhang, Jonathan P. Kastellec, and Gregory J. Wawro, "The Politics of Opinion Assignment and Authorship on the U.S. Courts of Appeals: Evidence from Sexual Harassment Cases," *Journal of Legal Studies* 44 (2015): S59.
16. Melinda Gann Hall, "Opinion Assignment Procedures and Conference Practices in State Supreme Courts," *Judicature* 73 (1989–1990): 209.
17. Adam Liptak, "As Justices Get Back to Business, Old Pro Reveals Tricks of the Trade," *New York Times*, October 3, 2011, A12.
18. Paul J. Wahlbeck, "Strategy and Constraints on Supreme Court Opinion Assignment," *University of Pennsylvania Law Review* 154 (2006): 1729.

19. Forrest Maltzman and Paul J. Wahlbeck, "May It Please the Chief? Opinion Assignments in the Rehnquist Court," *American Journal of Political Science* 40 (1996): 421.

20. Forrest Maltzman and Paul J. Wahlbeck, "A Conditional Model of Opinion Assignment on the Supreme Court," *Political Research Quarterly* 57 (2004): 557.

21. Id., 559–61.

22. Wahlbeck, "Strategy and Constraints on Supreme Court Opinion Assignment," 1742.

23. *See, for example*, Bush v. Vera, 518 U.S. 952 (1996) (in which Justice O'Connor concurred with her own majority opinion).

24. Forrest Maltzman, James F. Spriggs, and Paul J. Wahlbeck, *Crafting Law on the Supreme Court: The Collegial Game* (New York: Cambridge University Press, 2000); *see also* Paul J. Wahlbeck, James F. Spriggs, and Forrest Maltzman, "Marshalling the Court: Bargaining and Accommodation on the United States Supreme Court," *American Journal of Political Science* 42 (1998): 294.

25. Saul Brenner and Joseph M. Whitmeyer, *Strategy on the United States Supreme Court* (New York: Cambridge University Press, 2009).

26. Hein v. Freedom from Religion Foundation, 551 U.S. 587 (2007).

27. Flast v. Cohen, 392 U.S. 83 (1968).

28. James F. Spriggs II and David R. Stras, "Explaining Plurality Decisions," *Georgetown Law Journal* 99 (2011): 515.

29. H. W. Perry, *Deciding to Decide: Agenda Setting in the United States Supreme Court* (Cambridge, MA: Harvard University Press, 1991).

30. Robert L. Boucher Jr. and Jeffrey A. Segal, "Supreme Court Justices as Strategic Decision Makers: Aggressive Grants and Defensive Denials on the Vinson Court," *Journal of Politics* 57 (1995): 824; Sara C. Benesh, Saul Brenner, and Harold J. Spaeth, "Aggressive Grants by Affirm-Minded Justices," *American Politics Research* 30 (2002): 2019.

31. Sandy Adkins, "Iowa Legislature Threatens to Oust Four Supreme Court Justices," *National Center for States Courts*, available at http://www.ncsc.org/ newsroom/backgrounder/2010/judicial-impeachment.aspx.

32. *But see* Richard L. Hasen, "End of the Dialogue? Political Polarization, the Supreme Court, and Congress," *Southern California Law Review* 86 (2013): 205 (finding that Congress has become less likely to override the Supreme Court's statutory decisions).

33. Boumediene v. Bush, 553 U.S. 723 (2008).

34. Pablo T. Spiller and Rafael Gely, "Congressional Control or Judicial Independence: The Determinants of U.S. Supreme Court Labor Relations Decisions, 1949–1988," *RAND Journal of Economics* 23 (1992): 463.

35. Jeffrey A. Segal, "Separation of Power Games in the Positive Theory of Congress and Courts," *American Political Science Review* 91 (1997): 197.

36. Anna Harvey and Barry Friedman, "Ducking Trouble: Congressionally Induced Selection Bias in the Supreme Court's Agenda," *Journal of Politics* 71 (2009): 574.

37. Jeffrey A. Segal, Chad Westerland, and Stefanie A. Lindquist, "Congress, the Supreme Court, and Judicial Review: Testing a Constitutional Separation of Powers Model," *American Journal of Political Science* 55 (2011): 99.

38. Michael A. Bailey and Forrest Maltzman, *The Constrained Court: Law, Politics, and the Decisions Justices Make* (Princeton, NJ: Princeton University Press, 2011), 103–8.

39. Jack Knight and Lee Epstein, "The Norm of Stare Decisis," *American Journal of Political Science* 40 (1996): 1018.

40. Brenner and Whitmeyer, *Strategy on the United States Supreme Court*, 165.

41. Murphy, *Elements of Judicial Strategy*, 5.

42. Andrew D. Martin, Kevin M. Quinn, and Lee Epstein, "The Median Justice on the U.S. Supreme Court," *North Carolina Law Review* 83 (2005): 1275; *but see* Benjamin E. Lauderdale and Tom S. Clark, "The Supreme Court's Many Median Justices," *American Political Science Review* 106 (2012): 847 (noting that the median justice varies depending on the issue area); *and* Peter K. Enns and Patrick C. Wohlfarth, "The Swing Justice," *Journal of Politics* 75 (2013): 1089 (finding that the pivotal "swing" justice in a case is not necessarily the median).

43. *ScotusBlog* Stat Pack, available at http://www.scotusblog.com/reference/stat-pack/.

44. Chris W. Bonneau, Thomas H. Hammond, Forrest Maltzman, and Paul J. Wahlbeck, "Agenda Control, the Median Justice, and the Majority Opinion on the U.S. Supreme Court," *American Journal of Political Science* 51 (2007): 890; Tom S. Clark and Benjamin Lauderdale, "Locating Supreme Court Opinions in Doctrine Space," *American Journal of Political Science* 54 (2010): 871; Cliff Carrubba, Barry Friedman, Andrew D. Martin, and Georg Vanberg, "Who Controls the Content of Supreme Court Opinions?" *American Journal of Political Science* 56 (2012).

45. Frank B. Cross, *Decision Making on the U.S. Courts of Appeals* (Stanford, CA: Stanford University Press, 2007), 166.

46. Christina L. Boyd, Lee Epstein, and Andrew Martin, "Untangling the Causal Effects of Sex on Judging," *American Journal of Political Science* 54 (2010): 389; Sean Farhang and Gregory Wawro, "Institutional Dynamics on the U.S. Court of Appeals: Minority Representation under Panel Decision Making," *Journal of Law, Economics, and Organization* 20 (2004): 299; Jennifer L. Peresie, "Female Judges Matter: Gender and Collegial Decisionmaking in the Federal Appellate Courts," *Yale Law Journal* 114 (2005): 1759; Jonathan P. Kastellec, "Racial Diversity and Judicial Influence on Appellate Courts," *American Journal of Political Science* 57 (2012): 167.

47. Donald R. Songer, Jeffrey A. Segal, and Charles M. Cameron, "The Hierarchy of Justice: Testing a Principal-Agent Model of Supreme Court-Circuit Court Interactions," *American Journal of Political Science* 38 (1994): 673.

48. David E. Klein and Robert J. Hume, "Fear of Reversal as an Explanation of Lower Court Compliance," *Law & Society Review* 37 (2003): 579.

49. Virginia A. Hettinger, Stefanie A. Lindquist, and Wendy L. Martinek, "Comparing Attitudinal and Strategic Accounts of Dissenting Behavior on the U.S. Courts of Appeals," *American Journal of Political Science* 48 (2004): 123; *but see* Gregory A. Caldeira, John R. Wright, and Christopher J.W. Zorn, "Sophisticated Voting and Gate-Keeping in the Supreme Court," *Journal of Law, Economics, and Organization* 15 (1999): 549 (showing that the presence of a dissent does encourage higher-court review).

50. Melinda Gann Hall, "Electoral Politics and Strategic Voting in State Supreme Courts," *Journal of Politics* 54 (1992): 427.

51. Richard L. Vining Jr., and Teena Wilhelm, "Measuring Case Salience in State Courts of Last Resort," *Political Research Quarterly* 64 (2011): 559.

CASE ANALYSIS

Baker v. Vermont, 744 A.2d 864 (VT, 1999)

In Baker v. Vermont *(1999), the Vermont Supreme Court ruled that same-sex couples had to receive the same benefits and privileges as opposite-sex couples, but the justices stopped short of mandating full marriage equality. Why do you think they made this choice? Do Chief Justice Amestoy's remarks, in the next excerpt, persuade you that the court was being strategic?*

AMESTOY, C. J.

May the State of Vermont exclude same-sex couples from the benefits and protections that its laws provide to opposite-sex married couples? That is the fundamental question we address in this appeal, a question that the Court well knows arouses deeply-felt religious, moral, and political beliefs. Our constitutional responsibility to consider the legal merits of issues properly before us provides no exception for the controversial case. The issue before the Court, moreover, does not turn on the religious or moral debate over intimate same-sex relationships, but rather on the statutory and constitutional basis for the exclusion of same-sex couples from the secular benefits and protections offered married couples.

We conclude that under the Common Benefits Clause of the Vermont Constitution, which, in pertinent part, reads,

> That government is, or ought to be, instituted for the common benefit, protection, and security of the people, nation, or community, and not for the particular emolument or advantage of any single person, family, or set of persons, who are a part only of that community. . . .

Vt. Const., ch. I, art 7., plaintiffs may not be deprived of the statutory benefits and protections afforded persons of the opposite sex who choose to marry. We hold that the State is constitutionally required to extend to same-sex couples the common benefits and protections that flow from marriage under Vermont law. Whether this ultimately takes the form of inclusion within the marriage laws themselves or a parallel "domestic partnership" system or some equivalent statutory alternative, rests with the Legislature. Whatever system is chosen, however, must conform with the constitutional imperative to afford all Vermonters the common benefit, protection, and security of the law. . . .

In considering this issue, it is important to emphasize at the outset that it is the Common Benefits Clause of the Vermont Constitution we are construing, rather than its counterpart, the Equal Protection Clause of the Fourteenth Amendment to the United States Constitution. It is altogether fitting and proper that we do so. Vermont's constitutional commitment to equal rights was the product of the successful effort to create an independent republic and a fundamental charter of government, the Constitution of 1777, both of which preceded the adoption of the Fourteenth Amendment by nearly a century. As we explained in *State v. Badger*, 141 (1982), "our constitution is not a mere reflection of the federal charter. Historically and textually, it differs from the United States Constitution. It predates the federal counterpart, as it extends back to Vermont's days as an independent republic. It is an independent authority, and Vermont's fundamental law.". . .

While the laws relating to marriage have undergone many changes during the last century, largely toward the goal of equalizing the status of husbands and wives, the benefits of marriage have not diminished in value. On the contrary, the benefits and protections incident to a marriage license under Vermont law have never been greater. They include, for example, the right to receive a portion of the estate of a spouse who dies intestate and protection against disinheritance through elective share provisions; preference in being appointed as the personal representative of a spouse who dies intestate; the right to bring a lawsuit for the wrongful death of a spouse; the right to bring an action for loss of consortium; the right to workers' compensation survivor benefits; the right to spousal benefits statutorily guaranteed to public employees, including health, life, disability, and accident insurance; the opportunity to be covered as a spouse under group life insurance policies issued to an employee; the opportunity to be covered as the insured's spouse under an individual health insurance policy; the right to claim an evidentiary privilege for marital communications; homestead rights and protections; the presumption of joint ownership of property and the concomitant right of survivorship; hospital visitation and other rights incident to the medical treatment of a family member; and the right to receive, and the obligation to provide, spousal support, maintenance, and property division in the event of separation or divorce. Other courts and commentators have noted the collection of rights, powers, privileges, and responsibilities triggered by marriage. . . .

While other statutes could be added to this list, the point is clear. The legal benefits and protections flowing from a marriage license are of such significance that any statutory exclusion must necessarily be grounded on public concerns of sufficient weight, cogency, and authority that the justice of the deprivation cannot seriously be questioned. Considered in light of the extreme logical disjunction between the classification and the stated purposes of the law—protecting children and "furthering the link between procreation and child rearing"—the exclusion falls substantially short of this standard. The laudable governmental goal of promoting a commitment between married couples to promote the security of their children and the community as a whole provides no reasonable basis for denying the legal benefits and protections of marriage to same-sex couples, who are no differently situated with respect to this goal than their opposite-sex counterparts. Promoting a link between procreation and childrearing similarly fails to support the exclusion. . . .

Thus, viewed in the light of history, logic, and experience, we conclude that none of the interests asserted by the State provides a reasonable and just basis for the continued exclusion of same-sex couples from the benefits incident to a civil marriage license under Vermont law. Accordingly, in the faith that a case beyond the imagining of the framers of our Constitution may, nevertheless, be safely anchored in the values that infused it, we find a constitutional obligation to extend to plaintiffs the common benefit, protection, and security that

Vermont law provides opposite-sex married couples. It remains only to determine the appropriate means and scope of relief compelled by this constitutional mandate. . . .

We hold only that plaintiffs are entitled under Chapter I, Article 7, of the Vermont Constitution to obtain the same benefits and protections afforded by Vermont law to married opposite-sex couples. We do not purport to infringe upon the prerogatives of the Legislature to craft an appropriate means of addressing this constitutional mandate, other than to note that the record here refers to a number of potentially constitutional statutory schemes from other jurisdictions. These include what are typically referred to as "domestic partnership" or "registered partnership" acts, which generally establish an alternative legal status to marriage for same-sex couples, impose similar formal requirements and limitations, create a parallel licensing or registration scheme, and extend all or most of the same rights and obligations provided by the law to married partners. . . . We do not intend specifically to endorse any one or all of the referenced acts, particularly in view of the significant benefits omitted from several of the laws.

Further, while the State's prediction of "destabilization" cannot be a ground for denying relief, it is not altogether irrelevant. A sudden change in the marriage laws or the statutory benefits traditionally incidental to marriage may have disruptive and unforeseen consequences. Absent legislative guidelines defining the status and rights of same-sex couples, consistent with constitutional requirements, uncertainty and confusion could result. Therefore, we hold that the current statutory scheme shall remain in effect for a reasonable period of time to enable the Legislature to consider and enact implementing legislation in an orderly and expeditious fashion. . . . In the event that the benefits and protections in question are not statutorily granted, plaintiffs may petition this Court to order the remedy they originally sought.

Our colleague asserts that granting the relief requested by plaintiffs—an injunction prohibiting defendants from withholding a marriage license—is our "constitutional duty." (JOHNSON, J., concurring in part and dissenting in part). We believe the argument is predicated upon a fundamental misinterpretation of our opinion. It appears to assume that we hold plaintiffs are entitled to a marriage license. We do not. We hold that the State is constitutionally required to extend to same-sex couples the common benefits and protections that flow from marriage under Vermont law. That the State could do so through a marriage license is obvious. But it is not required to do so, and the mandate proposed by our colleague is inconsistent with the Court's holding. . . .

Our colleague greatly underestimates what we decide today and greatly overestimates the simplicity and effectiveness of her proposed mandate. First, our opinion provides greater recognition of—and protection for—same sex relationships than has been recognized by any court of final jurisdiction in this country with the instructive exception of the Hawaii Supreme Court in *Baehr*, 852 P.2d 44. See Hawaii Const., art. I, § 23 (state constitutional amendment overturned same-sex marriage decision in Baehr by returning power to legislature "to reserve marriage to opposite-sex couples"). Second, the dissent's suggestion that her mandate would avoid the "political caldron" of public debate is—even allowing for the welcome lack of political sophistication of the judiciary—significantly insulated from reality. See Hawaii Const., art. I, § 23; see also Alaska Const., art. I, § 25 (state constitutional amendment reversed trial court decision in favor of same-sex marriage, *Brause v. Bureau of Vital Statistics* [Alaska Super. Ct. Feb. 27, 1998], by providing that "a marriage may exist only between one man and one woman").

The concurring and dissenting opinion confuses decisiveness with wisdom and judicial authority with finality. Our mandate is predicated upon a fundamental respect for the ultimate source of constitutional authority, not a fear of decisiveness. No court was ever more decisive than the United States Supreme Court in *Dred Scott v. Sandford* (1857). Nor more wrong. Ironically it was a Vermonter, Stephen Douglas, who in defending the decision said—as the dissent in essence does here—"I never heard before of an appeal being taken from the Supreme Court." See A. Bickel, *The Morality of Consent* 101 (1975). But it was a profound understanding of the law and the "unruliness of the human condition," that prompted Abraham Lincoln to respond that the Court does not issue Holy Writ. Our colleague may be correct that a mandate intended to provide the Legislature with the opportunity to implement the holding of this Court in an orderly and expeditious fashion will have precisely the opposite effect. Yet it cannot be doubted that judicial authority is not ultimate authority. It is certainly not the only repository of wisdom.

When a democracy is in moral flux, courts may not have the best or the final answers. Judicial answers may be wrong. They may be counterproductive even if they are right. Courts do best by proceeding in a way that is catalytic rather than preclusive, and that is closely attuned to the fact that courts are participants in the system of democratic deliberation.

The implementation by the Vermont Legislature of a constitutional right expounded by this Court pursuant to the Vermont Constitution for the common benefit and protection of the Vermont community is not an abdication of judicial duty, it is the fulfillment of constitutional responsibility. . . .

JOHNSON, J., concurring in part and dissenting in part.
Plaintiffs come before this Court claiming that the State has unconstitutionally deprived them of the benefits of marriage based solely upon a discriminatory classification that violates their civil rights. They ask the Court to remedy the unlawful discrimination by enjoining the State and its municipalities from denying them the license that serves to identify the persons entitled to those benefits. The majority agrees that the Common Benefits Clause of the Vermont Constitution entitles plaintiffs to obtain the same benefits and protections as those bestowed upon married opposite-sex couples, yet it declines to give them any relief other than an exhortation to the Legislature to deal with the problem. I concur with the majority's holding, but I respectfully dissent from its novel and truncated remedy, which in my view abdicates this Court's constitutional duty to redress violations of constitutional rights. I would grant the requested relief and enjoin defendants from denying plaintiffs a marriage license based solely on the sex of the applicants.

The majority declares that the issue before this Court does not turn on the heated moral debate over intimate same-sex relationships, and further, that this

Court has a constitutional responsibility to consider the legal merits of even controversial cases. Yet, notwithstanding these pronouncements, the majority elects to send plaintiffs to an uncertain fate in the political caldron of that very same moral debate. And to what end? Passing this case on to the Legislature will not alleviate the instability and uncertainty that the majority seeks to avoid, and will unnecessarily entangle this Court in the Legislature's efforts to accommodate the majority's mandate within a "reasonable period of time." . . . Like the Hawaii Circuit Court in *Baehr v. Miike* (Haw.Cir.Ct., Dec. 3, 1996), which rejected the State's reasons for excluding same-sex couples from marriage, we should simply enjoin the State from denying marriage licenses to plaintiffs based on sex or sexual orientation. That remedy would provide prompt and complete relief to plaintiffs and create reliable expectations that would stabilize the legal rights and duties of all couples.

In Their Own Words:
Chief Justice Jeffrey L. Amestoy, Supreme Court of Vermont

In a speech delivered at Rutgers Law School on February 18, 2004, Chief Justice Jeffrey L. Amestoy discusses the strategic considerations that influenced the Vermont Supreme Court's decision in Baker v. Vermont *(1999). (See previous excerpt.) What do you think? Should these types of strategic considerations influence judging?*

Pragmatic Constitutionalism
Jeffrey L. Amestoy

Four years ago in the *Rutgers Law Journal*'s annual *Issue on State Constitutional Law*, Professor Douglas Reed proposed a theory of state constitutionalism asserting that the "processes of generating state constitutional meanings . . . are subject to much more intense political disputation by interests and coalitions of interests than is the Federal Constitution." Professor Reed labeled his theory "popular constitutionalism." After completion of his article—but prior to its publication—the Vermont Supreme Court issued its opinion in *Baker v. State.* Professor

Reed had time only to footnote a reference to *Baker*, which stated:

On December 20, 1999, the Vermont Supreme Court ruled that the Common Benefits Clause of the Vermont Constitution prevents the state from denying to the plaintiffs the statutory benefits and protections granted to married couples. It then ordered the state legislature to either enact "domestic partnership" legislation to confer those benefits or to allow same-sex partners to marry under the existing Vermont marriage statutes. In handing down this decision, it is clear that the Vermont Supreme Court learned from Hawaii's example, noting that a decision which mandated same-sex marriage outright might face intense opposition. Wrote the court: "It cannot be doubted that judicial authority is not ultimate authority." That, in a nutshell, is the lesson of popular constitutionalism.

Many of the insights in Professor Reed's article, *Popular Constitutionalism: Toward A Theory of State Constitutional Meanings*, are relevant to the Vermont experience in the wake of *Baker*. Indeed, although I do not know Professor Reed, I trust it is not too great a liberty to speculate that he was delighted to read a legal opinion that so closely corroborated aspects of his theory. Of course, his delight was matched by mine in reading a constitutional theory that mirrored aspects of my opinion. . . .

I have labeled my perspective "pragmatic constitutionalism.". . . Like "popular" or "strategic," "pragmatic" also has a vaguely unsettling connotation for it suggests considerations not normally associated with judicial decision-making. That connotation is one I hope these remarks refute for no sentence of the *Baker* majority opinion was more representative of how I perceive the court's responsibility than the one I wrote in response to my colleague Justice Johnson's view that failure to grant the plaintiffs immediate relief was "an abdication of judicial duty": "The implementation by the Vermont Legislature of a constitutional right expounded by this Court pursuant to the Vermont Constitution for the common benefit and protection of the Vermont community is not an abdication of judicial duty, it is the fulfillment of constitutional responsibility.". . .

When the *Baker* opinion was first issued, it prompted much comment, as decisions about controversial issues often do. It still does. I initially took comfort in knowing that many who were very critical of the opinion had not read it. That solace was offset, however, by the realization that many who praised the decision had not read it either. . . .

The opinion was, of course, not without its critics. Rather, too many, as those who processed the thousands of letters received by our court in the aftermath of its issuance would attest. Here, however, I am not examining the consequences of *Baker* in the context of "favorables" or "unfavorables"—the old standbys of public opinion polling. No justice on our court—nor on any appellate court of final jurisdiction, for that matter—would consider "popularity" in deciding a case. "Popular constitutionalism," as the phrase is used by Professor Reed, does not have its genesis in the "popularity" of constitutional opinions. Indeed, the "mobilized and politically active citizenry" that Professor Reed sees as characteristic of popular constitutionalism is more apt to be motivated by an appellate court's unpopular constitutional opinion. The passage of a state constitutional amendment effectively overturning the Hawaii Supreme Court decision granting marriage licenses to same-sex couples is illustrative.

In considering the impact of nonjudicial actors on the crafting of state constitutional law I do not mean to suggest that a state supreme court should abrogate its responsibility as a counter-majoritarian institution. Rather, I suggest that the court cannot ignore the presence of those nonjudicial actors. As Professor Reed astutely observes of the Hawaii experience, "the Hawaii Supreme Court's tremendous defeat at the hands of a majority of Hawaiian citizens did not stem from its institutional position as a counter-majoritarian body. Rather, its loss stemmed from its assumption that it alone could interpret the Hawaii Constitution and determine the range of constitutional discourse."

In other words, the architects assumed that the house could not be altered by those who lived in it. . . .

Considerations of strategy have long been held suspect by constitutional scholars—and . . . the suspicion that attaches to such factors in federal constitutionalism may be justified. But I cannot agree that the same skepticism ought to attach to the examination of strategic considerations in state constitutionalism. This is particularly so in jurisdictions like Vermont where an appeal is a matter of right; there is no intermediate appellate court; and no procedure to exercise case choice through a process of certiorari. . . .

I would add that not only are such judgments "natural and appropriate," but that the "strategic considerations" of constitutional decision-making in the state context, are a judicial responsibility as significant as considerations of history and textual analysis. I do not suggest that considerations of constitutional "strategy" will infuse every judicial opinion interpreting a state constitution. Indeed, "strategic considerations" . . . will seldom be a critical consideration in many state constitutional opinions. Yet it would be error to mistake its absence in most decisions for inappropriateness in any decision. . . .

If one accepts—and I understand that there are those who do not—the premise that sound state constitutionalism must acknowledge that judicial authority is not ultimate authority, then a paramount objective of a judicial opinion must be persuasiveness. By "persuasive" in this context, I mean more than the analytic rigor and sound legal reasoning that one should expect from a competent appellate court engaged in state constitutional interpretation. And I mean something other than the contribution one hopes a state constitutional opinion like *Baker* may make to a national dialogue about equality. The opinion must in its use of history, text, analysis, and language resonate with those who . . . live in the house and have the power to alter it. . . .

In the context of "pragmatic constitutionalism," one legitimate consideration in *Baker*—for this Justice at least—was the extent to which a state constitutional decision predicated upon a "suspect class/fundamental rights" test, would be persuasive to those with "extra-judicial authority" to change the result (i.e., the Legislature and citizens of Vermont). If, for example, an opinion premised on the rationale that gays in Vermont were a "suspect class" was likely to trigger a divisive legislative debate about whether the court had correctly concluded that homosexuals in Vermont were subject to animus and prejudice, or if a similar suspect class analysis concluding that the marriage statutes discriminated on the basis of sex was likely to prompt an extended public debate about the logic of the conclusion, one had to be supremely confident in the usefulness of federal constitutional doctrine to resolve an independent state constitutional claim of profound significance. That I was not is evident in the test adopted by the *Baker* majority, which rejected the suspect class/fundamental rights test in favor of a more flexible "weighing process," one which requires a "case specific analysis to ensure that any exclusion from the general benefit and protection of the law . . . bears a just and reasonable relation to the legislative goals." . . .

When confronted with such deeply divisive issues, a state constitutional opinion may not be persuasive with the extra judicial actors who can alter it if it does not acknowledge their legitimate constitutional role and engage them in finding a solution. . . . Whatever *Baker*'s ultimate fate as a statement of independent state constitutional jurisprudence, the experience of the Vermont community in responding to the opinion does demonstrate, I believe, that by conscious choice of language and analytic structure, a state appellate court may either arrest or advance the public debate even in such highly charged issues as same-sex marriage. . . .

Originally published as Jeffrey L. Amestoy, "Pragmatic Constitutionalism: Reflections on State Constitutional Theory and Same-Sex Marriage Claims," *Rutgers Law Journal* 35 (2004): 1249.

Part II

Judges in American Politics

5

Judicial Selection
and Retention

★ ★ ★

THE PREVIOUS CHAPTER explained how other actors influence judging, but it only scratched the surface, introducing you to just a few of the many ways in which other people influence judicial behavior and policymaking. The second half of the textbook explores the interactive nature of judging in greater detail, situating judges within a broader political context. We will look at how different methods of selecting and retaining judges affect judicial behavior, as well as the direct effects of public opinion on the choices that judges make. We will also study the impact of courts, identifying when judges are likely to bring about major policy change and how the people who interpret and implement court decisions can determine the amount of influence that judges have.

The subject of the next two chapters is the relationship between judges and the public. To what extent does public opinion shape judicial behavior? And how precisely does it matter? Many people believe that in a democracy judges should be accountable to the public, and in fact the evidence does suggest that judicial policy choices broadly reflect society's values. However, political scientists disagree about exactly how public opinion matters. (See Box 5.1.) Some say that public opinion has a *direct* impact on judging, which is to say that judges pay attention to what the public wants and change their behavior accordingly. But others maintain that the effects of public opinion are primarily *indirect*: judges do not think about public opinion, but the people's values still matter because they help to determine who gets to be a judge in the first place.

| TEXTBOX 5.1 | **Alternative Pathways for the Influence of Public Opinion on Judicial Behavior** |

What is the nature of the relationship between public opinion and judicial behavior? Political scientists have identified at least two alternative pathways of influence. The first specifies a *direct influence* of public opinion on judicial behavior. As the public mood becomes more liberal or conservative, judges change their behavior in response:

public opinion   →   judicial behavior

(X)   (Y)

The second alternative proposes an *indirect influence* of public opinion, with the selection and retention process acting as a **mediating variable** (Z). According to this approach, judges are not directly responsive to changes in the public mood, but the public has a say about who gets to be a judge, which in turn affects the types of policies that courts produce:

public opinion → selection and retention → judicial behavior

(X)   (Z)   (Y)

Which of these two alternatives seems more reasonable to you? Should we expect judges to pay attention to public opinion? Or is the selection process really the public's best chance to shape the judiciary? We will explore these possibilities over the next two chapters.

This chapter focuses on the indirect influences of public opinion by studying judicial selection and retention alternatives. As you will see, states use a variety of methods for selecting and retaining judges, and the procedures that they choose matter because they affect who sits on the bench and, by extension, what policies judges are likely to make. In fact, some would say that the selection process is the public's best opportunity to shape the contents of judicial policies, particularly in states that elect judges. However, it is unclear how responsive selection and retention systems actually are to public opinion, and whether it is even appropriate for the public to play an active role in choosing judges in the first place. How much influence is public opinion supposed to have over how judges decide cases?

OVERVIEW OF SELECTION AND
RETENTION ALTERNATIVES

Broadly speaking, **judicial selection** refers to the process by which candidates are initially chosen for judgeships, while **judicial retention** describes how judges are kept in office. Throughout the United States, judges are selected and retained with a variety of methods. The leading alternatives are in Table 5.1, which lists the methods of initial selection and terms of office of state supreme court justices. Looking at the list, you might be surprised at just how much variety there is in how states select and retain judges. Some states prefer to appoint judges, either by the governor or the legislature, while other states use partisan or nonpartisan elections. Still other states use a special committee to nominate the most qualified individuals for the bench.

States mix and match these selection and retention alternatives in different ways. For example, appointed judges might retain their offices through retention elections or by reappointment, depending on the judgeship. Elected judges might face contested partisan elections after short terms, or uncontested elections after long terms. States might use one method for selecting and retaining their state supreme court justices and another for retaining judges at other levels. Notably, however, no system precisely follows the federal model, with initial selection by the executive, confirmation by the legislature, and retention for life. A few states do permit governors to make the initial selection of candidates to their state supreme courts, but the justices do not have life tenure. Justices in California and Tennessee face the public in retention elections after their initial terms of office expire, while justices in Massachusetts and New Jersey have mandatory retirement at age seventy.

Why is there such a wide variety of judicial selection and retention alternatives? It is because states pursue a number of goals when they are designing their selection systems, and different systems emphasize different goals. (See Table 5.2.) Some states, for example, prioritize judicial *independence*, so their systems keep judges relatively free of electoral accountability. Systems that retain judges until age seventy, or that provide for their reappointment by governors or state legislators, emphasize electoral independence over other goals. The federal system is similarly meant to keep judges relatively independent from the electorate.

Other states, however, care more about *accountability*. They prefer to have judges who reflect public values, so they permit the public

Table 5.1 Methods of Initial Selection and Terms of Office for State Supreme Court Justices

Appointment		Partisan Elections		Nonpartisan Elections		Merit	
State	Term	State	Term	State	Term	State	Term
California (G)	12	Alabama	6	Arkansas	8	Alaska	10
Massachusetts (G)	to age 70	Illinois	10	Georgia	6	Arizona	6
New Jersey (G)	to age 70	Louisiana	10	Idaho	6	Colorado	10
South Carolina (L)	10	New Mexico	8	Kentucky	8	Connecticut	8
Tennessee (G)	8	Ohio	6	Michigan	8	Delaware	12
Virginia (L)	12	Pennsylvania	10	Minnesota	6	Florida	6
		Texas	6	Mississippi	8	Hawaii	10
				Montana	8	Indiana	10
				Nevada	6	Iowa	8
				North Carolina	8	Kansas	6
				North Dakota	10	Maine	7
				Oregon	6	Maryland	10
				Washington	6	Missouri	12
				West Virginia	12	Nebraska	6
				Wisconsin	10	New Hampshire	to age 70
						New York	14
						Oklahoma	6
						Rhode Island	Life
						South Dakota	8
						Utah	10
						Vermont	6
						Wyoming	8

Source: National Center for State Courts.

Note: (G) denotes gubernatorial appointment and (L) indicates legislative appointment. Many states that use merit selection have brief initial probationary terms of office for judges before their regular terms begin; the figures above reflect the lengths of their regular terms of office (in years). Methods of retention also vary by state. For more details, visit the National Center for State Courts' website (http://www.judicialselection.us/).

Table 5.2   The Goals of Judicial Selection Systems

		Appointment/ Life Tenure	Judicial Elections	Merit Selection
Goals	Independence	X		
	Accountability		X	
	Quality			X

to vote for judicial candidates. Some of these elections are contested, with at least two candidates running for the same office, while in other states elections are uncontested, with a single candidate running in a **retention election**. In contested election states, the candidates' party labels are sometimes on the ballot and sometimes not. Yet, in all of these systems, the goal is the same: to promote public accountability. States that use elections believe that the public should have a direct role in choosing judges, and that the public should be able to replace judges who make policy choices that they dislike.

Finally, a third group of states emphasizes appointing *qualified* judges. They use a system of **merit selection**, in which a nonpartisan commission nominates a slate of the most qualified candidates for judicial vacancies. The governor then selects a candidate from this list, and the successful candidate serves an initial term before facing the public in a retention election. This approach is sometimes referred to as the **Missouri Plan**, after the state that first adopted it. The goal is not to eliminate the public from the process, but to ensure that only the most qualified individuals will be contenders for judicial office.

In the rest of the chapter, we will explore how these different selection and retention alternatives affect judging. As you will see, critics are skeptical about whether any of these systems provide real opportunities for public feedback, but the nature of the critique varies with the system. For appointment and merit systems, the concern is that the public is too excluded from the process, whereas for systems that use judicial elections, critics maintain that public input is not meaningful because voters lack adequate knowledge and do not participate at sufficient levels. As it turns out, however, these critiques are flawed, and all selection systems permit a reasonable amount of public influence, to a greater or lesser degree. In this way, judicial selection provides an indirect pathway for the public to shape judicial behavior.

Appointment Systems

The first way of selecting judges is via appointment, either by the executive or, in some instances, the legislature. South Carolina and Virginia use legislative appointment for the selection and retention of judges at all levels of their state judiciaries. Appointment systems are designed to insulate judging from electoral politics, a tendency that is reinforced when judges have life tenure as well. The federal government uses this model for all federal judges, including Supreme Court justices. (See Judicial Process Box 5.1.) A few states also have appointment systems but do not provide life tenure, which means that judges are not as independent because they must maintain the support of the governor or the state legislature to remain in office.

Because appointment systems minimize opportunities for public influence, they raise questions about how democratic judging is, and

| JUDICIAL PROCESS BOX 5.1 | Selecting and Retaining Federal Judges |

The procedures for selecting and retaining federal judges are found in Articles II and III of the federal constitution. Article II focuses on the **initial selection** of judges, stating that the president "shall have power, by and with the advice and consent of the Senate, to . . . appoint . . . judges of the Supreme Court." Article III discusses judicial **retention**, specifying that "The judges, both of the supreme and inferior courts, shall hold their offices during good behavior."

Technically, the procedures for appointing and retaining all federal judges are identical. The president makes the appointment, subject to Senate confirmation, and the judges hold their offices for life. In practice, however, senators play a more active role in the selection of lower federal court judges. Under norms of senatorial courtesy, the Senate will not consider the nomination of a lower-court judge who is opposed by the home state senators from the president's party.

The procedures for selecting and retaining federal judges are probably familiar to you, but many people are surprised to learn that no other state uses the exact same methods for choosing judges. Most state judges are accountable to the public through some form of election, and hardly any state judges hold office for life. What do you think? Is the federal model the best way of selecting and retaining judges? Or should it be replaced with one of the alternative models that states employ?

whether it is appropriate for judges to review and invalidate the policies of elected branches. These concerns are heightened in the federal system whenever the Supreme Court strikes down acts of Congress. As law professor Alexander Bickel put it, "When the Supreme Court declares unconstitutional a legislative act or the action of an elected executive, it thwarts the will of representatives of the actual people of the here and now."[1] Bickel used the phrase the **counter-majoritarian difficulty** to describe the problem.

These worries might be reduced if there was reason to believe that appointed judges reflect public values. However, the amount of public influence over the selection process is uncertain. On the one hand, the public does choose the executives and legislators who select judicial candidates, which gives the public a chance to shape the judiciary with their votes. At the federal level, presidential candidates routinely talk about their judicial philosophies and point to specific judges whom they admire. Even if the public does not vote for presidents with the judiciary in mind, they are likely to know what they are getting, at least as far as the Supreme Court is concerned. President Donald Trump's election in 2016, for example, meant that the Court became more conservative than it would have been under a Hillary Clinton presidency. Instead of Merrick Garland, the more conservative Neil Gorsuch took a seat on the high court.

The appointment of lower federal courts is more complicated because the Senate plays a greater role in the initial selection of candidates. Under norms of senatorial courtesy, the Senate will not consider a candidate who is opposed by the home state senators from the president's party. Presidents often yield to Senate preferences on these occasions, permitting home state senators to propose nominees for the U.S. district courts and the U.S. courts of appeals. The public's vote for president therefore has less influence over the direction of the federal bench in many lower court appointments. Yet, because the public also votes for senators, there is still reason to be optimistic that public values will have an impact on the selection process.

On the other hand, it can be difficult to anticipate how judicial candidates will behave once they are on the bench, especially when they have the protections of life tenure. At the federal level, confirmation hearings only rarely provide meaningful information that the public can use to evaluate candidates. More typically, nominees for the Supreme Court give guarded answers that provide little insight into how they will decide cases. As Justice Ruth Bader Ginsburg stated at her confirmation hearings, there will be "no hints, no forecasts, no previews."[2] Sometimes these statements strain credulity, such as when Justice Clarence Thomas claimed that he could not remember personally discussing *Roe v. Wade* while he was in law school.[3]

An exception was the confirmation hearing of Robert Bork, whom President Ronald Reagan appointed to the Supreme Court in 1987. Bork spoke at length about his constitutional philosophy and offered detailed critiques of several Supreme Court precedents, including *Griswold v. Connecticut* (1965), which established the right to privacy. Bork said that the reasoning in *Griswold* was "utterly inadequate." He also criticized *Roe v. Wade* for having "almost no legal reasoning."[4] In return for his candor, the Democratic majority in the Senate refused to confirm Bork. To be sure, Bork might have fared better if Republicans had controlled the Senate, but his political opponents still likely would have used his remarks against him. After the Bork fiasco, candidates for federal judgeships learned that it was better not to say too much.

Another legacy of the Bork nomination is that presidents tend to choose judicial candidates who lack a clear record on important policy issues. The thinking is that if judicial candidates do not have a paper trail, then there will be less political ammunition for senators to use against them during the confirmation process, but occasionally the strategy backfires and presidents end up with judges who do not share their values. The most famous recent example was Justice David Souter, who had a much more liberal voting record than his appointing president, President George H. W. Bush, could have expected. Conservatives also point to Chief Justice John Roberts's votes to uphold the Affordable Care Act as a surprise to the Republicans who originally supported his nomination. If these surprises happen more frequently than not, then it would raise real questions about the capacity of the public to shape the appointment process because their votes for president would not necessarily change the direction of Supreme Court policymaking.

However, research indicates that presidents generally do get what they expect from their Supreme Court nominees. Political scientists Lee Epstein and Jeffrey Segal compared presidential values with the voting behavior of their appointees to the Supreme Court and found a high amount of correlation.[5] Figure 5.1 updates their findings with data on recent appointees through the Obama administration. In the figure, the line represents the ideologies of the appointing presidents, with the ideologies of the last five presidents marked on the line in bold for reference. Higher values are associated with more liberal

Figure 5.1   Presidential Ideology and Supreme Court Voting in Civil Liberties Cases, 1981–2014

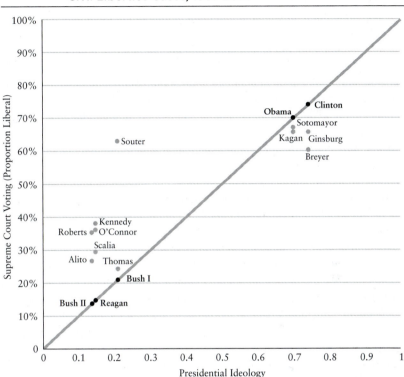

ideologies. Supreme Court nominees who voted more liberally than their appointing presidents in civil liberties cases are above the line, while nominees who were more conservative than their appointing presidents are below the line.

What do you think of the trends that you see? To what extent do presidents appoint justices who reflect their values? How much do justices deviate from presidential preferences? The data show that for the most part Supreme Court appointees vote consistently with the preferences of their appointing presidents. Over the past five presidencies, the only major outlier was Justice Souter, who was substantially more liberal in civil liberties cases than his appointing president, George H. W. Bush. Other appointees have been nearer the mark, with President Obama's nominees particularly close to his own ideology score. It would seem, then, that if the confirmation process is not as transparent as it could be, then at least the public can be assured that their votes for president will have a real impact on Supreme Court policymaking.

Judicial Elections

A second way of selecting and retaining judges is through elections, which give the public a more direct role in choosing judges than appointment systems do. Instead of having to trust that government officials will select judges who share their values, the public can make these choices themselves. The increased democratic accountability serves as a check on judicial power by permitting the public to remove unpopular judges from office. However, elections can also be a source of strength for the judiciary. The earliest supporters of judicial elections, in the middle of the nineteenth century, believed that judicial elections would enhance the power and prestige of the judiciary by giving it an independent foundation of public support.[6]

Judicial elections come in a variety of forms. In **contested elections,** several candidates compete for the same judicial office, while in retention elections a single judicial candidate is on the ballot. Judges might compete in **partisan elections**, with their party labels clearly identified, or **nonpartisan elections**, where they are not. As with other methods of selection and retention, states use different types of elections for different offices, or even for the same judgeships. For example, Illinois uses partisan elections for the initial selection of state supreme court justices, and then a retention election after a ten-year term. Merit selection systems also frequently use retention elections to retain judges after an initial term of office. The dynamics of retention elections are different from contested elections and will be considered in the next section.

Judicial elections are not available for federal judgeships, and other countries use them rarely, so readers might be surprised to learn how common judicial elections are in the states, and how long they have been in use. As early as 1812, Georgia amended its constitution to use partisan elections for certain judicial offices.[7] By 1850, two-thirds of the states in the union had adopted them, so that by the end of the nineteenth century, judicial elections were well established in the United States. States then began innovating with different forms of judicial elections and, for the most part, moved away from the partisan model. A number of states switched to nonpartisan elections to remove state judgeships from the control of party machines.[8] Merit selection systems, which states originally developed in the 1930s, favored uncontested retention elections.

The goal of all judicial elections is to increase the public's role in the selection and retention of judges. In theory, then, elections produce a more accountable, representative judiciary. But how effective are elections at achieving this goal? Do voters really end up getting a judiciary that reflects their values? One might assume that the answer is yes because elections obviously give voters a much greater opportunity to participate in selecting and retaining judges, but critics say that judicial elections do not work as intended because voters lack the knowledge that they need to make meaningful choices. The American Bar Association raised these concerns in a 2003 report chronicling the shortcomings of judicial elections. "Uninformed about the candidates' positions on relevant issues, uncertain about the candidates' qualifications or training, and unfamiliar with the candidates' job performance, voters are often unable to cast an informed ballot."[9]

Worse, some critics worry that voters fill in the gaps with information that is not relevant to judging, basing their votes on superficial qualities instead of considerations of law or policy. "Voters may be more motivated to vote," says one critic, "but not in the right ways."[10] The concern is that voters will reward such traits as "charisma, political savvy, connections to powerful interest groups and wealthy donors, a winning television appearance, and so on."[11] Two particularly vocal critics of judicial elections are retired Supreme Court Justice Sandra Day O'Connor and Chief Justice Ruth V. McGregor of the Arizona Supreme Court, who doubt that the public makes informed choices when they vote for judicial candidates. "Choosing judges through popular elections," they write, "always presented the danger that money and campaigning skills, rather than ability and merit, would determine who served as a judge."[12]

However, political science research indicates that these concerns about judicial elections are not valid. In fact, the public is fully capable of making meaningful choices in judicial elections, at least when certain conditions are met. One way of studying voter participation in judicial elections is by examining **roll-off**, which occurs when voters cast an incomplete ballot. For example, a voter might select a choice for president but not mark a preference for judicial candidates who are listed further down the ballot. The assumption is that when levels of roll-off are high, it is because voters are not prepared to participate in judicial elections. Voters do not know who to select for judicial offices, so they leave those sections of the ballot blank.

Figure 5.2 looks at roll-off levels by election type and, as you can see, there is considerable variation. What do you think about the

Figure 5.2 Average Roll-Off in State Supreme Court Elections, 1990–2004

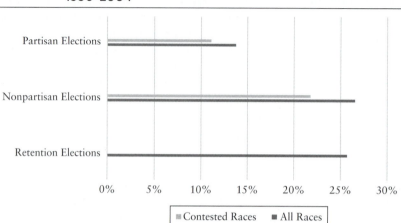

Source: Chris W. Bonneau and Melinda Gann Hall, *In Defense of Judicial Elections* (New York: Routledge, 2009), 27.

trends that you observe? What conclusions can you make about when the public is most likely to participate in judicial elections? When is the public less likely to participate? The data show that levels of roll-off are the lowest in states that use partisan elections to retain judges. Roll-off levels are at 11.1 percent in contested partisan elections, compared to 21.8 percent in contested nonpartisan elections and 25.7 percent in retention elections. The public, in other words, is the most prepared to vote for judicial candidates in states that use partisan elections.

Why does voter participation in judicial elections vary by election type? It is because party identification provides information to voters that they need to make informed choices. This information is the most readily available to voters in partisan election states because party labels are on the ballot. Nonpartisan elections do not provide this information, but as long as elections are contested, campaigns can give voters clues about the candidates' preferences. Chris Bonneau and Damon Cann found that voters in nonpartisan elections can sometimes guess candidates' party identifications from their campaign statements. "When the signal is strong," they wrote, "voters were able to identify the candidate who is their co-partisan."[13] However, the researchers still found roll-off levels to be higher in nonpartisan elections than partisan elections because when voters cannot guess a candidate's partisan identification, they do not vote.

Retention elections have among the highest roll-off levels because they provide the least information to voters. Without other candidates to challenge them, incumbent judges have fewer incentives to campaign or to talk about their judicial philosophies. The implication is that a movement back to contested elections, especially partisan ones, could enhance democratic accountability by giving voters the information that they need to make rational voting decisions. The irony is that many of the reforms that were intended to make judicial elections less political have ended up making it more difficult for voters to participate in elections. Retention elections are particularly problematic because there is so little campaign activity to keep voters informed.

On balance, then, the evidence suggests that contested elections enhance accountability, but despite these benefits, critics point to several disadvantages that they say should discourage their more widespread use. First, critics say that contested elections damage public confidence in courts by requiring judges to engage in campaign activity that makes them look less impartial. For example, critics say that it is problematic for judicial candidates to announce their views on disputed legal and political issues such as crime, welfare, and abortion. Yet, when states such as Minnesota tried to restrict the campaign speech of judicial candidates, the U.S. Supreme Court struck down the policy in *Republican Party of Minnesota v. White* (2002).[14] The justices ruled that, as long as judges do not pledge to decide particular cases in certain ways, judicial candidates have free speech rights that must be respected. (See case excerpt at the end of the chapter.)

Political scientists who have studied the issue have found no evidence that campaign statements cause public confidence in courts to decline. James Gibson analyzed public attitudes about courts in states that elect judges and concluded that many of the concerns that critics raise about judicial elections have no foundation. "When citizens hear issue-based speech from candidates for judicial office, court legitimacy does *not* suffer," Gibson concluded. "It seems that many Americans . . . are not at all uncomfortable when candidates for the bench announce how they feel about the sorts of sociopolitical issues coming before courts these days."[15] On the contrary, Gibson found that elections generally increase public confidence in courts, "most likely by reminding citizens that their courts are accountable to their constituents, the people."[16]

The major exception is campaign contributions. According to Gibson, "Contributions to candidates for judicial office imply for many a conflict of interest, even a *quid pro quo* relationship between the donor and the judge, which undermines perceived impartiality and legitimacy."[17] Even the appearance of bias could be enough to damage legitimacy if the public thinks that judges are unprincipled. Several of the justices in *Republican Party of Minnesota v. White* were concerned that campaign contributions would damage public confidence in this way. In a concurring opinion, Justice O'Connor worried that "campaign donations may leave judges feeling indebted to certain parties or interest groups." She wrote, "Even if judges were able to refrain from favoring donors, the mere possibility that judges' decisions may be motivated by the desire to repay campaign contributors is likely to undermine the public's confidence in the judiciary."[18] It is unclear how much these concerns are grounded in reality. While some studies have found that elected judges systematically favor their campaign contributors, others have not.[19]

A second concern about judicial elections is that campaign activity will lead to a greater number of judicial **recusals**: the withdrawal of judges from cases because of bias or the appearance of bias. As campaigns for judicial office have become more expensive in recent years, and money more prevalent, it increases the likelihood that the litigants and lawyers who appear before judges are also campaign donors. One such controversy arose in *Caperton v. Massey* (2009), when a justice on West Virginia's high court declined to recuse himself from a dispute involving one of his top contributors.[20] Justice Brent Benjamin received $3 million from Don Blankenship, whose company had just suffered a $50 million jury verdict for "fraudulent misrepresentation, concealment, and tortious interference with existing contractual relations."[21] It seemed clear that Blankenship was expecting his sponsored candidate, Justice Benjamin, to reverse the jury's verdict on appeal. And Justice Benjamin did, by a 3–2 vote.

The case eventually made its way to the U.S. Supreme Court, which ruled that Justice Benjamin's failure to recuse himself had deprived the litigants of due process.[22] (See case excerpt at the end of the chapter.) "We conclude that there is a serious risk of actual bias—based on objective and reasonable perceptions—when a person with a personal stake in a particular case had a significant and disproportionate influence in placing the judge on the case by raising funds or directing the judge's election campaign when the case was pending or imminent."[23] After *Caperton*, a number of states considered revising their recusal policies to reduce the appearance of bias stemming from campaign contributions. For example, a New York State judicial board required the recusal of any judge who had received at least

$2,500 from the lawyers or other parties to a case within the past two years.[24] The reforms were meant to combat a culture in which lawyers would try to gain influence with judges by contributing to their campaigns.

Despite these concerns, supporters of contested elections say that they are a net benefit to the public—and for courts—because campaign activity increases voter knowledge about the judiciary and improves the public's ability to keep judges accountable to them. Moreover, the public, when asked, tends to favor judicial elections over other selection and retention methods.[25] What do you think? Do you agree that it is better for the public to have a direct role in the selection and retention of judges? Or do elections carry too much of a risk that judges will not be impartial? Is it possible to elect judges without making them look like politicians in robes?

Merit Selection

The third method of choosing judges, favored by almost half of the states, is merit selection, which prioritizes appointing qualified judges. This approach is sometimes referred to as the Missouri Plan in recognition of the state that first adopted it, in 1940. States vary in precisely how they approach merit selection, but Missouri's own nonpartisan court plan is a typical model. (See Figure 5.3.) When a vacancy occurs, candidates apply to a nonpartisan commission, which interviews the applicants and submits three names to the governor for consideration. The governor then selects a nominee from the list, and that candidate serves for an initial term of office. Finally, the public decides whether to maintain the appointment by voting in an uncontested retention election. In this way, merit selection combines features of other systems, but with a focus on the candidates' qualifications instead of their political connections, issue positions, or party loyalties.

It is an open question whether merit selection actually results in a more qualified judiciary. Certainly, states try to design nominating commissions that are fair and balanced. For example, in Missouri, the Appellate Judicial Commission that reviews candidates for appellate courts is composed of three lawyers elected by the Missouri

Figure 5.3 The Missouri Plan

nonpartisan commission →	governor →	public
selects three candidates for a judicial appointment	chooses one of the candidates	votes in retention election at next general election

bar, three citizens chosen by the governor, and the chief justice of the state supreme court.[26] Yet, there is no guarantee that nominating commissions will end up choosing more qualified judges, because the commissioners might wish to advance goals and preferences of their own. Some research indicates that nominating commissions reflect the liberal, elite preferences of state bar associations,[27] while other research has found that bar associations tend to rate minority applicants as less qualified.[28] In general, however, political scientists who have compared the qualifications of judges across multiple selection systems have found little evidence that merit selection produces more qualified judges.[29]

From the standpoint of democratic accountability, it does seem clear that merit systems make it more difficult for the public to influence the composition of their state judiciaries. Even though retention elections technically give the public an opportunity to recall judges who make choices that they dislike, in practice it is very rare for a judge to lose a retention election. Table 5.3 shows the average retention election results for state appellate court judges in 2016, and as you can see, the typical incumbent won reelection by a vote of about 69.6 percent.[30] In fact, no appellate judge lost reelection that year.

Table 5.3   Results for 2016 Judicial Retention Elections, State Appellate Courts

State	Number of Seats	Average Retention Vote
Alaska	3	59.0%
Arizona	7	77.2%
Colorado	11	68.5%
Florida	31	69.3%
Illinois	7	77.3%
Indiana	4	71.5%
Iowa	7	67.9%
Kansas	11	61.3%
Maryland	5	83.7%
Missouri	3	61.6%
Nebraska	7	74.7%
New Mexico	4	70.8%
Oklahoma	7	60.5%
Tennessee	10	71.3%
Wyoming	3	76.5%
TOTAL	**120**	**69.6%**

Source: Ballotpedia, https://ballotpedia.org/.

Political scientists agree that these high success rates do not occur because voters actually approve of the jobs that their judges are doing, but because voters do not know much about them. With no other candidates to run against incumbents and highlight their faults, voters lack knowledge about judges' records that might prompt negative votes.

Nevertheless, voters still can and do use retention elections to remove judges who make choices that depart too far from public values. Perhaps the most famous example was the reaction of Iowa voters to a 2009 state supreme court decision legalizing same-sex marriage in that state. Public opinion in Iowa was not receptive to the state supreme court's decision at the time. A poll released by the University of Iowa just a day before found that only 26.2 percent of citizens in the state favored same-sex marriage.[31] After the Iowa Supreme Court unanimously mandated marriage equality anyway, in *Varnum v. Brien*, interest groups mobilized against three of the justices who were up for reelection in the next retention election, including Chief Justice Marsha Ternus.[32] Because of the backlash, all three justices lost their jobs. While cases such as *Varnum* are surely the exception—no other justice had lost a retention election in Iowa before—they are an important reminder that judges in merit selection systems are not necessarily safe from popular recall.

DISCUSSION QUESTIONS

1. How much influence should the public have over choosing judges? Do any of our methods of selecting and retaining judges give the public enough of a voice? Why or why not?
2. Some critics of judicial elections claim that they make judges less impartial. Do you share these concerns? Do any systems of selection and retention do a good job of promoting impartiality, based on what you know about judging?
3. How much campaigning is it appropriate for judicial candidates to do? Should any subjects be off limits to them? Do you agree with how the U.S. Supreme Court addressed this issue in *Republican Party of Minnesota v. White*?
4. Should judges recuse themselves from cases whenever one of their campaign donors appears before them, or only sometimes? What other types of ethical problems might judges face, besides those mentioned in *Caperton v. Massey*?

KEY TERMS

mediating variable
judicial selection
judicial retention
retention election
merit selection
Missouri Plan
initial selection

counter-majoritarian difficulty
contested elections
partisan elections
nonpartisan elections
roll-off
recusals

FURTHER READING

Epstein, Lee, and Jeffrey A. Segal. 2007. *Advice and Consent: The Politics of Judicial Appointments*. New York: Oxford University Press.

Bonneau, Chris W., and Melinda Gann Hall. 2009. *In Defense of Judicial Elections*. New York: Routledge.

Bonneau, Chris W., and Damon M. Cann. 2015. *Voters' Verdicts: Citizens Campaigns, and Institutions in State Supreme Courts*. Charlottesville: University of Virginia Press.

NOTES

1. Alexander M. Bickel, *The Least Dangerous Branch*, second edition (New Haven, CT: Yale University Press, 1986), 16–17.

2. Transcript, "Nomination of Ruth Bader Ginsburg, to be Associate Justice of the Supreme Court of the United States," Government Printing Office (1994), at 323, available at https://www.loc.gov/law/find/nominations/ginsburg/hearing .pdf.

3. Transcript, "Nomination of Judge Clarence Thomas to be Associate Justice of the Supreme Court of the United States," Part 1 of 4, Government Printing Office (1993), 222, available at https://www.loc.gov/law/find/nominations /thomas/hearing-pt1.pdf.

4. Transcript, "Nomination of Robert H. Bork to be Associate Justice of the Supreme Court of the United States," Part 1 of 5, Government Printing Office (1989), 184, available at https://www.loc.gov/law/find/nominations/bork/hearing -pt1.pdf.

5. Lee Epstein and Jeffrey A. Segal, *Advice and Consent: The Politics of Judicial Appointments* (New York: Oxford University Press, 2005). It should be noted that the ideology and voting scores are measured differently and so are not precisely equivalent. Presidential ideology is based on the DW-NOMINATE common-space scores. *See* Royce Carroll, Jeff Lewis, James Lo, Nolan McCarty, Keith Poole, and Howard Rosenthal, "'Common Space' DW-NOMINATE Scores with Bootstrapped Standard Errors," available at https://legacy.voteview.com /dwnomin_joint_house_and_senate.htm. Supreme Court voting in civil liberties cases is from the Supreme Court database, available at http://scdb.wustl.edu/.

6. Kermit L. Hall, "Progressive Reform and the Decline of Democratic Accountability: The Popular Election of State Supreme Court Judges, 1850–1920," *American Bar Foundation Research Journal* 9 (1984): 347–48.

7. Larry C. Berkson, Rachel Caufield, and Malia Reddick, "Judicial Selection in the United States: A Special Report," *American Judicature Society* (2004), available at http://judicialselection.us/uploads/documents/Berkson_1196091951709 .pdf.

8. Id.

9. Alfred P. Carlton Jr., *Justice in Jeopardy: Report of the American Bar Association Commission on the 21st Century Judiciary* (Chicago: The American Bar Association, 2003), 27, available at http://www.americanbar.org/content/dam/ aba/migrated/judind/jeopardy/pdf/report.authcheckdam.pdf.

10. David E. Pozen, "The Irony of Judicial Elections," *Columbia Law Review* 108 (2008): 304.

11. Ibid.

12. Sandra Day O'Connor and Ruth V. McGregor, "Judicial Selection Principles: A Perspective," *Albany Law Review* 75 (2012): 1742.

13. Chris W. Bonneau and Damon M. Cann, *Voters' Verdicts: Citizens, Campaigns, and Institutions in State Supreme Court Elections* (Charlottesville: University of Virginia Press, 2015), 102.

14. Republican Party of Minnesota v. White, 536 U.S. 765 (2002).

15. James L. Gibson, "'New-Style' Judicial Campaigns and the Legitimacy of State High Courts," *Journal of Politics* 71 (2009): 1277–88.

16. James L. Gibson, *Electing Judges: The Surprising Effects of Campaigning on Judicial Legitimacy* (Chicago: University of Chicago Press, 2012), 130; *but see* Sara C. Benesh, "Understanding Public Confidence in American Courts," *Journal of Politics* 68 (2006): 697 (finding that judicial elections reduce confidence in courts).

17. Gibson, "New Style Judicial Campaigns," 1288.

18. *White*, at 790 (O'Connor, J., concurring).

19. *Compare* Damon M. Cann, "Campaign Contributions and Judicial Behavior," *American Review of Politics* 23 (2002): 261 (finding no effect of campaign contributions on judicial behavior in Wisconsin) *with* Damon M. Cann, "Justice for Sale? Campaign Contributions and Judicial Decisionmaking," *State Politics and Policy Quarterly* 7 (2007): 281 (finding an effect of campaign contributions on judicial behavior in Georgia).

20. Caperton v. Massey, 556 U.S. 868 (2009). *See also* Tumey v. Ohio, 273 U.S. 510 (1927).

21. *Caperton*, at 872.

22. Id., at 868.

23. Id., at 884.

24. William Glaberson, "New York Takes Step on Money in Judicial Elections," *New York Times*, February 14, 2011, A1.

25. Chris W. Bonneau and Melinda Gann Hall, *In Defense of Judicial Elections* (New York: Routledge), 47; *see also* Chris W. Bonneau and Damon M. Cann, "Party Identification and Vote Choice in Partisan and Nonpartisan Elections," *Political Behavior* 37 (2015), 44 (describing failed efforts to switch merit

selection in Minnesota and Nevada); *and* "Nevada Voters Reject Judicial Ballot Measures," *Las Vegas Sun*, November 3, 2010, available at http://m.lasvegassun. com/news/2010/nov/03/nv-nevada-measures-2nd-ld-writethru/.

26. Missouri Courts, "Missouri Nonpartisan Court Plan," available at https:// www.courts.mo.gov/page.jsp?id=297.

27. Brian T. Fitzpatrick, "The Politics of Merit Selection," *Missouri Law Review* 74 (2009): 675.

28. Maya Sen, "Minority Judicial Candidates Have Changed: The ABA Ratings Gap Has Not," *Judicature* 98 (2014): 46; *but see* Mark S. Hurwitz and Drew Noble Lanier, "Diversity in State and Federal Appellate Courts: Change and Continuity across 20 Years," *Justice System Journal* 29 (2008): 47 (finding no evidence that the diversity of state judiciaries varies by selection system).

29. Henry R. Glick and Craig F. Emmert, "Selection Systems and Judicial Characteristics: The Recruitment of State Supreme Court Judges," *Judicature* 70 (1987): 228 (examining differences in the education and experience of judicial candidates across selection systems); Stephen J. Choi, G. Mitu Gulati, and Eric A. Posner, "Professionals or Politicians: The Uncertain Empirical Case for an Elected Rather Than Appointed Judiciary," *Journal of Law, Economics, and Organization* 26 (2008): 290.

30. Cindy Kehler, "Incumbents Overwhelmingly Prevail in State Courts in 2016 Elections," *Ballotpedia*, November 11, 2016, available at https://ballotpedia.org/ Incumbents_overwhelmingly_prevail_in_state_courts_in_2016_elections.

31. *See* University of Iowa Hawkeye Poll, "Iowans' Views on Gay Marriage and Civil Unions" (April 2, 2009).

32. Varnum v. Brien, 763 N.W.2d 862 (Iowa 2009).

CASE ANALYSIS

Republican Party of Minnesota v. White, 536 U.S. 765 (2002)

*In a 5–4 opinion, the U.S. Supreme Court struck down a state policy pro-
hibiting judicial candidates from "announcing their views on disputed legal
and political issues." Some of the justices also used the occasion to comment on the desirability of judicial elections in general. What do you think?
Should judicial candidates be able to discuss their views on disputed issues? Should we expect judges to behave differently from candidates for
other elected offices?*

JUSTICE SCALIA delivered the opinion of the Court.

The question presented in this case is whether the First Amendment permits the
Minnesota Supreme Court to prohibit candidates for judicial election in that
State from announcing their views on disputed legal and political issues.

I

Since Minnesota's admission to the Union in 1858, the State's Constitution has
provided for the selection of all state judges by popular election. Since 1912,
those elections have been nonpartisan. Since 1974, they have been subject to
a legal restriction which states that a "candidate for a judicial office, including
an incumbent judge," shall not "announce his or her views on disputed legal
or political issues." This prohibition, promulgated by the Minnesota Supreme
Court and based on Canon 7(B) of the 1972 American Bar Association (ABA)
Model Code of Judicial Conduct, is known as the "announce clause." Incumbent
judges who violate it are subject to discipline, including removal, censure, civil
penalties, and suspension without pay. Lawyers who run for judicial office also
must comply with the announce clause. Those who violate it are subject to, *inter
alia*, disbarment, suspension, and probation.

In 1996, one of the petitioners, Gregory Wersal, ran for associate justice of
the Minnesota Supreme Court. In the course of the campaign, he distributed literature criticizing several Minnesota Supreme Court decisions on issues such as
crime, welfare, and abortion. . . . In 1998, Wersal ran again for the same office.
Early in that race, he sought an advisory opinion from the Lawyers Board with
regard to whether it planned to enforce the announce clause. The Lawyers Board
responded equivocally, stating that, although it had significant doubts about the
constitutionality of the provision, it was unable to answer his question because
he had not submitted a list of the announcements he wished to make. Shortly
thereafter, Wersal filed this lawsuit in Federal District Court against respondents,
seeking, *inter alia*, a declaration that the announce clause violates the First
Amendment and an injunction against its enforcement. . . .

II

Before considering the constitutionality of the announce clause, we must be
clear about its meaning. Its text says that a candidate for judicial office shall
not "announce his or her views on disputed legal or political issues." We know

that "announcing . . . views" on an issue covers much more than *promising* to decide an issue a particular way. The prohibition extends to the candidate's mere statement of his current position, even if he does not bind himself to maintain that position after election. All the parties agree this is the case, because the Minnesota Code contains a so-called "pledges or promises" clause, which *separately* prohibits judicial candidates from making "pledges or promises of conduct in office other than the faithful and impartial performance of the duties of the office,"—a prohibition that is not challenged here and on which we express no view. . . .

III

As the Court of Appeals recognized, the announce clause both prohibits speech on the basis of its content and burdens a category of speech that is "at the core of our First Amendment freedoms"—speech about the qualifications of candidates for public office. The Court of Appeals concluded that the proper test to be applied to determine the constitutionality of such a restriction is what our cases have called strict scrutiny; the parties do not dispute that this is correct. Under the strict-scrutiny test, respondents have the burden to prove that the announce clause is (1) narrowly tailored, to serve (2) a compelling state interest. In order for respondents to show that the announce clause is narrowly tailored, they must demonstrate that it does not "unnecessarily circumscribe protected expression." The Court of Appeals concluded that respondents had established two interests as sufficiently compelling to justify the announce clause: preserving the impartiality of the state judiciary and preserving the appearance of the impartiality of the state judiciary. . . . Respondents are rather vague, however, about what they mean by "impartiality." Indeed, although the term is used throughout the Eighth Circuit's opinion, the briefs, the Minnesota Code of Judicial Conduct, and the ABA Codes of Judicial Conduct, none of these sources bothers to define it. Clarity on this point is essential before we can decide whether impartiality is indeed a compelling state interest, and, if so, whether the announce clause is narrowly tailored to achieve it.

One meaning of "impartiality" in the judicial context—and of course its root meaning—is the lack of bias for or against either *party* to the proceeding. . . . We think it plain that the announce clause is not narrowly tailored to serve impartiality (or the appearance of impartiality) in this sense. Indeed, the clause is barely tailored to serve that interest *at all*, inasmuch as it does not restrict speech for or against particular *parties*, but rather speech for or against particular *issues*. To be sure, when a case arises that turns on a legal issue on which the judge (as a candidate) had taken a particular stand, the party taking the opposite stand is likely to lose. But not because of any bias against that party, or favoritism toward the other party. *Any* party taking that position is just as likely to lose. The judge is applying the law (as he sees it) evenhandedly.

It is perhaps possible to use the term "impartiality" in the judicial context (though this is certainly not a common usage) to mean lack of preconception in favor of or against a particular *legal view*. This sort of impartiality would be concerned, not with guaranteeing litigants equal application of the law, but rather with guaranteeing them an equal chance to persuade the court on the legal points in their case. Impartiality in this sense may well be an interest served by the announce clause, but it is not a *compelling* state interest, as strict scrutiny requires. A judge's lack of predisposition regarding the relevant legal issues in a case has never been thought a necessary component of equal justice, and with good reason. For one thing, it is virtually impossible to find a judge who does not have preconceptions about the law. . . . And since avoiding judicial preconceptions on legal issues is neither possible nor desirable, pretending otherwise by attempting to preserve the "appearance" of that type of impartiality can hardly be a compelling state interest either.

A third possible meaning of "impartiality" (again not a common one) might be described as openmindedness. This quality in a judge demands, not that he have no preconceptions on legal issues, but that he be willing to consider views that oppose his preconceptions, and remain open to persuasion, when the issues arise in a pending case. This sort of impartiality seeks to guarantee each litigant, not an *equal* chance to win the legal points in the case, but at least *some* chance of doing so. It may well be that impartiality in this sense, and the appearance of it, are desirable in the judiciary, but we need not pursue that inquiry, since we do not believe the Minnesota Supreme Court adopted the announce clause for that purpose.

Respondents argue that the announce clause serves the interest in openmindedness, or at least in the appearance of openmindedness, because it relieves a judge from pressure to rule a certain way in order to maintain consistency with statements the judge has previously made. The problem is, however, that statements in election campaigns are such an infinitesimal portion of the public commitments to legal positions that judges (or judges-to-be) undertake, that this object of the prohibition is implausible. Before they arrive on the bench (whether by election or otherwise) judges have often committed themselves on legal issues that they must later rule upon. . . .

The short of the matter is this: In Minnesota, a candidate for judicial office may not say "I think it is constitutional for the legislature to prohibit same-sex marriages." He may say the very same thing, however, up until the very day before he declares himself a candidate, and may say it repeatedly (until litigation is pending) after he is elected. As a means of pursuing the objective of open-mindedness that respondents now articulate, the announce clause is so woefully underinclusive as to render belief in that purpose a challenge to the credulous. . . .

* * *

There is an obvious tension between the article of Minnesota's popularly approved Constitution which provides that judges shall be elected, and the Minnesota Supreme Court's announce clause which places most subjects of interest to the voters off limits. That opposition may be well taken (it certainly had the support of the Founders of the Federal Government), but the First Amendment does not permit it to achieve its goal by leaving the principle of elections in place while preventing candidates from discussing what the elections are about. . . .

The Minnesota Supreme Court's canon of judicial conduct prohibiting candidates for judicial election from announcing their views on disputed legal and political issues violates the First Amendment. Accordingly, we reverse the grant of summary judgment to respondents and remand the case for proceedings consistent with this opinion.

It is so ordered.

JUSTICE O'CONNOR, concurring.

I join the opinion of the Court but write separately to express my concerns about judicial elections generally. Respondents claim that "the Announce Clause is necessary . . . to protect the State's compelling governmental interest in an actual and perceived . . . impartial judiciary." I am concerned that, even aside from what judicial candidates may say while campaigning, the very practice of electing judges undermines this interest.

We of course want judges to be impartial, in the sense of being free from any personal stake in the outcome of the cases to which they are assigned. But if judges are subject to regular elections they are likely to feel that they have at least some personal stake in the outcome of every publicized case. Elected judges cannot help being aware that if the public is not satisfied with the outcome of a particular case, it could hurt their reelection prospects. Even if judges were able to suppress their awareness of the potential electoral consequences of their decisions and refrain from acting on it, the public's confidence in the judiciary could be undermined simply by the possibility that judges would be unable to do so. Moreover, contested elections generally entail campaigning. And campaigning for a judicial post today can require substantial funds. Even if judges were able to refrain from favoring donors, the mere possibility that judges' decisions may be motivated by the desire to repay campaign contributors is likely to undermine the public's confidence in the judiciary.

Despite these significant problems, 39 States currently employ some form of judicial elections for their appellate courts, general jurisdiction trial courts, or both. Judicial elections were not always so prevalent. The first 29 States of the Union adopted methods for selecting judges that did not involve popular elections. As the Court explains, however, beginning with Georgia in 1812, States began adopting systems for judicial elections. From the 1830's until the 1850's, as part of the Jacksonian movement toward greater popular control of public office, this trend accelerated. By the beginning of the 20th century, however, elected judiciaries increasingly came to be viewed as incompetent and corrupt, and criticism of partisan judicial elections mounted. In 1906, Roscoe Pound gave a speech to the American Bar Association in which he claimed that "compelling judges to become politicians, in many jurisdictions has almost destroyed the traditional respect for the bench."

In response to such concerns, some States adopted a modified system of judicial selection that became known as the Missouri Plan (because Missouri was the first State to adopt it for most of its judicial posts). Under the Missouri Plan, judges are appointed by a high elected official, generally from a list of nominees put together by a nonpartisan nominating commission, and then subsequently stand for unopposed retention elections in which voters are asked whether the judges should be recalled. If a judge is recalled, the vacancy is filled through a new nomination and appointment. This system obviously reduces threats to judicial impartiality, even if it does not eliminate all popular pressure on judges. The Missouri Plan is currently used to fill at least some judicial offices in 15

States. Thirty-one States, however, still use popular elections to select some or all of their appellate and/or general jurisdiction trial court judges, who thereafter run for reelection periodically. Of these, slightly more than half use nonpartisan elections, and the rest use partisan elections. Most of the States that do not have any form of judicial elections choose judges through executive nomination and legislative confirmation.

Minnesota has chosen to select its judges through contested popular elections instead of through an appointment system or a combined appointment and retention election system along the lines of the Missouri Plan. In doing so the State has voluntarily taken on the risks to judicial bias described above. As a result, the State's claim that it needs to significantly restrict judges' speech in order to protect judicial impartiality is particularly troubling. If the State has a problem with judicial impartiality, it is largely one the State brought upon itself by continuing the practice of popularly electing judges.

JUSTICE GINSBURG, with whom JUSTICE STEVENS, JUSTICE SOUTER, and JUSTICE BREYER join, dissenting.
Whether state or federal, elected or appointed, judges perform a function fundamentally different from that of the people's elected representatives. Legislative and executive officials act on behalf of the voters who placed them in office; "judges represent the Law." Unlike their counterparts in the political branches, judges are expected to refrain from catering to particular constituencies or committing themselves on controversial issues in advance of adversarial presentation. Their mission is to decide "individual cases and controversies" on individual records, neutrally applying legal principles, and, when necessary, "standing up to what is generally supreme in a democracy: the popular will.". . .

I would differentiate elections for political offices, in which the First Amendment holds full sway, from elections designed to select those whose office it is to administer justice without respect to persons. Minnesota's choice to elect its judges, I am persuaded, does not preclude the State from installing an election process geared to the judicial office.

Legislative and executive officials serve in representative capacities. They are agents of the people; their primary function is to advance the interests of their constituencies. Candidates for political offices, in keeping with their representative role, must be left free to inform the electorate of their positions on specific issues. . . . Judges, however, are not political actors. They do not sit as representatives of particular persons, communities, or parties; they serve no faction or constituency. . . . Thus, the rationale underlying unconstrained speech in elections for political office—that representative government depends on the public's ability to choose agents who will act at its behest—does not carry over to campaigns for the bench. . . .

For more than three-quarters of a century, States like Minnesota have endeavored, through experiment tested by experience, to balance the constitutional interests in judicial integrity and free expression within the unique setting of an elected judiciary. I would uphold it as an essential component in Minnesota's accommodation of the complex and competing concerns in this sensitive area. Accordingly, I would affirm the judgment of the Court of Appeals for the Eighth Circuit.

CASE ANALYSIS

Caperton v. Massey, 556 U.S. 868 (2009)

In Caperton v. Massey *(2009), the U.S. Supreme Court ruled that it violated the due process clause for state supreme court justices to decide cases involving their major campaign donors. Do you agree with Justice Kennedy's majority opinion? When are campaign contributions likely to cause bias or the appearance of bias? Does the dissent persuade you that an increase in the number of recusal motions would do more to undermine public confidence in courts?*

JUSTICE KENNEDY delivered the opinion of the Court.

In this case the Supreme Court of Appeals of West Virginia reversed a trial court judgment, which had entered a jury verdict of $50 million. Five justices heard the case, and the vote to reverse was 3 to 2. The question presented is whether the Due Process Clause of the Fourteenth Amendment was violated when one of the justices in the majority denied a recusal motion. The basis for the motion was that the justice had received campaign contributions in an extraordinary amount from, and through the efforts of, the board chairman and principal officer of the corporation found liable for the damages. Under our precedents there are objective standards that require recusal when "the probability of actual bias on the part of the judge or decisionmaker is too high to be constitutionally tolerable." Applying those precedents, we find that, in all the circumstances of this case, due process requires recusal.

I

In August 2002 a West Virginia jury returned a verdict that found respondents A. T. Massey Coal Co. and its affiliates (hereinafter Massey) liable for fraudulent misrepresentation, concealment, and tortious interference with existing contractual relations. The jury awarded petitioners Hugh Caperton, Harman Development Corp., Harman Mining Corp., and Sovereign Coal Sales (hereinafter Caperton) the sum of $50 million in compensatory and punitive damages. . . .

Don Blankenship is Massey's chairman, chief executive officer, and president. After the verdict but before the appeal, West Virginia held its 2004 judicial elections. Knowing the Supreme Court of Appeals of West Virginia would consider the appeal in the case, Blankenship decided to support an attorney who sought to replace Justice McGraw. Justice McGraw was a candidate for reelection to that court. The attorney who sought to replace him was Brent Benjamin.

In addition to contributing the $1,000 statutory maximum to Benjamin's campaign committee, Blankenship donated almost $2.5 million to "And For The Sake Of The Kids," a political organization formed under 26 U.S.C. §527. The §527 organization opposed McGraw and supported Benjamin. Blankenship's donations accounted for more than two-thirds of the total funds it raised. This was not all. Blankenship spent, in addition, just over $500,000 on independent expenditures—for direct mailings and letters soliciting donations as well as television and newspaper advertisements—"to support . . . Brent Benjamin." To provide some perspective, Blankenship's $3 million in contributions were more than the total amount spent by all other Benjamin supporters and three times the amount spent by Benjamin's own committee. Caperton contends that Blankenship spent $1 million more than the total amount spent by the campaign committees of both candidates combined.

Benjamin won. He received 382,036 votes (53.3%), and McGraw received 334,301 votes (46.7%). In October 2005, before Massey filed its petition for appeal in West Virginia's highest court, Caperton moved to disqualify now-Justice Benjamin under the Due Process Clause and the West Virginia Code of Judicial Conduct, based on the conflict caused by Blankenship's campaign involvement. Justice Benjamin denied the motion in April 2006. He indicated that he "carefully considered the bases and accompanying exhibits proffered by the movants." But he found "no objective information . . . to show that this Justice has a bias for or against any litigant, that this Justice has prejudged the matters which comprise this litigation, or that this Justice will be anything but fair and impartial.". . . In November 2007 that court reversed the $50 million verdict against Massey. . . .

II

It is axiomatic that "[a] fair trial in a fair tribunal is a basic requirement of due process." As the Court has recognized, however, "most matters relating to judicial disqualification [do] not rise to a constitutional level." The early and leading case on the subject is *Tumey v. Ohio*, 273 U.S. 510 (1927). There, the Court stated that "matters of kinship, personal bias, state policy, remoteness of interest, would seem generally to be matters merely of legislative discretion." The *Tumey* Court concluded that the Due Process Clause incorporated the common-law rule that a judge must recuse himself when he has "a direct, personal, substantial, pecuniary interest" in a case. This rule reflects the maxim that "[n]o man is allowed to be a judge in his own cause; because his interest would certainly bias his judgment, and, not improbably, corrupt his integrity.". . .

As new problems have emerged that were not discussed at common law, however, the Court has identified additional instances which, as an objective matter, require recusal. These are circumstances "in which experience teaches that the probability of actual bias on the part of the judge or decisionmaker is too high to be constitutionally tolerable." To place the present case in proper context, two instances where the Court has required recusal merit further discussion.

A

The first involved the emergence of local tribunals where a judge had a financial interest in the outcome of a case, although the interest was less than what would have been considered personal or direct at common law. This was the problem addressed in *Tumey*. There, the mayor of a village had the authority to sit as a judge (with no jury) to try those accused of violating a state law prohibiting the possession of alcoholic beverages. Inherent in this structure were two potential conflicts. First, the mayor received a salary supplement for performing judicial duties, and the funds for that compensation derived from the fines assessed in a case. No fines were assessed upon acquittal. The mayor-judge thus received a salary supplement only if he convicted the defendant. Second, sums from the criminal fines were deposited to the village's general treasury fund for village improvements and repairs. The Court held that the Due Process Clause required disqualification "both because of [the mayor-judge's] direct pecuniary interest in the outcome, and because of his official motive to convict and to graduate the fine to help the financial needs of the village."

B

The second instance requiring recusal that was not discussed at common law emerged in the criminal contempt context, where a judge had no pecuniary interest in the case but was challenged because of a conflict arising from his participation in an earlier proceeding. This Court characterized that first proceeding (perhaps pejoratively) as a "one-man grand jury."

In that first proceeding, and as provided by state law, a judge examined witnesses to determine whether criminal charges should be brought. The judge called the two petitioners before him. One petitioner answered questions, but the judge found him untruthful and charged him with perjury. The second declined to answer on the ground that he did not have counsel with him, as state law seemed to permit. The judge charged him with contempt. The judge proceeded to try and convict both petitioners. This Court set aside the convictions on grounds that the judge had a conflict of interest at the trial stage because of his earlier participation followed by his decision to charge them. The Due Process Clause required disqualification. . . .

III

Based on the principles described in these cases we turn to the issue before us. This problem arises in the context of judicial elections, a framework not presented in the precedents we have reviewed and discussed. Caperton contends that Blankenship's pivotal role in getting Justice Benjamin elected created a constitutionally intolerable probability of actual bias. Though not a bribe or criminal influence, Justice Benjamin would nevertheless feel a debt of gratitude to Blankenship for his extraordinary efforts to get him elected. . . .

We conclude that there is a serious risk of actual bias—based on objective and reasonable perceptions—when a person with a personal stake in a particular case had a significant and disproportionate influence in placing the judge on the case by raising funds or directing the judge's election campaign when the case was pending or imminent. The inquiry centers on the contribution's relative size in comparison to the total amount of money contributed to the campaign, the total amount spent in the election, and the apparent effect such contribution had on the outcome of the election.

Applying this principle, we conclude that Blankenship's campaign efforts had a significant and disproportionate influence in placing Justice Benjamin on the case. Blankenship contributed some $3 million to unseat the incumbent and replace him with Benjamin. His contributions eclipsed the total amount spent by all other Benjamin supporters and exceeded by 300% the amount spent by Benjamin's campaign committee. Caperton claims Blankenship spent $1 million more than the total amount spent by the campaign committees of both candidates combined. . . .

Whether Blankenship's campaign contributions were a necessary and sufficient cause of Benjamin's victory is not the proper inquiry. Much like determining whether a judge is actually biased, proving what ultimately drives the electorate to choose a particular candidate is a difficult endeavor, not likely to lend itself to a certain conclusion. This is particularly true where, as here, there is no procedure for judicial factfinding and the sole trier of fact is the one accused of bias. Due process requires an objective inquiry into whether the contributor's influence on the election under all the circumstances "would offer a possible temptation to the average . . . judge to . . . lead him not to hold the balance nice, clear and true." Blankenship's campaign contributions—in comparison to the total amount contributed to the campaign, as well as the total amount spent in the election—had a significant and disproportionate influence on the electoral outcome. And the risk that Blankenship's influence engendered actual bias is sufficiently substantial that it "must be forbidden if the guarantee of due process is to be adequately implemented."

The temporal relationship between the campaign contributions, the justice's election, and the pendency of the case is also critical. It was reasonably foreseeable, when the campaign contributions were made, that the pending case would be before the newly elected justice. The $50 million adverse jury verdict had been entered before the election, and the Supreme Court of Appeals was the next step once the state trial court dealt with post-trial motions. So it became at once apparent that, absent recusal, Justice Benjamin would review a judgment that cost his biggest donor's company $50 million. Although there is no allegation of a *quid pro quo* agreement, the fact remains that Blankenship's extraordinary contributions were made at a time when he had a vested stake in the outcome. Just as no man is allowed to be a judge in his own cause, similar fears of bias can arise when—without the consent of the other parties—a man chooses the judge in his own cause. And applying this principle to the judicial election process, there was here a serious, objective risk of actual bias that required Justice Benjamin's recusal. . . .

IV

Our decision today addresses an extraordinary situation where the Constitution requires recusal. Massey and its *amici* predict that various adverse consequences will follow from recognizing a constitutional violation here—ranging from a flood of recusal motions to unnecessary interference with judicial elections. We disagree. The facts now before us are extreme by any measure. The parties point to no other instance involving judicial campaign contributions that presents a potential for bias comparable to the circumstances in this case. . . .

The judgment of the Supreme Court of Appeals of West Virginia is reversed, and the case is remanded for further proceedings not inconsistent with this opinion.

It is so ordered.

CHIEF JUSTICE ROBERTS, with whom JUSTICE SCALIA, JUSTICE THOMAS, and JUSTICE ALITO join, dissenting.

I, of course, share the majority's sincere concerns about the need to maintain a fair, independent, and impartial judiciary—and one that appears to be such. But I fear that the Court's decision will undermine rather than promote these values.

Until today, we have recognized exactly two situations in which the Federal Due Process Clause requires disqualification of a judge: when the judge has a financial interest in the outcome of the case, and when the judge is trying a defendant for certain criminal contempts. Vaguer notions of bias or the appearance of bias were never a basis for disqualification, either at common law or under our constitutional precedents. Those issues were instead addressed by legislation or court rules.

Today, however, the Court enlists the Due Process Clause to overturn a judge's failure to recuse because of a "probability of bias." Unlike the established grounds for disqualification, a "probability of bias" cannot be defined in any limited way. The Court's new "rule" provides no guidance to judges and litigants about when recusal will be constitutionally required. This will inevitably lead to an increase in allegations that judges are biased, however groundless those charges may be. The end result will do far more to erode public confidence in judicial impartiality than an isolated failure to recuse in a particular case. . . .

There is a "presumption of honesty and integrity in those serving as adjudicators." All judges take an oath to uphold the Constitution and apply the law impartially, and we trust that they will live up to this promise. We have thus identified only *two* situations in which the Due Process Clause requires disqualification of a judge: when the judge has a financial interest in the outcome of the case, and when the judge is presiding over certain types of criminal contempt proceedings. . . . Subject to the two well-established exceptions described above, questions of judicial recusal are regulated by "common law, statute, or the professional standards of the bench and bar.". . .

It is true that Don Blankenship spent a large amount of money in connection with this election. But this point cannot be emphasized strongly enough: Other than a $1,000 direct contribution from Blankenship, *Justice Benjamin and his campaign had no control over how this money was spent.* Campaigns go to great lengths to develop precise messages and strategies. An insensitive or ham-handed ad campaign by an independent third party might distort the campaign's message or cause a backlash against the candidate, even though the candidate was not responsible for the ads. . . . It is also far from clear that Blankenship's expenditures affected the outcome of this election. Justice Benjamin won by a comfortable 7-point margin (53.3% to 46.7%). Many observers believed that Justice Benjamin's opponent doomed his candidacy by giving a well-publicized speech that made several curious allegations; this speech was described in the local media as "deeply disturbing" and worse. Justice Benjamin's opponent also refused to give interviews or participate in debates. All but one of the major West Virginia newspapers endorsed Justice Benjamin. Justice Benjamin just might have won because the voters of West Virginia thought he would be a better judge than his opponent. Unlike the majority, I cannot say with any degree of certainty that

Blankenship "cho[se] the judge in his own cause." I would give the voters of West Virginia more credit than that.

It is an old cliché but sometimes the cure is worse than the disease. I am sure there are cases where a "probability of bias" should lead the prudent judge to step aside, but the judge fails to do so. Maybe this is one of them. But I believe that opening the door to recusal claims under the Due Process Clause, for an amorphous "probability of bias," will itself bring our judicial system into undeserved disrepute, and diminish the confidence of the American people in the fairness and integrity of their courts. I hope I am wrong.

I respectfully dissent.

6

Courts and the Public

★ ★ ★

SO FAR WE have examined the indirect impact of public opinion on
judging by studying methods of judicial selection and retention, but
what about the direct effects? How much do judges pay attention to
public attitudes once they are on the bench? The answer may well
vary with the court, and with the judge. As we saw in the last chapter,
most judges in this country are directly accountable to the public in
one way or another, either in contested elections or uncontested retention elections. When judges know that the public can vote them out
of office, they have incentives to consult public opinion and to make
choices that the public supports.

However, the effects of public opinion are not limited to elected
courts. Even judges who have life tenure say that public opinion influences them from time to time. For example, in *Roper v. Simmons*
(2005), the U.S. Supreme Court was deciding whether the Eighth
Amendment prohibited states from executing people who were under
the age of eighteen when they committed their crimes.[1] Christopher
Simmons was only seventeen when he abducted and murdered a Missouri woman, but the state tried him as an adult and sought to impose
the death penalty. To determine whether it was "cruel" or "unusual"
to execute juveniles, the Court looked at public opinion, asking
whether these executions offended "evolving standards of decency
that mark the progress of a maturing society."[2] (See case excerpt at
the end of the chapter.)

How did the justices know what the public thought about juvenile executions? In *Roper*, Justice Anthony Kennedy consulted two
primary sources of information in his majority opinion. (See Judicial

Process Box 6.1.) First, he looked at trends in state legislation, noting that over the past fifteen years, five states had revised their laws to prohibit juvenile executions, so that by 2005, thirty states banned the practice.[3] Second, Justice Kennedy looked at actual sentencing practices in death penalty cases and discovered that, even when it was permissible to execute juveniles, the practice was rare, with only three states carrying out such executions in the previous decade.[4] Altogether, the evidence persuaded the Court that society's attitudes were changing, and that the public now believed that the execution of juveniles was a cruel and unusual punishment.

Judges also use other sources of information to identify public attitudes about legal questions. For example, in a second death penalty case, *Atkins v. Virginia* (2002), the Supreme Court looked at polling data to learn whether the public supported the execution of mentally disabled criminal defendants. The Court also consulted trends in world opinion, observing that there was widespread

---

JUDICIAL PROCESS BOX 6.1 | Gauging Public Opinion

How do judges know what the public thinks about an issue? What sources of information do they consult? Generally speaking, judges use four primary resources:

polling data	What do opinion polls reveal about public attitudes about the issue?
legislative trends	How have states legislated recently on the issue, and is there an emerging consensus?
sentencing practices	In criminal cases, which sentences do prosecutors request, and which penalties do judges and juries actually impose?
international law	How do practices in this country compare with those in the world community?

Some people say that it is good for judges to use all of these sources of information to determine what the public thinks about legal questions, but other people are not so sure that this is the proper role for a judge. What do you think? Are some sources more appropriate for judges to consult than others? Should judges take public opinion into account at all? Why or why not?

international disapproval of the practice. "Although these factors are by no means dispositive," the Court wrote, "their consistency with the legislative evidence lends further support to our conclusion that there is a consensus among those who have addressed the issue."[5] Following *Atkins*, Justice Kennedy also cited the laws of other countries in his decision in *Roper.*

Cases such as *Roper* and *Atkins* suggest that judges sometimes do consult public opinion when they are making decisions, but how common is the practice, and how much does it really influence judicial behavior? This chapter takes up these questions, examining what political scientists have learned about the impact of public opinion on judging. As you will see, there is some evidence of a direct effect of public opinion, but researchers doubt that it matters to judges most of the time, even on elected courts. The majority of cases are simply not visible enough for the public to take notice, or to possess attitudes. It is only in the most high-profile cases, involving issues such as the death penalty, abortion, and same-sex marriage, that the public has the strongest opinions and judges have the most incentives to be responsive.

Even in these cases, however, not every judge believes that public opinion is relevant to their decision making. In both *Roper* and *Atkins*, some members of the Court were skeptical that it was their job to keep the Constitution up to date with the times. Justice Scalia in *Roper* was particularly critical of the majority's reliance on international law.[6] Judges who support an originalist constitutional philosophy are unlikely to think that laws mean anything different today than they once did, even if public opinion has changed. When you are thinking about judicial behavior, it is important to consider how much you actually want judges to take public opinion into account. How responsive to the public do you think judges ought to be? When would it be better for judges to make choices that are different from what the public wants?

THEORETICAL JUSTIFICATIONS FOR THE IMPACT OF PUBLIC OPINION ON JUDGING

There are a number of theoretical reasons for hypothesizing a direct link between public opinion and judging. To begin with, it should be remembered that judges are not separate from society but part of it and share many of the same cultural and political attitudes as their constituents. In an influential article about the U.S. Supreme Court, political scientist Robert Dahl suggested that, more often than not, justices were likely to be members of the governing majority. "Except for short-lived transitional period when the old alliance is disintegrating and the new one is struggling to take control of political institutions, the Supreme Court is inevitably part of the dominant national alliance," Dahl wrote. "As an element in the political leadership of the dominant alliance, the Court of course supports the major policies of the alliance."[7]

Even when judges disagree with public opinion, they have incentives to be responsive to it. For elected judges, there is the possibility of direct electoral sanctions. Judges know that they can be voted out of office when they differ from their constituents on high-profile issues that the public cares about, such as death penalty cases. As you will read about below, the **electoral connection** between judges and their constituents is particularly strong in states that use contested partisan elections. To a lesser degree, judges who are appointed but lack life tenure might also think about public opinion because there is a chance that governors or state legislators will decline to reappoint judges who make choices that are inconsistent with public values.

Another incentive for all judges—not just elected ones—to follow public opinion is to preserve their institutional **legitimacy**. All judges know that, to at least some degree, their authority depends on maintaining public confidence in courts. Without other resources to secure compliance, judges draw upon the strength of their reputations to be effective. Research is divided over just how much legitimacy is damaged when judges make decisions that the public dislikes. On the U.S. Supreme Court, while there is evidence that unpopular decisions can produce temporary declines in public confidence,[8] over the long term the Court's legitimacy has been resilient,[9] capable of withstanding short-term bursts of disapproval of the justices' behavior.[10] You will spend more time reading about the subject of legitimacy in the next chapter.

Judges might also choose to follow public opinion to enhance their personal reputations or to solicit favorable media coverage. Economist Thomas Sowell hypothesized that, like many of us, "judges are swayed by a desire for praise."[11] Sowell said that some judges like to see flattering coverage about themselves in newspapers, which leads them to make choices that will burnish their image. Sowell termed this phenomenon the **Greenhouse Effect** after *New York Times* reporter Linda Greenhouse. It is unknown how much the Greenhouse Effect is an actual phenomenon—Greenhouse herself has described it as a "snarky phrase"—but the broader point, that judges care about their legacies, could lead judges to favor positions that the public supports.[12]

On the other hand, there are also reasons for thinking that judges are not responsive to public opinion. Perhaps the most powerful is the fact that many judges do not believe that public attitudes are appropriate to consider when answering legal questions. In fact, some would say that the whole point of giving life tenure to federal judges was to reduce the impact of routine political considerations on the resolution of important legal questions, such as the interpretation of the U.S. Constitution. Even elected judges do not necessarily believe that public opinion ought to guide their decision making, even if they are sometimes swayed by it. Many judges would say that the time for public input is at the moment of their selection or retention, not when deciding cases.

Another problem is that most cases are not visible to the public, so it would not be coherent for judges to expect the public to be aware of them or to have opinions about them. Even on the U.S. Supreme Court, it is the rare case that makes the front page of the newspaper, and a rarer one that captures the public's imagination. It could be, then, that if public opinion does influence judicial behavior, it is only in exceptional cases, and only at the margins. When you are reviewing the evidence below about the impact of public opinion on judging, take some time to think about what your theoretical expectations are. When would you expect public opinion to influence judging? Do you expect it to matter all the time, or only sometimes? Are you persuaded that judges are likely to take public opinion into account at all? Why or why not?

EVIDENCE FOR THE IMPACT OF PUBLIC OPINION ON THE U.S. SUPREME COURT

The U.S. Supreme Court is designed to be independent from electoral politics, but cases such as *Atkins* and *Roper* show that Supreme Court justices do look at public opinion from time to time, even though the justices have life tenure and do not depend upon the public's support to retain office. The question is how frequently this behavior occurs. Are *Roper* and *Atkins* special cases, or does public opinion routinely factor into Supreme Court decision making? Another question is whether public opinion has a *meaningful* influence on judicial behavior, or if the Court just pays lip-service to it. Supreme Court justices might say that they are following public opinion, but in reality, they are using public opinion to justify outcomes that they already support.

A common way of evaluating the impact of public opinion on judging is to compare trends in judicial voting behavior with changes in the **public mood**. Compiled by political scientist James Stimson, the public policy mood index is a composite measure of public support for government programs across a range of domestic policy issues over time.[13] Figure 6.1 illustrates trends in the public mood between 1952 and 2014 and contrasts it with Supreme Court voting behavior during the same period, using data taken from the Supreme Court Database. Higher values are associated with more liberal voting behavior, and a more liberal public mood. What do you think about the trends that you see? To what extent are the data consistent with the hypothesis that U.S. Supreme Court justices are responsive to variations in the public mood? To what extent are the data inconsistent with the hypothesis?

A review of the data indicates that the evidence is mixed. For a period of about thirty years, from the 1950s through the 1970s, Supreme Court justices did seem to react to changes in the public mood. When the public became more liberal in the 1950s, Supreme Court justices became more liberal in response. Then, when the public mood turned in a more conservative direction in the 1960s, the Supreme Court followed. Political scientists William Mishler and Reginald Sheehan

Figure 6.1   Liberalism of the Public Mood and Supreme Court Decisions, All Cases (1952–2014)

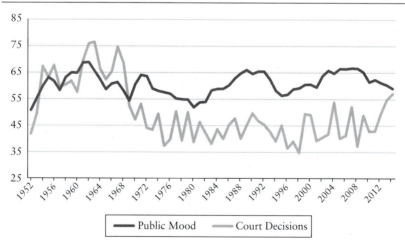

determined that the timing of the justices' responsiveness was approximately five years.[14] That is to say, when there was a liberal swing in the public mood, the justices would take about five years to absorb the trend before responding. Mishler and Sheehan confirmed that variations in Supreme Court voting behavior were not merely attributable to membership changes on the Court. Public attitudes about government policies had an independent influence on judging.

However, the relationship between the public mood and judicial behavior broke down during the 1980s. As the public mood became more liberal during the late 1980s and 1990s, the Supreme Court remained conservative, and when the public mood became more conservative in the 2010s, the Supreme Court actually became more liberal, in opposition to the public mood. It would appear, then, that for the past several decades, Supreme Court justices have been out-of-step with public opinion—and they are no more responsive in visible cases. Figure 6.2 reports Supreme Court voting behavior in civil liberties cases and reveals a similar disconnect.[15]

What explains the variations in the responsiveness of justices to the public mood? One possibility is that particular justices have had different attitudes over time about how much weight to give public opinion. During the Warren Court, for example, many justices believed that it was the role of the Supreme Court to keep the Constitution up-to-date with the times, so it makes sense that these justices

Figure 6.2 Liberalism of the Public Mood and Civil Liberties Decisions (1952–2014)

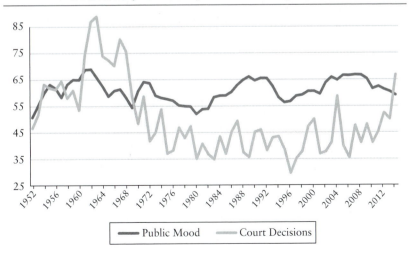

would have been more responsive to the public mood. It was the Warren Court that determined, in *Trop v. Dulles* (1958), that courts should identify cruel and unusual punishments by looking at "evolving standards of decency."[16] In contrast, the conservative justices who were appointed to the Court in the 1980s were committed to originalist constitutional philosophies, which place less emphasis on public opinion.

Social science research affirms that not all justices react equally to public opinion. Political scientists Roy Flemming and Dan Wood found that, at least in civil rights cases, there have been significant differences in how the justices have responded to changes in the public mood. Among the most responsive were Hugo Black, Potter Stewart, and Lewis Powell, who had all retired by the 1980s.[17] Justices who were on the court after that point, such as Rehnquist, O'Connor, and Scalia, were more counter-majoritarian. The implication is that future membership changes could make the Supreme Court become responsive once again to the public mood, assuming that the new justices believe that it is appropriate for them to consider public attitudes.

Yet, even among justices who are attentive to the public mood, the degree of responsiveness has been relatively small. Flemming and Wood found that, on average, a 29 percent shift in the public mood only yields about a 2 percent change in the liberalism of Supreme Court decisions. Certain issue areas produce larger effects, and there will always be exceptional cases in which public attitudes are decisive. *Roper* and *Atkins* might be among them. But, overall, the evidence indicates that when justices do listen to the public, it only changes the outcomes in a handful of close cases, if at all. A better way for the public to alter the direction of policy on the Supreme Court is to replace its members, voting for presidents who will nominate justices who share their values.

EVIDENCE FOR THE IMPACT OF PUBLIC OPINION ON ELECTED COURTS

A more likely place to look for a direct impact of public opinion is on elected courts, where the electoral connection between judges and their constituents is well documented. Research has shown that elected judges have special incentives to be responsive to public opinion, particularly when judges must face opponents in contested partisan elections. Strategic judges will change their behavior to accommodate their constituents' preferences on legal questions that the public cares about. Death penalty cases and other cases involving visible policy issues, such as same-sex marriage, provide the greatest incentives for judges to be strategic.

We know that elected judges engage in this behavior because they tell us that they do. In some of her earliest work on the subject, political scientist Melinda Gann Hall described an interview with a member of the Louisiana Supreme Court, which uses partisan elections.[18] The justice personally opposed the death penalty but was reluctant to vote in a way that went against his constituents' preferences. "Since a liberal voting pattern in this highly visible and emotional set of decisions would place the justice at odds with his more conservatively oriented constituency," Hall reported, the justice "stated that he does not dissent in death penalty cases against an opinion of the court to affirm a defendant's conviction and sentence, expressly because of a perceived voter sanction, in spite of his deeply felt personal preferences to the contrary."[19]

Subsequent work with Paul Brace affirmed that this behavior is common among judges in states with contested elections.[20] To stay in office, judges make compromises to accommodate their constituents. As one might expect, these tendencies are the strongest when judges are the most at risk of losing their jobs. Hall and Brace found that, in death penalty cases, state supreme court justices are more responsive to public opinion when they are in electorally competitive districts or have shorter terms. They concluded, "Having to face voters more frequently, thereby risking the chance of being removed from office, encourages justices in state supreme courts, who otherwise might vote consistently to overturn death sentences instead, to manifest conservative voting patterns in these cases."[21] Research on trial courts has also found that elected judges impose more punitive sentences the closer they are to reelection.[22]

Yet, public opinion does not influence judicial behavior in every case, or even most cases. Like U.S. Supreme Court justices, elected judges are more responsive to public opinion when cases are visible to the public. Notably, Hall and Brace's original work was in death penalty cases, which they described as "a highly salient issue where multiple political and legal forces are likely to be at play."[23] Not every issue raises the same level of public awareness or concern. Even many death penalty cases might not be visible by conventional standards—only rarely do they appear on the front pages of their states' most circulated newspapers.[24] Damon Cann and Teena Wilhelm found that when cases are less visible, state supreme court justices are less responsive to public opinion.[25] Judges might not even be aware of their constituents' preferences in less visible cases.

Judges might also deliberately choose to disregard public opinion, even when their jobs are at risk. Certainly, the Iowa Supreme Court justices understood the stakes in *Varnum v. Brien* (2009) when they legalized same-sex marriage despite public opposition. "I can assure you that the members of our court were very much aware when we issued our decision in *Varnum* that we could lose our jobs because of our vote on that case," Chief Justice Marsha Ternus later said in remarks delivered at Albany Law School.[26] Ternus voted for same-sex marriage anyway, and the people voted her out. The incident shows that even when there is a strong possibility of electoral sanctions, certain judges will continue to answer legal questions in the ways they think best. Sometimes judges think that standing against the public is the right thing to do.

HAVES V. HAVE-NOTS

So far this chapter has assumed that public opinion is a single entity, but the truth is that the American public is highly diverse, and not everyone has an equal voice. Even when judges are listening, some people are heard more loudly than others and are more likely to get rules and judgments that reflect their values. People who have resources, or who litigate frequently, know how to get their messages out and to use legal rules to their advantage. To understand more fully the influence of the public, it is important to consider how these disparities affect judging.

The most influential work on this subject is by Marc Galanter, who in a classic article titled "Why the 'Haves' Come Out Ahead" (1974), theorized about how **litigant status** influences the development of legal rules and, by implication, the choices that judges make. Galanter believed that litigants could be divided into two primary categories: **repeat players**, who participate regularly in the legal system, and **one-shotters**, who litigate occasionally.[27] Examples of repeat players include prosecutors, landlords, insurance companies, and governments, while one-shotters include criminal defendants, tenants, consumers, and other individuals. (See Methodological Note 6.1.) Galanter explained that repeat players have certain systematic advantages that help them to make effective legal arguments and to win more cases over the long term.

METHODOLOGICAL NOTE 6.1 | Measuring Litigant Status

Marc Galanter hypothesized that repeat players have certain advantages over one-shotters in the American legal system. But what do we mean by a repeat player? What is a one-shotter? Political scientists frequently use typologies such as the one below to measure litigant status. The higher the score, the greater advantage a litigant is likely to have:

1. poor individuals
2. minorities
3. individuals
4. unions
5. small businesses
6. businesses
7. corporations
8. local governments
9. state governments
10. the federal government

What do you think? Is this a good way of measuring litigant status? Would you change the ranking in any way? Are there any categories of litigants who are missing from the list?

Source: Kevin T. McGuire, "Repeat Players in the Supreme Court: The Role of Experienced Lawyers in Litigation Success," *Journal of Politics* 57 (1995): 187.

To begin with, repeat players benefit from their familiarity with the legal process. They know the judges and the other officers of the court, and they know how to put together winning arguments. For some repeat players, such as prosecutors, litigating is their full-time job. Other repeat players, such as landlords and insurance executives, might not be attorneys themselves but have access to in-house counsel. Because they know how the process works, repeat players can learn from their experiences and structure their affairs to increase their chances of winning. "It is the RP who writes the form contract, requires the security deposit, and the like," Galanter writes.[28] In contrast, one-shotters may have never been in court before. They probably do not know their attorneys well, if they have counsel at all, and they do not know how the system works.

Galanter's most important insight, however, was that repeat players are able to change legal rules to improve their chances of winning cases. One way of doing so is by directly lobbying legislators and other public office holders, asking them to write laws that advance their interests. Another way is through litigation strategies. Because repeat players care about their long-term success rate, they can afford to lose cases from time to time if it serves their broader interests. Repeat players can **play the odds**, finding legal strategies that help them win more often than not, even if the strategies do not suit every case. They can also **play for rules**, securing legal judgments that establish the most favorable precedents moving forward. To achieve these goals, repeat players only bring to court cases that they think they can win. Otherwise, repeat players settle and, in this way, avoid having judges set precedents that are unfavorable to them. Over the long term, this strategy makes it harder for one-shotters to win cases.

In fact, one-shotters might often choose not to litigate in the first place. Without sufficient resources, or good attorneys, the costs of pressing one's case in court might be too much. Political scientist Christina Boyd found that the likelihood of an appeal from the federal district courts is 66 percent higher when the federal government loses to a private individual than when an individual loses to the government. According to Boyd, this finding "confirms the great strengths held by government parties, particularly when facing individual adversaries."[29] This problem is heightened with indigent defendants, who are the least likely to be able to afford an appeal.

For their part, most judges do not have time to give their full attention to every case, and it might not surprise you to learn that litigants who have greater resources tend to get better treatment. In both the state and federal judicial systems, judges have staggering caseloads, with the typical lower federal court judge deciding far more cases than the seventy or so that Supreme Court justices decide each year. One estimate puts the workload of the average judge on the U.S. Courts of Appeals at over three hundred cases per year.[30] To manage this work, judges decide most cases summarily and with no oral arguments.

It is the repeat players who end up getting the judges' full attention. According to law professors William Richman and William Reynolds in their book *Injustice on Appeal* (2012), litigants in "important" cases who have "serious counsel" get first-class treatment from the Courts of Appeals. "There will be oral argument, an opinion prepared by the judges and her staff, and the result will contain a sufficiently detailed explanation so that the whole world can second-guess the result."[31] In contrast, litigants who are "poor, without counsel, and with a boring repetitive problem," get no opinions or oral arguments. Richman and Reynolds do not maintain that judges deliberately set out to deny due process to indigent defendants, but the legal claims are more routine and fail to capture the judges' interest. The authors conclude that "judges are simply less likely to devote serious effort and attention to the routine veterans' benefit denial appeal than to the interesting corporate tax case."[32]

Among the most disadvantaged litigants are noncitizens who are facing deportation or seeking asylum in immigration court. With a backlog of about a half million cases, delays in immigration court are the norm, and many noncitizens cannot afford the costs of sustaining litigation.[33] (See Figure 6.3.) Although the government provides attorneys for defendants in criminal cases, individuals who are facing deportation must pay for their own, or go without counsel, and argue against seasoned government attorneys. When noncitizens lose their cases, appeals are often too expensive to pursue, which limits opportunities for correction and oversight.

The reality, then, is that even if public opinion does influence judicial behavior, judges are not necessarily hearing the voices of the whole public. The most marginalized among us frequently lack the resources that they need to make effective legal arguments. They are also the least likely to vote and the most likely to be missed by pollsters. Not surprisingly, these individuals are often characterized by their poor economic status, their race, and their age. When you are thinking about judicial behavior, take some time to reflect on the

Figure 6.3 Immigration Court Pending Cases

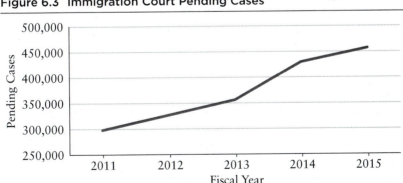

Source: Executive Office for Immigration Review.

injustices that are embedded in the system. What obligation do judges have to ensure that all people get an equal voice? What obligation do you have, as someone who might be thinking about law school?

THE INFLUENCE OF LAWYERS
AND INTEREST GROUPS

You might think that a good lawyer could reduce or eliminate the advantages that repeat players have over one-shotters in the legal system, and to a certain extent you would be right. Public defenders, as well as other public-interest lawyers and interest groups, do play a role in giving voice to the disadvantaged. Research has demonstrated that one-shotters fare better in court when experienced litigators represent them and devote time to their cases.

The problem is that repeat players have lawyers too, and often these attorneys are more experienced and have better resources. According to Galanter, many of the lawyers who represent one-shotters represent the "lower echelons" of the profession and may provide their clients with **ineffective assistance of counsel**. (See Judicial Process Box 6.2.) "Compared to the lawyers who provide services to RPs," Galanter writes, "lawyers in these specialties tend to be drawn from lower socio-economic origins, to have attended local, proprietary or part-time law schools, to practice alone rather than in large firms, and to possess low prestige within the profession."[34] Galanter also points out that it would be unethical for the lawyers of one-shotters to use many of the same litigation strategies that repeat players use. Public defenders cannot settle if their clients want to go to court, for example, even if the attorneys fear that bad precedents will be set.

Research has identified two qualities that can help to make attorneys more effective advocates for one-shotters. The first is attorney experience. In a series of articles, political scientist Kevin McGuire found that when litigators argue more frequently before the U.S. Supreme Court, they are more likely to win. McGuire theorized that experienced advocates help the Court by fulfilling certain "informational needs," providing justices with "a clear and faithful focus on the issues presented in a case, an understanding of the relationship of those issues to existing law, a clarification of uncertainties, and a view of the implications of a decision for public policy, tempered with candor."[35] Even when justices are inclined to vote their policy preferences, experienced attorneys can frame cases in ways to make it look like the

JUDICIAL PROCESS BOX 6.2 | **Ineffective Assistance of Counsel**

The Sixth Amendment of the U.S. Constitution guarantees defendants in criminal cases the right "to have the assistance of counsel," but it does not promise everyone a *good* lawyer. For the most part, repeat players are able to afford better, more experienced attorneys than one-shotters can.

Sometimes, however, the quality of advocacy for one-shotters is so low that it qualifies as a violation of defendants' Sixth Amendment rights. In *Padilla v. Kentucky* (2010), for example, a lawyer neglected to inform a noncitizen that he would be deported if he pleaded guilty for distributing marijuana. (See case excerpt in this chapter.) Too often, noncitizens and other indigent defendants find themselves making poor choices because of bad legal advice.

In *Strickland v. Washington* (1984), the U.S. Supreme Court established a two-pronged test for determining whether litigants have received ineffective assistance of counsel. A court must find (1) that counsel's representation "fell below an objective standard of reasonableness"; and (2) that "but for counsel's unprofessional errors, the result of the proceeding would have been different."

What do you think? What types of errors do you think should qualify as ineffective assistance of counsel? Can legal advice ever be so bad that convictions should be tossed out?

justices' attitudes support their clients' views. Importantly, however, McGuire did not find that attorney experience completely eliminated the role of litigant status on judging. Although experienced attorneys do tend to win in court, repeat players still retain advantages before the justices.

One of the most experienced attorneys is the **solicitor general**, who is responsible for representing the United States government at the Supreme Court. The solicitor general's office participates in approximately two-thirds of the cases that the Supreme Court decides on the merits each year, and it wins most of them.[36] Research is divided over why the solicitor general is so effective. McGuire suggested that the office's success is a function of the amount of experience that it has litigating before the Court.[37] However, other research indicates that the quality of advocacy might simply be better, and that the justices think of the solicitor general as a peer. Political scientists Ryan Black and Ryan Owens observe that the solicitor general's office has a reputation for being staffed by professionals who have many of the same goals as the justices, such as protecting the institution of the Court.[38] Regardless of the explanation, when the solicitor general's office advocates on behalf of one-shotters, they obtain a powerful ally.

A second hallmark of effective advocacy is the willingness of attorneys to devote resources to their clients. Even when one-shotters have experienced lawyers, there is no guarantee that the attorneys will pay much attention to them. Public defenders are very experienced but severely overworked and can only commit a limited amount of time to each case. Research affirms that when one-shotters get more time and attention from counsel, they are more likely to win. For example, one study of state trial courts found that representation by a larger law firm did not, by itself, eliminate the advantages of repeat-player status, but when lawyers at these firms devoted more time to cases, one-shotters were more likely to obtain favorable outcomes. The authors concluded, "When a larger number of attorneys represents the plaintiff compared to the defendant, the plaintiff's likelihood of receiving compensation increases by 6 percent."[39]

This finding relates to work by Paul Brace and Melinda Gann Hall, who found that when state supreme courts are more professionalized, they are also more likely to side with one-shotters. **Professionalization** measures the capacity of courts "to generate and evaluate information."[40] A professionalized court tends to have more staff, and the judges generally decide fewer cases each year because they have greater control over their dockets. These features give judges more time to focus on cases concerning the disadvantaged. As Brace and Hall explain, "More highly professionalized state supreme courts will have greater liberty to consider have/have-not cases than courts with fewer staff resources or support."[41] The implication is that disadvantaged litigants will do better in court when judges, as well as attorneys, have more time to devote to their cases.

One-shotters have also benefited from the development of public interest groups that advocate on behalf of the disadvantaged. Typically, these groups participate in the form of **amicus curiae**, or "friend of the court," briefs that reinforce or supplement arguments that the litigants' attorneys have raised. However, sometimes public interest groups file the litigation themselves and represent disadvantaged parties directly. Research has shown that interest group participation can help to level the playing field between repeat players and one-shotters. For example, Paul Collins found that filing amicus briefs improves litigation success rates in the U.S. Supreme Court.[42] Other work has shown that amicus participation improves success rates in state supreme courts.[43]

Yet, just as the quality of lawyers is variable, inequalities exist among public interest groups. As one study concluded about the influence of interest groups on the U.S. Supreme Court, "well-connected and powerful groups are considerably more likely to have the experience, name recognition, and resources necessary to be recognized as experts in a given policy area by the Court, and thus exert a greater influence on the final decision on the merits."[44] One-shotters might do better if their causes are taken up by powerful interest groups, such as the American Civil Liberties Union, the American Farm Bureau, or the National Wildlife Federation. Yet, these groups can only take part in a tiny fraction of the litigation that occurs each year.

What can you do to assist one-shotters? Galanter encouraged all new attorneys to become more aware of the injustices that are present in the legal system and to take action to represent the less fortunate. The rise of public interest litigation has helped to correct the imbalance, but there is still much work left to do. Immigration law in particular is an area in which many voices are left out. When you are thinking about judging, reflect on what responsibility you have to make sure that every voice has an equal say in our legal system. What can be done to empower all of our citizens, and noncitizens, so that our laws truly reflect the interests of all?

DISCUSSION QUESTIONS

1. Should judges take public opinion into account when they are deciding cases? Is public opinion more relevant in some types of cases than others?
2. Did the U.S. Supreme Court make good use of public opinion in *Roper v. Simmons* (2005)? What are the strengths and weaknesses of the Court's argument?
3. Does Marc Galanter's research about the relative advantages of repeat players over one-shotters make you question the fairness of the justice system? What advantages and disadvantages would you have if you ever went to court?
4. What obligation do lawyers have to provide legal services to the disadvantaged? Do you think good attorneys can give effective assistance to one-shotters? Why or why not?

KEY TERMS

electoral connection
legitimacy
Greenhouse Effect
public mood
litigant status
repeat players
one-shotters

play the odds
play for rules
ineffective assistance of counsel
solicitor general
professionalization
amicus curiae

FURTHER READING

Galanter, Marc. 1974. "Why the 'Haves' Come Out Ahead: Speculations on the Limits of Legal Change." *Law & Society Review* 9: 95–160.
Richman, William M., and William L. Reynolds. 2012. *Injustice on Appeal: The United States Courts of Appeals in Crisis*. New York: Oxford University Press.

NOTES

1. Roper v. Simmons, 543 U.S. 551 (2005).
2. Trop v. Dulles, 356 U.S. 86 (1958), at 101.
3. *Roper*, at 565.
4. Id., at 564.
5. Atkins v. Virginia, 536 U.S. 304 (2002), at 316 (note 21).
6. *Roper*, at 622 (Scalia, J., dissenting).
7. Robert A. Dahl, "Decision-Making in a Democracy: The Supreme Court as a National Policy-Maker," *Journal of Public Law* 6 (1957): 293; *see also* Barry Friedman, *The Will of the People: How Public Opinion Has Influenced the Supreme Court and Shaped the Meaning of the Constitution* (New York: Farrar, Straus, and Giroux, 2009); *and* Lee Epstein and Andrew D. Martin, "Does Public Opinion Influence the Supreme Court? Possibly Yes (But We're Not Sure Why)," *University of Pennsylvania Journal of Constitutional Law* 13 (2010): 263.
8. Anke Grosskopf and Jeffrey J. Mondak, "Do Attitudes toward Specific Supreme Court Decisions Matter? The Impact of Webster and *Texas v. Johnson* on Public Confidence in the Supreme Court," *Political Research Quarterly* 51, no. 3 (1998): 633–54.
9. *But see* Brandon L. Bartels and Christopher D. Johnston, "On the Ideological Foundations of Supreme Court Legitimacy in the American Public," *American Journal of Political Science* 57, no. 1 (2013): 184–99 (finding that "ideological disagreement exhibits a potent, deleterious impact on legitimacy").
10. Gregory A. Caldeira and James L. Gibson, "The Etiology of Public Support for the Supreme Court," *American Journal of Political Science* 36 (1992): 635; James L. Gibson and Gregory A. Caldeira, "Blacks and the United States Supreme Court: Models of Diffuse Support," *Journal of Politics* 54, no. 4 (1992):

1120–45; and Vanessa A. Baird, "Building Institutional Legitimacy: The Role of Procedural Justice," *Political Research Quarterly* 54, no. 2 (2001): 333–54.

11. Thomas Sowell, "The Greenhouse Effect," *Times Union* (Albany, NY), March 8, 1994, A10.

12. Linda Wertheimer, "Supreme Court Reporter Linda Greenhouse Retires," NPR, July 12, 2008, available at http://www.npr.org/templates/story/story.php ?storyId=92489115.

13. James A. Stimson, *Public Opinion in America: Mood, Cycles, and Swings* (New York: Westview Press, 1991). Data available at http://stimson.web.unc.edu /data/.

14. William Mishler and Reginald S. Sheehan, "The Supreme Court as a Countermajoritarian Institution? The Impact of Public Opinion on Supreme Court Decisions," *American Political Science Review* 87, no. 1 (1993): 87–101; *but see* Helmut Norpoth and Jeffrey A. Segal, "Popular Influence on Supreme Court Decisions: Comment," *American Political Science Review* 88 (1994): 711 (questioning Mishler and Sheehan's procedures and findings).

15. Civil liberties cases included the categories of civil rights, criminal procedure, due process, First Amendment, and privacy.

16. Trop v. Dulles, 356 U.S. 86 (1958), at 101.

17. Roy B. Flemming and B. Dan Wood, "The Public and the Supreme Court: Individual Justice Responsiveness to American Policy Moods," *American Journal of Political Science* 41 (1997): 490–91; *see also* Michael W. Giles, Bethany Blackstone, and Richard L. Vining Jr., "The Supreme Court in American Democracy: Unraveling the Linkages between Public Opinion and Judicial Decision Making," *Journal of Politics* 70 (2008): 293.

18. Melinda Gann Hall, "Constituent Influence in State Supreme Courts: Conceptual Notes and a Case Study," *Journal of Politics* 49 (1987): 1117.

19. Id., 1120.

20. *See* Paul Brace and Melinda Gann Hall, "Neo-Institutionalism and Dissent in State Supreme Courts," *Journal of Politics* 52 (1990): 54; Melinda Gann Hall, "Electoral Politics and Strategic Voting in State Supreme Courts," *Journal of Politics* 54 (1992): 427; Paul Brace and Melinda Gann Hall, "Integrated Models of Judicial Dissent," *Journal of Politics* 55 (1993): 914.

21. Paul Brace and Melinda Gann Hall, "The Interplay of Preferences, Case Facts, Context, and Rules in the Politics of Judicial Choice," *Journal of Politics* 59 (1997): 1223.

22. Gregory A. Huber and Sanford C. Gordon, "Accountability and Coercion: Is Justice Blind When It Runs for Office?," *American Journal of Political Science* 48 (2004): 247.

23. Id., 1208–9.

24. Richard L. Vining Jr. and Teena Wilhelm, "Measuring Case Salience in State Courts of Last Resort," *Political Research Quarterly* 64, no. 3 (2011): 564. "Interestingly, we find that popular notions about the salience of death penalty appeals may be mistaken. While 25.62 percent . . . of criminal appeals cases on the front page involved capital punishment, only 2.31 percent of death penalty appeals received front-page coverage. . . . Attentiveness to death penalty decisions

may be a state-specific phenomenon related to the relative frequency of the death penalty itself." They found that among the most salient state supreme court cases are civil government appeals, which involve "elections, First Amendment issues, government regulation, the practice of law, public contracts, privacy issues, or torts involving government" (565).

25. *See* Damon M. Cann and Teena Wilhelm, "Case Visibility and the Electoral Connection in State Supreme Courts," *American Politics Research* 39 (2011):557.

26. Marsha Ternus, "Remarks," *Albany Law Review* 74 (2011): 1569.

27. Marc Galanter, "Why the 'Haves' Come Out Ahead: Speculations on the Limits of Legal Change," *Law & Society Review* 9 (1974): 95.

28. Id., at 98.

29. Christina L. Boyd, "Litigant Status and Trial Court Appeal Mobilization," *Law & Policy* 37 (2015): 312.

30. Marin K. Levy, "Judging Justice on Appeal," *Yale Law Journal* 123, no. 7 (2014): 2134–2573.

31. William M. Richman and William L. Reynolds, *Injustice on Appeal: The United States Courts of Appeals in Crisis* (New York: Oxford University Press, 2012): 119–20; William M. Richman and William L. Reynolds, "Elitism, Expediency, and the New Certiorari: Requiem for the Learned Hand Tradition," *Cornell Law Review* 81 (1996): 273–342.

32. Richman and Reynolds, *Injustice on Appeal*, 120.

33. Julia Preston, "Deluged Immigration Courts, Where Cases Stall for Years, Begin to Buckle," *New York Times*, December 1, 2016, A1; *see also* Executive Office for Immigration Review, *FY 2015 Statistics Yearbook*, available at https://www.justice.gov/eoir/page/file/fysb15/download.

34. Galanter, "Why the 'Haves' Come Out Ahead," 116.

35. Kevin T. McGuire, "Repeat Players in the Supreme Court: The Role of Experienced Lawyers in Litigation Success," *Journal of Politics* 57 (1995): 189.

36. Andrew Pincus, "The Solicitor General's Report Card," *ScotusBlog*, July 2, 2014, available at http://www.scotusblog.com/2014/07/the-solicitor-generals-report-card/.

37. Kevin T. McGuire, "Explaining Executive Success in the U.S. Supreme Court," *Political Research Quarterly* 51 (1998): 505.

38. Ryan C. Black and Ryan J. Owens, "A Built-In Advantage: The Office of the Solicitor General and the U.S. Supreme Court," *Political Research Quarterly* 66 (2013): 455–56.

39. Tao L. Dumas, Stacia L. Haynie, and Dorothy Daboval, "Does Size Matter? The Influence of Law on Litigant Success Rates," *Justice System Journal* 36 (2015): 349.

40. Peverill Squire, "Measuring the Professionalization of State Courts of Last Resort," *State Politics and Policy Quarterly* 8 (2008): 223.

41. Paul Brace and Melinda Gann Hall, "'Haves' versus 'Have Nots' in State Supreme Courts: Allocating Docket Space and Wins in Power Asymmetric Cases," *Law & Society Review* 35 (2001): 402.

42. Paul M. Collins Jr., "Friends of the Court: Examining the Influence of Amicus Curiae Participation in U.S. Supreme Court Litigation," *Law & Society*

Review 38 (2004): 807; Paul M. Collins Jr., "Lobbyists before the U.S. Supreme Court: Investigating the Influence of Amicus Curiae Briefs," *Political Research Quarterly* 60 (2007): 55; Paul M. Collins, *Friends of the Supreme Court: Interest Groups and Judicial Decision Making* (New York: Oxford University Press, 2008).

43. Donald Songer, Ashlyn Kuersten, and Erin Kaheny, "Why the Haves Don't Always Come Out Ahead: Repeat Players Meet Amici Curiae for the Disadvantaged," *Political Research Quarterly* 53 (2000): 537.

44. Janet M. Box-Steffensmeier, Dino P. Christenson, and Matthew P. Hitt, "Quality Over Quantity: Amici Influence and Judicial Decision Making," *American Political Science Review* 107 (2013): 448.

CASE ANALYSIS

Roper v. Simmons, 543 U.S. 551 (2005)

In Roper v. Simmons *(2005), the U.S. Supreme Court overturned a death sentence imposed on a defendant who was seventeen when he committed his crime. To justify his decision, Justice Anthony Kennedy looked for evidence of a national consensus on the subject of juvenile executions. What do you think? Do you find Justice Kennedy's evidence persuasive? Is it ever appropriate for judges to consult public opinion when making decisions? Why or why not?*

JUSTICE KENNEDY delivered the opinion of the Court.

This case requires us to address, for the second time in a decade and a half, whether it is permissible under the Eighth and Fourteenth Amendments to the Constitution of the United States to execute a juvenile offender who was older than 15 but younger than 18 when he committed a capital crime. In *Stanford v. Kentucky*, 492 U.S. 361 (1989), a divided Court rejected the proposition that the Constitution bars capital punishment for juvenile offenders in this age group. We reconsider the question.

I

At the age of 17, when he was still a junior in high school, Christopher Simmons, the respondent here, committed murder. About nine months later, after he had turned 18, he was tried and sentenced to death. There is little doubt that Simmons was the instigator of the crime. Before its commission Simmons said he wanted to murder someone. In chilling, callous terms he talked about his plan, discussing it for the most part with two friends, Charles Benjamin and John Tessmer, then aged 15 and 16 respectively. Simmons proposed to commit burglary and murder by breaking and entering, tying up a victim, and throwing the victim off a bridge. Simmons assured his friends they could "get away with it" because they were minors. . . .

II

The Eighth Amendment provides: "Excessive bail shall not be required, nor excessive fines imposed, nor cruel and unusual punishments inflicted.". . . The prohibition against "cruel and unusual punishments," like other expansive language in the Constitution, must be interpreted according to its text, by considering history, tradition, and precedent, and with due regard for its purpose and function in the constitutional design. To implement this framework we have established the propriety and affirmed the necessity of referring to "the evolving standards of decency that mark the progress of a maturing society" to determine which punishments are so disproportionate as to be cruel and unusual. *Trop v. Dulles*, 356 U.S. 86, 100–101 (1958) (plurality opinion).

In *Thompson v. Oklahoma*, 487 U.S. 815 (1988), a plurality of the Court determined that our standards of decency do not permit the execution of any offender under the age of 16 at the time of the crime. The next year, in *Stanford v. Kentucky*, 492 U.S. 361 (1989), the Court, over a dissenting opinion joined by four Justices, referred to contemporary standards of decency in this country and concluded the Eighth and Fourteenth Amendments did not proscribe the execution of juvenile offenders over 15 but under 18. The Court noted that 22 of the 37 death penalty States permitted the death penalty for 16-year-old offenders, and, among these 37 States, 25 permitted it for 17-year-old offenders. These numbers, in the Court's view, indicated there was no national consensus "sufficient to label a particular punishment cruel and unusual." . . .

[W]e now reconsider the issue decided in *Stanford*. The beginning point is a review of objective indicia of consensus, as expressed in particular by the enactments of legislatures that have addressed the question. This data gives us essential instruction. We must then determine, in the exercise of our own independent judgment, whether the death penalty is a disproportionate punishment for juveniles.

III
A

The evidence of national consensus against the death penalty for juveniles is . . . sufficient to demonstrate a national consensus. . . . 30 States prohibit the juvenile death penalty, comprising 12 that have rejected the death penalty altogether and 18 that maintain it but, by express provision or judicial interpretation, exclude juveniles from its reach. . . . In the present case, too, even in the 20 States without a formal prohibition on executing juveniles, the practice is infrequent. Since *Stanford*, six States have executed prisoners for crimes committed as juveniles. In the past 10 years, only three have done so: Oklahoma, Texas, and Virginia. In December 2003 the Governor of Kentucky decided to spare the life of Kevin Stanford, and commuted his sentence to one of life imprisonment without parole, with the declaration that "[w]e ought not be executing people who, legally, were children." By this act the Governor ensured Kentucky would not add itself to the list of States that have executed juveniles within the last 10 years even by the execution of the very defendant whose death sentence the Court had upheld in *Stanford v. Kentucky*. . . .

Five States that allowed the juvenile death penalty at the time of *Stanford* have abandoned it in the intervening 15 years—four through legislative enactments and one through judicial decision. . . . Since *Stanford*, no State that previously prohibited capital punishment for juveniles has reinstated it. This fact, coupled with the trend toward abolition of the juvenile death penalty, carries special force in light of the general popularity of anticrime legislation, and in light of the particular trend in recent years toward cracking down on juvenile crime in other respects. . . . [T]he objective indicia of consensus in this case—the rejection of the juvenile death penalty in the majority of States; the infrequency of its use even where it remains on the books; and the consistency in the trend toward abolition of the practice—provide sufficient evidence that today our society views juveniles . . . as "categorically less culpable than the average criminal."

B

A majority of States have rejected the imposition of the death penalty on juvenile offenders under 18, and we now hold this is required by the Eighth Amendment. Because the death penalty is the most severe punishment, the Eighth Amendment applies to it with special force. Capital punishment must be limited to those offenders who commit "a narrow category of the most serious crimes" and whose extreme culpability makes them "the most deserving of execution."

Three general differences between juveniles under 18 and adults demonstrate that juvenile offenders cannot with reliability be classified among the worst offenders. First, as any parent knows and as the scientific and sociological studies respondent and his *amici* cite tend to confirm, "[a] lack of maturity and an underdeveloped sense of responsibility are found in youth more often than in adults and are more understandable among the young. These qualities often result in impetuous and ill-considered actions and decisions.". . . The second area of difference is that juveniles are more vulnerable or susceptible to negative influences and outside pressures, including peer pressure. . . . The third broad difference is that the character of a juvenile is not as well formed as that of an adult. The personality traits of juveniles are more transitory, less fixed. These differences render suspect any conclusion that a juvenile falls among the worst offenders. . . . Their own vulnerability and comparative lack of control over their immediate surroundings mean juveniles have a greater claim than adults to be forgiven for failing to escape negative influences in their whole environment. . . . Once the diminished culpability of juveniles is recognized, it is evident that the penological justifications for the death penalty apply to them with lesser force than to adults. . . .

IV

Our determination that the death penalty is disproportionate punishment for offenders under 18 finds confirmation in the stark reality that the United States is the only country in the world that continues to give official sanction to the juvenile death penalty. This reality does not become controlling, for the task of interpreting the Eighth Amendment remains our responsibility. Yet at least from the time of the Court's decision in *Trop*, the Court has referred to the laws of other countries and to international authorities as instructive for its interpretation of the Eighth Amendment's prohibition of "cruel and unusual punishments." As respondent and a number of *amici* emphasize, Article 37 of the United Nations Convention on the Rights of the Child, which every country in the world has ratified save for the United States and Somalia, contains an express prohibition on capital punishment for crimes committed by juveniles under 18. No ratifying country has entered a reservation to the provision prohibiting the execution of juvenile offenders. Parallel prohibitions are contained in other significant international covenants.

Respondent and his *amici* have submitted, and petitioner does not contest, that only seven countries other than the United States have executed juvenile offenders since 1990: Iran, Pakistan, Saudi Arabia, Yemen, Nigeria, the Democratic Republic of Congo, and China. Since then each of these countries has either abolished capital punishment for juveniles or made public disavowal of the practice. In sum, it is fair to say that the United States now stands alone in a world that has turned its face against the juvenile death penalty.

Though the international covenants prohibiting the juvenile death penalty are of more recent date, it is instructive to note that the United Kingdom abolished the juvenile death penalty before these covenants came into being. The United Kingdom's experience bears particular relevance here in light of the historic ties between our countries and in light of the Eighth Amendment's own origins. The Amendment was modeled on a parallel provision in the English Declaration of Rights of 1689, which provided: "[E]xcessive Bail ought not to be required nor excessive Fines imposed; nor cruel and unusuall Punishments inflicted." As of now, the United Kingdom has abolished the death penalty in its entirety; but, decades before it took this step, it recognized the disproportionate nature of the juvenile death penalty; and it abolished that penalty as a separate matter. . . . In the 56 years that have passed since the United Kingdom abolished the juvenile death penalty, the weight of authority against it there, and in the international community, has become well established.

It is proper that we acknowledge the overwhelming weight of international opinion against the juvenile death penalty, resting in large part on the understanding that the instability and emotional imbalance of young people may often be a factor in the crime. The opinion of the world community, while not controlling our outcome, does provide respected and significant confirmation for our own conclusions. . . .

* * *

The Eighth and Fourteenth Amendments forbid imposition of the death penalty on offenders who were under the age of 18 when their crimes were committed. The judgment of the Missouri Supreme Court setting aside the sentence of death imposed upon Christopher Simmons is affirmed.

It is so ordered.

JUSTICE O'CONNOR, dissenting.

The Court's decision today establishes a categorical rule forbidding the execution of any offender for any crime committed before his 18th birthday, no matter how deliberate, wanton, or cruel the offense. Neither the objective evidence of contemporary societal values, nor the Court's moral proportionality analysis, nor the two in tandem suffice to justify this ruling.

Although the Court finds support for its decision in the fact that a majority of the States now disallow capital punishment of 17-year-old offenders, it refrains from asserting that its holding is compelled by a genuine national consensus. Indeed, the evidence before us fails to demonstrate conclusively that any such consensus has emerged in the brief period since we upheld the constitutionality of this practice in *Stanford v. Kentucky*, 492 U.S. 361 (1989).

Instead, the rule decreed by the Court rests, ultimately, on its independent moral judgment that death is a disproportionately severe punishment for any 17-year-old offender. I do not subscribe to this judgment. Adolescents *as a class* are undoubtedly less mature, and therefore less culpable for their misconduct, than adults. But the Court has adduced no evidence impeaching the seemingly reasonable conclusion reached by many state legislatures: that at least *some* 17-year-old murderers are sufficiently mature to deserve the death penalty in an appropriate case. Nor has it been shown that capital sentencing juries are incapable of accurately assessing a youthful defendant's maturity or of giving due weight to the mitigating characteristics associated with youth.

On this record—and especially in light of the fact that so little has changed since our recent decision in *Stanford*—I would not substitute our judgment about the moral propriety of capital punishment for 17-year-old murderers for the judgments of the Nation's legislatures. Rather, I would demand a clearer showing that our society truly has set its face against this practice before reading the Eighth Amendment categorically to forbid it.

JUSTICE SCALIA, with whom THE CHIEF JUSTICE and JUSTICE THOMAS join, dissenting. In urging approval of a constitution that gave life-tenured judges the power to nullify laws enacted by the people's representatives, Alexander Hamilton assured the citizens of New York that there was little risk in this, since "[t]he judiciary . . . ha[s] neither FORCE nor WILL but merely judgment." The Federalist No. 78, p. 465 (C. Rossiter ed. 1961). But Hamilton had in mind a traditional judiciary, "bound down by strict rules and precedents which serve to define and point out their duty in every particular case that comes before them." Bound down, indeed. What a mockery today's opinion makes of Hamilton's expectation, announcing the Court's conclusion that the meaning of our Constitution has changed over the past 15 years—not, mind you, that this Court's decision 15 years ago was *wrong*, but that the Constitution *has changed*.

The Court reaches this implausible result by purporting to advert, not to the original meaning of the Eighth Amendment, but to "the evolving standards of decency," of our national society. It then finds, on the flimsiest of grounds, that a national consensus which could not be perceived in our people's laws barely 15 years ago now solidly exists. . . . The Court thus proclaims itself sole arbiter of our Nation's moral standards—and in the course of discharging that awesome responsibility purports to take guidance from the views of foreign courts and legislatures. Because I do not believe that the meaning of our Eighth Amendment, any more than the meaning of other provisions of our Constitution, should be determined by the subjective views of five Members of this Court and like-minded foreigners, I dissent.

CASE ANALYSIS

Padilla v. Kentucky, 559 U.S. 356 (2010)

Noncitizens and other indigent defendants frequently receive bad legal advice, which can have disastrous consequences. In Padilla v. Kentucky *(2010), Jose Padilla faced deportation because his attorney did not tell him he would have to leave the country if he pleaded guilty to a drug charge, but the Supreme Court ruled that Padilla had received ineffective assistance of counsel, in violation of the Sixth Amendment. Do you agree with the Court's decision? What obligations do lawyers have to their clients? When does bad legal advice become a constitutional harm?*

JUSTICE STEVENS delivered the opinion of the Court.

Petitioner Jose Padilla, a native of Honduras, has been a lawful permanent resident of the United States for more than 40 years. Padilla served this Nation with honor as a member of the U.S. Armed Forces during the Vietnam War. He now faces deportation after pleading guilty to the transportation of a large amount of marijuana in his tractor-trailer in the Commonwealth of Kentucky.

In this postconviction proceeding, Padilla claims that his counsel not only failed to advise him of this consequence prior to his entering the plea, but also told him that he "did not have to worry about immigration status since he had been in the country so long." Padilla relied on his counsel's erroneous advice when he pleaded guilty to the drug charges that made his deportation virtually mandatory. He alleges that he would have insisted on going to trial if he had not received incorrect advice from his attorney. . . .

We granted certiorari to decide whether, as a matter of federal law, Padilla's counsel had an obligation to advise him that the offense to which he was pleading guilty would result in his removal from this country. We agree with Padilla that constitutionally competent counsel would have advised him that his conviction for drug distribution made him subject to automatic deportation. Whether he is entitled to relief depends on whether he has been prejudiced, a matter that we do not address.

I

The landscape of federal immigration law has changed dramatically over the last 90 years. While once there was only a narrow class of deportable offenses and judges wielded broad discretionary authority to prevent deportation, immigration reforms over time have expanded the class of deportable offenses and limited the authority of judges to alleviate the harsh consequences of deportation. The "drastic measure" of deportation or removal, *Fong Haw Tan v. Phelan*, 333 U.S. 6, 10 (1948), is now virtually inevitable for a vast number of noncitizens convicted of crimes. . . . These changes to our immigration law have dramatically raised the stakes of a noncitizen's criminal conviction. The importance of accurate legal advice for noncitizens accused of crimes has never been more important. These changes confirm our view that, as a matter of federal law, deportation is an integral part—indeed, sometimes the most important part—of the penalty that may be imposed on noncitizen defendants who plead guilty to specified crimes.

II

Before deciding whether to plead guilty, a defendant is entitled to "the effective assistance of competent counsel." *McMann v. Richardson*, 397 U.S. 759, 771 (1970). The Supreme Court of Kentucky rejected Padilla's ineffectiveness claim on the ground that the advice he sought about the risk of deportation concerned only collateral matters, *i.e.*, those matters not within the sentencing authority of the state trial court. In its view, "collateral consequences are outside the scope of representation required by the Sixth Amendment," and, therefore, the "failure of defense counsel to advise the defendant of possible deportation consequences is not cognizable as a claim for ineffective assistance of counsel." The Kentucky high court is far from alone in this view. . . .

We have long recognized that deportation is a particularly severe "penalty," but it is not, in a strict sense, a criminal sanction. Although removal proceedings are civil in nature, deportation is nevertheless intimately related to the criminal process. Our law has enmeshed criminal convictions and the penalty of deportation for nearly a century. And, importantly, recent changes in our immigration law have made removal nearly an automatic result for a broad class of noncitizen offenders. Thus, we find it "most difficult" to divorce the penalty from the conviction in the deportation context. Moreover, we are quite confident that noncitizen defendants facing a risk of deportation for a particular offense find it even more difficult. . . .

III

Under *Strickland* [*v. Washington*, 466 U.S. 668, at 688 (1984)], we first determine whether counsel's representation "fell below an objective standard of reasonableness." Then we ask whether "there is a reasonable probability that, but for counsel's unprofessional errors, the result of the proceeding would have been different." The first prong—constitutional deficiency—is necessarily linked to the practice and expectations of the legal community: "The proper measure of attorney performance remains simply reasonableness under prevailing professional norms." We long have recognized that "[p]revailing norms of practice as reflected in American Bar Association standards and the like . . . are guides to determining what is reasonable. . . ." Although they are "only guides," and not "inexorable commands," these standards may be valuable measures of the prevailing professional norms of effective representation, especially as these standards have been adapted to deal with the intersection of modern criminal prosecutions and immigration law.

The weight of prevailing professional norms supports the view that counsel must advise her client regarding the risk of deportation. . . . In the instant case, the terms of the relevant immigration statute are succinct, clear, and explicit in defining the removal consequence for Padilla's conviction. Padilla's counsel could have easily determined that his plea would make him eligible for deportation simply from reading the text of the statute, which addresses not some broad classification of crimes but specifically commands removal for all controlled substances convictions except for the most trivial of marijuana possession offenses. Instead, Padilla's counsel provided him false assurance that his conviction would not result in his removal from this country. This is not a hard case in which to find deficiency: The consequences of Padilla's plea could easily be determined from reading the removal statute, his deportation was presumptively mandatory, and his counsel's advice was incorrect.

Immigration law can be complex, and it is a legal specialty of its own. Some members of the bar who represent clients facing criminal charges, in either state or federal court or both, may not be well versed in it. There will, therefore, undoubtedly be numerous situations in which the deportation consequences of a particular plea are unclear or uncertain. The duty of the private practitioner in such cases is more limited. When the law is not succinct and straightforward, . . . a criminal defense attorney need do no more than advise a noncitizen client that pending criminal charges may carry a risk of adverse immigration consequences. But when the deportation consequence is truly clear, as it was in this case, the duty to give correct advice is equally clear. . . .

The judgment of the Supreme Court of Kentucky is reversed, and the case is remanded for further proceedings not inconsistent with this opinion.

It is so ordered.

JUSTICE ALITO, with whom THE CHIEF JUSTICE joins, concurring in the judgment.
I concur in the judgment because a criminal defense attorney fails to provide effective assistance within the meaning of *Strickland v. Washington*, 466 U.S. 668 (1984), if the attorney misleads a noncitizen client regarding the removal consequences of a conviction. In my view, such an attorney must (1) refrain from unreasonably providing incorrect advice and (2) advise the defendant that a criminal conviction may have adverse immigration consequences and that, if the alien wants advice on this issue, the alien should consult an immigration attorney. I do not agree with the Court that the attorney must attempt to explain what those consequences may be. As the Court concedes, "[i]mmigration law can be complex"; "it is a legal specialty of its own"; and "[s]ome members of the bar who represent clients facing criminal charges, in either state or federal court or both, may not be well versed in it." The Court nevertheless holds that a criminal defense attorney must provide advice in this specialized area in those cases in which the law is "succinct and straightforward"—but not, perhaps, in other situations. This vague, halfway test will lead to much confusion and needless litigation.

JUSTICE SCALIA, with whom JUSTICE THOMAS joins, dissenting.
In the best of all possible worlds, criminal defendants contemplating a guilty plea ought to be advised of all serious collateral consequences of conviction, and surely ought not to be misadvised. The Constitution, however, is not an all-purpose tool for judicial construction of a perfect world; and when we ignore its text in order to make it that, we often find ourselves swinging a sledge where a tack hammer is needed.

The Sixth Amendment guarantees the accused a lawyer "for his defense" against a "criminal prosecutio[n]"—not for sound advice about the collateral consequences of conviction. For that reason, and for the practical reasons set forth in . . . Justice Alito's concurrence, I dissent from the Court's conclusion that the Sixth Amendment requires counsel to provide accurate advice concerning the potential removal consequences of a guilty plea. For the same reasons, but unlike the concurrence, I do not believe that affirmative misadvice about those consequences renders an attorney's assistance in defending against the prosecution constitutionally inadequate; or that the Sixth Amendment requires counsel to warn immigrant defendants that a conviction may render them removable. Statutory provisions can remedy these concerns in a more targeted fashion, and without producing permanent, and legislatively irreparable, overkill.

7

The Impact of Courts

COURT DECISIONS CAN have policy implications that extend beyond the litigants who are involved in disputes. In fact, social reform groups frequently litigate specifically for this purpose, to achieve policy change with a nationwide impact.[1] The U.S. Supreme Court has played a major role in shaping national policy on issues such as school desegregation, abortion, and criminal procedure, among many others, and in recent years, state courts have assumed a policymaking role as well, particularly in same-sex marriage policy. Because of the important consequences that their decisions can have, judges have incentives to think about the impact of their rulings, to consider the real-world consequences for the people who must live with their decisions and put them into effect.

Consider, for example, how the U.S. Supreme Court handled the desegregation of Southern schools following the landmark decision *Brown v. Board of Education* (1954).[2] After concluding in *Brown* that "in the field of public education the doctrine of 'separate but equal' has no place," the justices had to decide how quickly Southern school districts would need to implement the ruling.[3] The justices could have required an immediate end to school segregation, but they did not. When the justices made their implementation order a year later, in *Brown II* (1955), they mandated only that schools desegregate with "all deliberate speed."[4] (See case excerpt at the end of the chapter.) Why do you think the justices asked for so little? Why did

Portions of this chapter appeared as Chapter 2 in *Courthouse Democracy and Minority Rights: Same Sex Marriage in the States*, Oxford University Press, 2013.

they not require all school districts to admit students on a nonracial basis right away?

Quite possibly, the justices understood that if they asked for more, the decision would not have been implemented. During oral arguments in *Brown II*, attorney S. Emory Rogers made clear that his school district would not comply with a stronger mandate. (See Box 7.1.) "I am frank to tell you, right now," said Rogers, "in our district I do not think that we will send—the white people of the district will send their children to the Negro schools." The justices themselves also acknowledged that there were likely to be logistical problems with implementing their order. In *Brown II*, Chief Justice Warren described "problems related to administration, arising from the physical condition of the school plant, the school transportation system, personnel, revision of school districts and attendance areas into compact units . . . and revision of local laws and regulations."[5] When faced with these challenges, it was probably wise for the justices not to request immediate desegregation.

TEXTBOX 7.1	Oral Argument Excerpt from Brown v. Board of Ed. (Brown II), 349 U.S. 294 (1955)

Chief Justice Earl Warren: Is your request for an open decree predicated upon the assumption that your school district will immediately undertake to conform to the opinion of this Court of last year and to the decree, or is it on the basis—

Attorney S. Emory Rogers (Clarendon County, South Carolina): Mr. Chief Justice, to say we will conform depends on the decree handed down. I am frank to tell you, right now in our district I do not think that we will send—the white people of the district will send their children to the Negro schools. It would be unfair to tell the Court that we are going to do that. I do not think it is. But I do think that something can be worked out. We hope so.

Warren: It is not a question of attitude; it is a question of conforming to the decree. Is there any basis upon which we can assume that there will be an immediate attempt to comply with the decree of this Court, whatever it may be?

Rogers: Mr. Chief Justice, I would say that we would present our problem, as I understand it, if the decree is sent out, that we would present our problem to the district court, and we are in the Fourth Circuit. . . . I feel we can expect the courts in the

TEXTBOX 7.1 | **Continued**

Fourth Circuit and the people of the district to work out something in accordance with your decree.

Warren: Don't you believe that the question as to whether the district will attempt to comply should be considered in any such decree?

Rogers: Not necessarily, sir. I think that should be left to the lower court.

Warren: And why?

Rogers: Your Honors, we have laid down here in this Court the principle that segregation is unconstitutional. The lower court, we feel, is the place that the machinery should be set in motion to conform to that.

Warren: But you are not willing to say here that there would be an honest attempt to conform to this decree, if we did leave it to the district court?

Rogers: No, I am not. Let us get the word "honest" out of there.

Warren: No, leave it in.

Rogers: No, because I would have to tell you that right now we would not conform; we would not send our white children to the Negro schools.

Warren: Thank you.

Source: Phillip B. Kurland and Gerhard Casper, *Landmark Briefs and Arguments of the Supreme Court of the United States* (Arlington, VA: University Publications of America, 1975).

The truth is that court decisions are not self-implementing, and some judges might think about how the people who are responsible for interpreting and implementing their policy choices are likely to react. Among the most important of these groups is the **implementing population**, the nonjudicial actors who have the responsibility for putting court decisions into effect.[6] The people who compose the implementing population are different in each case. For school desegregation, the primary members of the implementing population were school districts. In criminal procedure cases, they have frequently been police officers or prosecutors, while for same-sex marriage, they were county clerks. What these actors have in common is their location outside of the judicial hierarchy and their power to determine whether and how court decisions go into effect.

Also central to implementation is the **interpreting population,** the lower-court judges who interpret the holdings of other courts and decide how to apply them. Technically, lower-court judges must follow the precedents of their superiors in the judicial hierarchy, but precedents are not always clear. Think about how challenging it must have been for lower-court judges in the years after *Brown II* to decide what the Supreme Court meant by "all deliberate speed."[7] How much time was too much to give the school districts? What accommodations would it be reasonable for judges to make? The Supreme Court's mandate did not say. Lower-court judges might also sometimes disagree with precedents and try to interpret them as narrowly as possible. Higher courts can overrule these decisions, but they have no power to fire lower-court judges who are insubordinate.

In addition to these groups, the impact of courts can be shaped by the **consumer population,** which is composed of the people who make use of judicial policies. (See Judicial Process Box 7.1.) In *Brown*, for example, the primary consumers were the families who lived in segregated school districts. In criminal procedure cases, the consumers are often criminal defendants. Also potentially relevant are the reactions of the **secondary population,** made up of other interested parties who are not directly affected by a court's decision. Members of the secondary population might include the public at large, the media, interest groups, and other government officials.

Political scientists disagree about how much judges depend on these other actors to be effective. Some researchers see courts as dynamic institutions that can bring about significant policy change on their own, but others think of courts as more constrained institutions. Still other researchers believe that court decisions tend to inspire a backlash, leaving reform groups worse off than they were before by mobilizing opposing groups. The more constrained that courts are, the more incentives that judges have to anticipate the reactions of interpreting and implementing populations when making decisions. To understand judicial behavior more fully, then, it is necessary to study the impact of courts and to think about how concerns about implementation might influence judicial behavior. It could be that, much like in *Brown II*, judges are reluctant to venture further than where they can be effective. If judges anticipate resistance to their orders or other practical problems with implementation, it might affect the choices they make.

Judges routinely depend on other actors to carr   ir judg-ments. Political scientists Bradley Canon and C   ohnson developed a typology of key actors who are centr   imple-mentation and interpretation of judicial policies:

implementing population — nonjudicial actors who ha responsibility for putting court decisions into effect

interpreting population — lower-court judges who interpret court decisions and decide how to apply them

consumer population — the people who use judicial policies

secondary population — other interested parties who are not directly affected by a Court's decision (e.g., the public at large, the media, interest groups, and other elected officials)

What do you think about this list? Are some of these actors likely to be more central to the impact of court decisions than others? Are any key actors missing from the list?

See Bradley C. Canon and Charles A. Johnson, *Judicial Policies: Implementation and Impact*, second edition (Washington, DC: CQ Press, 1999).

THE DYNAMIC COURT MODEL

The first theory of judicial impact is the **dynamic court model,** which holds that courts are capable of producing major policy change. The theory suggests that social reform groups and other litigants can use courts to achieve policy goals that they cannot achieve elsewhere. In *Brown*, for example, the National Association for the Advancement of Colored People (NAACP) turned to courts to desegregate the schools. In same-sex marriage litigation, the goal was marriage equality. When legislatures are unwilling or unable to make policy, the dynamic court model maintains that litigation can be an effective alternative. In fact, the model suggests that courts are better than other institutions at achieving policy change in some circumstances.

The reason that courts have so much potential to be dynamic is because of their institutional legitimacy. People tend to trust courts, even when they disagree with the choices that they make. Judges benefit from a **positivity bias**, which makes the public think about judicial decision making as a principled process that is worthy of their respect. According to political scientists James Gibson and Gregory Caldeira, who have conducted extensive research about public attitudes about courts, this positivity bias exists "even during conflicts, and even among the losers in such conflicts."[8] As one illustration of the positivity bias, Figure 7.1 reports the approval ratings of the Supreme Court, the president, and Congress since 2000.[9] How does the Supreme Court compare to these other institutions? What do you think? As the data show, the Supreme Court generally enjoys higher approval ratings compared to the other branches, particularly Congress. For most of this century, public approval of the Supreme Court has been above 50 percent, occasionally topping 60 percent. Although public approval of the Supreme Court has been declining in recent years, it still far exceeds Congressional approval, which fell to 13 percent in 2012. Presidential approval has been more variable, consistently above Congress but generally below the approval ratings

Figure 7.1   Public Approval of Government Institutions

Do you approve of the way the [Supreme Court/President/Congress] is handling its job?

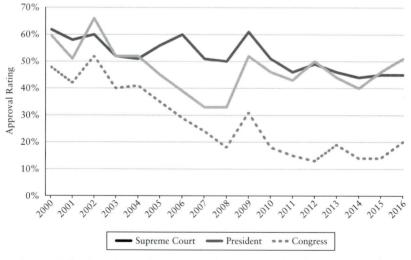

Source: Gallup Organization.

for the Supreme Court, except for a few years when approval of the president was higher.

These positive attitudes about courts are not based on an unsophisticated view of how judges do their jobs. Research has found that support for the U.S. Supreme Court actually becomes stronger when people become more educated about it. As political scientists often put it, "to know courts is to love them."[10] Gibson and Caldeira's research has shown that the public is aware that Supreme Court justices have discretion and that judicial decisions can be motivated by policy considerations. Nevertheless, Gibson and Caldeira have found that the public thinks that judging is different from other political behavior, "that discretion is being exercised in a principled, rather than strategic, way."[11] This perception is reinforced by judicial symbols such as the robes judges wear, honorific forms of addressing judges, and the courtroom setting.[12]

Research also indicates that legitimacy remains robust despite public disapproval of particular decisions. That is to say, the public distinguishes between **diffuse support** for courts as institutions and **specific support** for the policies that judges make. Research has consistently found that the legitimacy of the U.S. Supreme Court is capable of weathering public disapproval of particular decisions. For example, after *Bush v. Gore* (2000), which decided the 2000 presidential election, many commentators assumed that the Court's legitimacy would be damaged because the decision was so visible and so politicized.[13] However, researchers did not find a sustained negative impact on legitimacy.[14] Although there is some evidence that unpopular decisions produce short-term declines in public confidence,[15] and other research questions how resilient legitimacy really is,[16] for the most part diffuse support for courts remains high.

One consequence of the positivity bias is that courts can function as a **republican schoolmaster**. That is to say, judges can *change* public opinion, increasing support for policies on the strength of their judgments alone. Laboratory experiments have found that people are more likely to support a policy when a court endorses it than when it is attributed to another institution, such as Congress or a nonpartisan think tank.[17] Political scientists Valerie Hoekstra and Jeffrey Segal found evidence of the republican schoolmaster effect in polls taken at the time of the Supreme Court's decision in *Lamb's Chapel v. Center Moriches Union Free School District* (1993).[18] In *Lamb's Chapel*, the justices ruled that religious groups could use public school facilities for their own religious events after hours. Hoekstra and Segal showed that local public attitudes about the policy changed immediately following the decision.[19] (See Figure 7.2.) In the town of Center Moriches, where the public school was located, as well as in surrounding Suffolk County, people became less opposed to using public school facilities by religious groups.

Yet Hoekstra and Segal's research also highlights some of the limitations on the ability of judges to function as republican schoolmasters. The data show that the Court's impact on public opinion was weaker in Center Moriches than in the surrounding Suffolk County. Most likely, the difference occurred because the people in Center Moriches, who were directly affected by the ruling, had already made up their minds about it. In contrast, people in Suffolk County were more open-minded, although they were still aware of the decision because of local media coverage about it. Hoekstra and Segal concluded that "the more immediate the situation is to one's personal life, the less likely one is to defer to the judgment of some other source, even one thought to be highly credible."[20] The implication is that judges are more capable of being dynamic policymakers when the public is paying attention to their decisions but lacks strong preexisting attitudes about them.[21]

Figure 7.2 Public Attitudes about Religious Accommodation Pre- and Post-*Lamb's Chapel*

Do you feel that a religious group ought to be allowed to use public school facilities after school hours if other community groups are allowed to use the facilities, or do you believe that a church should not be allowed to use the school facilities?

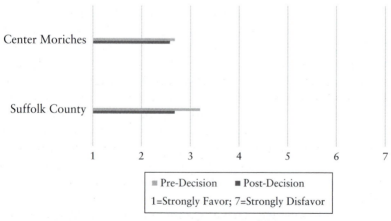

■ Pre-Decision   ■ Post-Decision

1=Strongly Favor; 7=Strongly Disfavor

Source: Valerie J. Hoekstra and Jeffrey A. Segal, "The Shepherding of Local Public Opinion: The Supreme Court and *Lamb's Chapel*," *Journal of Politics* 58 (1996): 1091.

Judges are also more likely to be dynamic policymakers when lower courts can implement their decisions directly. In his study of the impact of U.S. Supreme Court decisions, political scientist Matthew E. K. Hall distinguishes between **vertical issues**, which lower courts can implement, and **lateral issues**, which must be implemented by officials outside of the judicial hierarchy such as school boards, city councils, and police officers.[22] Hall finds that when justices are less dependent on extra-judicial actors, they are more likely to be effective, even when their decisions are unpopular. Hall points to flag burning, obscenity, and death penalty cases as examples of unpopular vertical issues in which the justices managed to have an impact.

Another way that courts can be dynamic is by acting as a **veto point**, blocking policies that other actors would like to put into effect. Imagine, for example, if Chief Justice Roberts had voted to strike down the Affordable Care Act ("Obamacare") in *National Federation of Independent Business v. Sebelius* (2012). The decision would have had an immediate and profound impact on health care coverage in the country. In a similar way, judges managed to block President Obama's executive orders on immigration, which sought to shield undocumented immigrants from deportation.[23] More recently, President Donald Trump has encountered judicial challenges to his own immigration orders.[24] When you are thinking about judicial behavior, consider what other types of resources that judges have that can make them effective policymakers. Under what circumstances are judges most likely to be dynamic? When are they less likely to be so?

THE CONSTRAINED COURT MODEL

A second theory of judicial impact, the **constrained court model**, is more skeptical that courts can produce major policy change. The model traces back at least to Alexander Hamilton, who in *Federalist 78* described the judiciary as the "least dangerous branch" because it lacks the power to enforce its decisions. (See reading at the end of the chapter.) As Hamilton put it, the judiciary has "neither force, nor will, but merely judgment."[25] Judges depend primarily on their institutional legitimacy, and the persuasiveness of their written opinions, to be effective policymakers. In contrast, Congress can enforce its policies by making use of its taxing and spending powers, while the president can muster the resources of the military and the executive bureaucracy.

The most famous contemporary exponent of the constrained court model is Gerald Rosenberg, who in a 1991 landmark study

The Hollow Hope concluded that litigation was not the best way for reform groups to advance their causes.[26] Rosenberg described litigation as a "hollow hope" because he saw judges as essentially powerless to bring about social change without the support of the public or the other branches of government. Rosenberg thought that it would be much better for groups to seek policy reforms from legislatures, or to change hearts and minds in society at large. The problem with a litigation strategy, Rosenberg wrote, is that "not only does litigation steer activists to an institution that is constrained from helping them, but also it siphons off crucial resources and talent, and runs the risk of weakening political efforts."[27]

Rosenberg argues that judges are constrained because of three structural limitations on their power. The first is the limited nature of rights. Rosenberg explains that for judges to make policy, they must establish a new right or expand the application of an existing one. Either approach requires judges to ground their actions in a plausible interpretation of the Constitution, their own precedents, or some other legal authority. Judges cannot create new constitutional rights out of whole cloth, not if they want their decisions to be accepted by other political actors and the legal community. Judges must achieve their policy goals within the existing legal framework.

A second constraint that Rosenberg describes is the lack of judicial independence. Courts operate in a system of checks and balances in which other government actors have resources to limit the effects of judicial decisions that they dislike. Many of these constraints on courts are described in chapter 4 and include the ability of other branches to amend the Constitution, to impeach judges, and to threaten to withhold pay raises and other budget requests. These institutional checks and balances matter because they provide leverage for the other branches to correct what they perceive to be excesses of judicial power. Although policymakers rarely use court-curbing measures at the federal level, the fact that they exist might be sufficient to discourage judges from pushing their power too far beyond what the elected branches will accept.

Finally, and perhaps most important, judges lack formal implementation powers, depending on other actors to interpret and implement their decisions consistently with their intent. Because these actors are likely to have their own attitudes about policies, they might not be willing to implement judicial decisions faithfully, and there is little that higher courts can do about it. As discussed above, judges cannot remove insubordinate actors from office. When interpreting and implementing populations shirk their responsibilities, judges must wait for litigants to bring cases to them so that they can issue new mandates, perhaps more strongly worded than before. Yet, these new decisions are just as vulnerable to defiance or evasion, leaving judges once again in the position of having to clarify their intentions. Rosenberg maintains that, to overcome the constraints on their power, judges need the support of other actors outside of the judicial branch.

Rosenberg tests his theory by focusing primarily on the impact of two landmark Supreme Court decisions, *Brown v. Board of Education* (1954) and *Roe v. Wade* (1973). The Supreme Court is credited in *Brown* with bringing about an end to segregation in the public schools, whereas *Roe* is said to have liberalized national abortion policy. However, Rosenberg argues that neither case actually brought about the changes that reform groups sought. As an illustration, Figure 7.3 reports the number of black schoolchildren attending school with whites in the Deep South from 1954 to 1966.[28] What do you think of the trends that you see? To what extent are the data consistent with the hypothesis that the Supreme Court's impact on school desegregation in the South was constrained? To what extent are the data inconsistent?

Figure 7.3 Number of Black Schoolchildren Attending School with Whites, Deep South Only

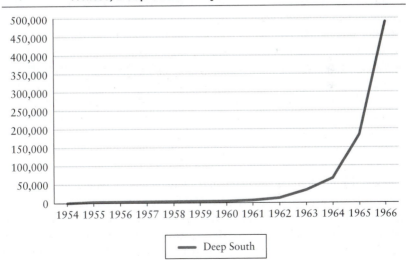

Source: Gerald Rosenberg, *The Hollow Hope: Can Courts Bring About Social Change?*, second edition (Chicago: University of Chicago Press, 2008).

Looking only at the Deep South, Rosenberg does appear to have strong support for his hypothesis. For about a decade after *Brown*, virtually no black schoolchildren attended school with whites. Meaningful integration occurred only after Congress intervened with the passage of the 1964 Civil Rights Act. The Act authorized the federal government to file lawsuits on behalf of families denied access to schools, and it permitted the Department of Health, Education, and Welfare to cut off federal funds to schools that did not integrate. With the addition of these congressional sanctions, the mandate in *Brown* ultimately did go into effect, but by itself the Supreme Court had virtually no direct impact on the integration of Southern schools.

The analysis becomes more complicated, however, when one looks at rates of integration outside of the Deep South. Figure 7.4 reports the number of black schoolchildren attending schools with whites in the Border States, which include Delaware, Kentucky, Maryland, Missouri, Oklahoma, and West Virginia. The data show that, contrary to Rosenberg's hypothesis, integration did occur at a steady pace in the decade after *Brown*, without any intervention from Congress. What can account for the difference? One explanation might relate to Hoekstra and Segal's research on public reactions to court decisions, which you read about earlier. If you recall, Hoekstra and Segal found, in their research on the *Lamb's Chapel* decision, that people were more resistant to judicial policies when they already had strong opinions about them. For court decisions to have a persuasive effect, it was necessary for the public to have an open mind. Perhaps a similar dynamic was at work in the aftermath of *Brown*. In areas of the Deep South where public attitudes about segregation were the strongest and the most entrenched, the justices could not persuade school districts to desegregate without the support of Congress and the president. Outside of the Deep South, where the decision was still visible but the public was less committed to segregation, school districts responded and integration occurred.

Another thing to keep in mind is that the Supreme Court did not ask for immediate desegregation in *Brown II*. When the justices issued their desegregation order in 1955, they only required the South to desegregate with "all deliberate speed." Of course, the justices were probably expecting more of a response than what they got from the Deep South—no doubt the rate of implementation in the Border States better reflects their intent. But the mandate left a lot of room for school districts to evade the order, and the vague language made it

Figure 7.4 Number of Black Schoolchildren Attending School with Whites, with Border States

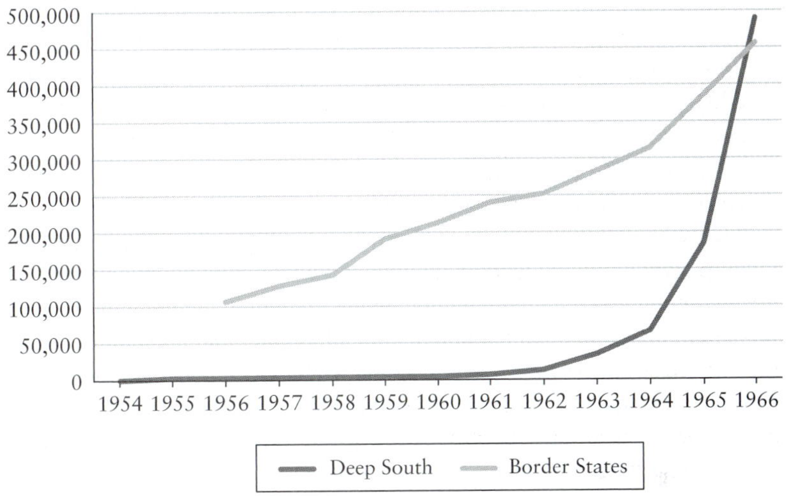

Source: Gerald Rosenberg, *The Hollow Hope: Can Courts Bring About Social Change?*, second edition (Chicago: University of Chicago Press, 2008).

more difficult for federal trial judges to enforce it. In his classic book *58 Lonely Men* (1971), Jack Peltason documents the social pressures that Southern district judges faced to slow the pace of integration. "A judge who makes rulings adverse to integration," he writes, "is not so likely to be honored by testimonial dinners, or to read flattering editorials in the local press, or to partake of the fellowship at the club. He will no longer be invited to certain homes; former friends will avoid him when they meet on the street."[29] A clearer mandate in *Brown II* would have given cover for these judges to take a firmer stance and say that they were simply following the Supreme Court's orders.

Rosenberg's account of judicial impact has received considerable scholarly attention, as well as its share of criticism.[30] Perhaps the most prominent critic is political scientist Michael W. McCann, who maintains that Rosenberg overstates his argument, missing some of the less-tangible ways in which judges have influenced reform movements. Particularly important is the potential for judges to legitimize unpopular policy alternatives. If the *Brown* decision did not bring about an immediate end to segregation, it still might have helped to validate the civil rights movement, encouraging further public support and laying the groundwork for future policy victories. Favorable court decisions might have also empowered supporters to stand up and fight for needed change. McCann observes that Rosenberg's own data show that enrollment in the NAACP increased significantly in the years following the *Brown* decision.[31] The increase in registration rates might have been spurred by the Supreme Court's endorsement of civil rights causes in *Brown*.

More broadly, McCann argues that Rosenberg overstates the weaknesses of judges compared to other branches. No institution of government is likely to have a meaningful impact on society without public or elite support. "My reading of scholarly literature, and the newspapers for that matter," McCann writes, "suggests an overwhelming consensus that executive and legislative institutions at all levels have trouble translating their will into effective social change."[32] The American constitutional system of separation of powers and checks and balances ensures that all national institutions will have difficulty making policy unilaterally. Meaningful social change almost always requires coordination and cooperation across branches. When you are thinking about judicial behavior, reflect on how the constraints on judges compare to those on the other branches. Can any branch of government achieve significant policy change on its own?

THE BACKLASH THESIS

A third approach to the impact of courts is the **backlash thesis**, which maintains that a major consequence of judicial policymaking is to mobilize the opponents of court decisions. For example, *Roe v. Wade* (1973) sparked the growth of the prolife movement, while early same-sex marriage litigation encouraged the passage of state constitutional amendments limiting marriage to one man and one woman.[33] The backlash thesis differs from the constrained court model because it suggests that court decisions do have an effect, but unlike the dynamic court model, it is not what judges intend. In fact, reform groups might end up *worse off* than they were before by providing rallying points to the opponents of the policy changes they seek.

The leading exponent of the backlash thesis is legal historian Michael Klarman, who in an influential article showed that the immediate impact of *Brown v. Board of Education* (1954) was to radicalize Southern racial politics and to spark massive resistance. *Brown* had this effect, Klarman writes, because it expected Southerners to do too much too quickly. "*Brown* was an unambiguous, highly salient pronouncement that southern race relations were destined to change. It could not easily be ignored or discounted as gradual, diffuse, and less salient changes could be."[34] Moreover, *Brown* represented interference by the federal government in Southern politics on an extremely sensitive issue: race relations in public education. The result was an increase in racial violence and an immediate setback to racial progress in the South.

The backlash thesis maintains that court decisions routinely have this sort of effect, at once increasing the visibility of issues and imposing solutions that opponents are not ready to accept. In this way, the intervention of courts on major policy questions can end up being counterproductive to reform efforts. Ironically, Klarman finds that in the long run the backlash to *Brown* actually helped to secure the passage of the 1964 Civil Rights Act. The "nationally televised scenes of southern law enforcement officers using police dogs, high-pressure fire hoses, tear gas, and truncheons against peaceful, prayerful black demonstrators (often children) . . . converted millions of previously indifferent northern whites into enthusiastic proponents of civil rights legislation."[35] In a roundabout way, then, the backlash to *Brown* ended up advancing the cause of civil rights, but not in a way that the original litigants could have intended.

Critics of the backlash thesis suggest that court decisions do not just mobilize the opponents of court decisions, but the supporters as well. That is to say, court decisions have a polarizing effect.[36] As discussed above, Rosenberg's own data suggest that there was an increase in the mobilization of supporters of civil rights in the years after *Brown*. Other research indicates that cases such as *Roe v. Wade* have had a similar impact on supporters.[37] Additionally, critics maintain that the backlash thesis has limited application because not every court decision is likely to invoke such a strong reaction. The theory might help us to understand how people respond to highly visible and divisive cases such as *Brown* and *Roe*, but not routine matters where the public is less engaged. When you are thinking about the impact of courts, take some time to consider which types of policies are likely to prompt the strongest public reactions. When is a backlash more likely to occur? When do you think that court decisions are less likely to be polarizing?

THE IMPACT OF STATE COURTS

Much of the research on judicial impact has focused on the U.S. Supreme Court, but state courts also engage in policymaking and face unique institutional constraints that shape their impact. Many of these constraints became clear in the early 2000s, when state courts were innovating in the area of same-sex marriage policy.[38] Some court decisions resulted in marriages: in states such as Massachusetts, Connecticut, and Iowa, county clerks issued marriage licenses to same-sex couples under court order despite public opposition. Yet, in other states, courts had less of an impact, with marriage equality rulings overturned by state constitutional amendments in California, Hawaii, and Alaska. The variation in the effectiveness of these rulings suggests that state courts are not similarly situated in their capacity to bring about major policy change.

Among the reasons that state court decisions are less secure is that many states make it much easier for their citizens to amend their state constitutions. In California, for example, citizens can get a state constitutional amendment on the ballot with a petition drive. The amendment then only needs the support of a simple majority of voters in the state to become law. In this way, opponents of same-sex marriage secured the passage of Proposition 8 in 2008 to overturn a California Supreme Court decision striking down the state's same-sex marriage ban that same year. Other states make use of these **initiative amendment** procedures as well. (See Judicial Process Box 7.2.) Even when states do not let citizens propose constitutional amendments directly, they almost always let them vote on amendments that their state legislators have proposed.[39] With state constitutional amendments so much easier to obtain, state court decisions are more vulnerable and state judges are less likely to secure the implementation of policies that the public opposes. Notably, constitutional amendments prohibiting same-sex marriage passed in sixteen of the eighteen states that permit initiative amendments (88.9 percent), and only fifteen of the thirty-two states that do not (46.9 percent).[40] In contrast, it is very difficult to overturn a constitutional judgment of the U.S. Supreme Court. In the federal system, an amendment needs an extraordinary level of support, including the approval of two-thirds of both houses of Congress, or a national convention, before it is sent for ratification by at least three-quarters of the states. For this reason, Supreme Court decisions have more resilience than many state court decisions do. Despite the widespread criticism that *Roe v. Wade* (1973) has received, the only time that *Roe* has actually been in jeopardy is when the justices themselves have considered overturning it. Other actors know that, for the most part, they must learn to live with Supreme Court precedents or else work around them.

JUDICIAL PROCESS BOX 7.2	State Constitutional Amendment Procedures

States use a variety of methods for amending their state constitutions. In most states, the legislatures propose amendments, which are then put before the public for a vote, but some states give citizens a more active role. States with **direct initiatives** permit citizens to propose amendments directly using a petition drive, while states with **indirect initiatives** let citizens propose amendments, but only subject to legislative approval. What do you think? Should citizens have a direct role in amending their state constitutions? Why or why not? What do you see as the costs and benefits of initiative amendment procedures?

Direct Initiatives	Indirect Initiatives	No Initiatives	
AR	MA	AL	NJ
CA	MS	AK	NM
CO		CT	NY
FL		DE	NC
IL		GA	PA
MI		HI	RI
MO		ID	SC
MT		IN	TN
NE		IA	TX
NV		KS	UT
ND		KY	VT
OH		LA	VA
OK		ME	WA
OR		MD	WV
SD		MN	WI
		NH	WY
16 states	**2 states**	**32 states**	

Source: Initiative and Referendum Institute, http://www.iandrinstitute.org/.

Another important difference between state supreme courts and the U.S. Supreme Court is that state courts are not limited by the text or the interpretive history of the U.S. Constitution. Each state has its own constitution and precedents that judges can use to justify case outcomes. Under principles of **judicial federalism**, state court judges are free to use their own constitutions to supplement federal rights, as long as they do not take away rights guaranteed by federal law. Yet, the legal resources that judges have to work with vary from state to state. Depending on what their state constitutions, precedents, and other sources of law say about a subject, state judges might find that they have a harder time having an impact on some issue areas.

For example, many state constitutions include language that specifically protects citizens against sex discrimination, language that the federal constitution does not contain. The Fourteenth Amendment to the U.S. Constitution is gender neutral, providing "persons" in the several states with equal protection and due process rights. The federal Equal Rights Amendment, which would have specifically prohibited sex discrimination, was never ratified, but a number of states enacted equal rights amendments of their own. (See Judicial Process Box 7.3.) These "mini-ERAs" can provide cover for judges to innovate in certain policy areas. For example, when state supreme court justices in Hawaii first ruled, in the 1990s, that state laws prohibiting same-sex marriage were probably unconstitutional, they relied on their state equal rights amendment. The justices in *Baehr v. Lewin* (1993) ruled that it was sex discrimination to deny couples the right to marry based solely on the sex of their partners.[41] As it turns out, all four state supreme courts that provided for full marriage equality after *Baehr v. Lewin* also had mini-ERAs on the books.[42]

A third factor that can influence the impact of state courts is variation in the selection and retention of judges. Like initiative amendment procedures, judicial elections give the opponents of court decisions an opportunity to mobilize against judges, replacing them with candidates who pledge to interpret the law more consistently with the public will. We learned in chapter 5 that judges in Iowa faced removal for legalizing same-sex marriage in that state. Even appointed judges are vulnerable to replacement when they lack life tenure and depend on the continuing support of their governors or state legislators. It is difficult for judges to have a lasting impact on legal policy when they cannot stay on the bench to oversee the implementation of their decisions.

JUDICIAL IMPACT AND JUDICIAL BEHAVIOR

What, if any, effect do concerns about implementation have on judicial behavior? Certainly, judges seem to indicate, in their writings and other public remarks, that they think about practical problems relating to implementation when they are making decisions. During oral arguments, for example, U.S. Supreme Court justices frequently pose hypothetical

JUDICIAL PROCESS BOX 7.3 | **State Equal Rights Amendments**

The Fourteenth Amendment of the U.S. Constitution protects our "liberty" and guarantees us the "equal protection of the laws," but it does not specifically mention sex discrimination. Congress passed the federal Equal Rights Amendment in 1972, but only thirty-five states ratified it, three short of the three-fourths majority required. The amendment would have read, "Equality of rights under the law shall not be denied or abridged in the United States or by any state on account of sex."

However, a number of states have amended their state constitutions to feature their own equal rights amendments. A sample of these provisions is below:

Hawaii. "Equality of rights under the law shall not be denied or abridged by the State on account of sex. The legislature shall have the power to enforce, by appropriate legislation, the provisions of this section." Hawaii Constitution, Article I, §3 (1972).

Iowa: "All men and women are, by nature, free and equal and have certain inalienable rights—among which are those of enjoying and defending life and liberty, acquiring, possessing and protecting property, and pursuing and obtaining safety and happiness." Iowa Constitution, Article I, §1 (1998).

Massachusetts: "All people are born free and equal, and have certain natural, essential, and unalienable rights; among which may be reckoned the right of enjoying and defending their lives and liberties; that of acquiring, possessing and protecting property; in fine, that of seeking and obtaining their safety and happiness. Equality under the law shall not be denied or abridged because of sex, race, color, creed or national origin." Massachusetts Constitution, Part 1, Article 1 (1976).

What do you think? In what other ways should states amend their constitutions to give their citizens more generous rights protections than the federal constitution provides?

Source: Leslie W. Gladstone, "Equal Rights Amendments: State Provisions," in *Congressional Research Service Report for Congress* (Washington, DC: The Library of Congress, 2004).

scenarios to attorneys to assess what the broader policy consequences of their rulings will be. Occasionally, as in *Brown II*, the justices learn that there will be resistance to their orders. But are judges really less likely to seek policy change when they anticipate noncompliance?

Systematic research on this question is limited, but at least one study has found evidence of an effect. Political scientist Matthew E. K. Hall discovered that U.S. Supreme Court justices are more attentive to the preferences of external actors, such as members of Congress and the public, when nonjudicial actors are responsible for implementing their decisions.[43] The justices have less control over the administration of legal policies on these lateral issues, so they are more likely to listen to what others want. Yet, the justices' motivations change when lower courts are able to implement the Court's policies directly. With these vertical issues, which include criminal prosecutions, civil liability, and judicial administration, the justices have more control and can behave more independently. Hall concludes that "the fear of nonimplementation is a critical factor motivating the Supreme Court's response to external pressure," and that "the Court is more constrained when trying to alter policy beyond the control of lower courts."[44]

As we have learned throughout this textbook, judges are immersed in politics, so it makes sense to learn that practical considerations sometimes guide their decision making. Judges understand that the choices that they make can have profound consequences for all of us. Before deciding cases on public policy issues such as abortion, affirmative action, or school prayer, judges have incentives to take the long-term view and to think about what the effects of their decisions are likely to be. Part of this process involves anticipating how other actors are likely to react to their decisions. Otherwise, judges might find that their rulings have little effect, or that they have different consequences from what they intended.

But not every case is a landmark, and not every judge has the power to enact substantial policy change. In more routine disputes, what matters the most to judges is the impact on the litigants who appear before them. Day by day, judges make choices that affect people in ways great and small. Maybe you have come into contact with a judge yourself at some point. The everyday impact of courts is felt in the traffic disputes, minor drug offenses, and routine civil proceedings in which we find ourselves from time to time. When you are thinking about judicial impact, it is important to remember that every act of judging is consequential to someone. Even if a judge's decision does not change society, it probably still has a major impact on someone's life.

DISCUSSION QUESTIONS

1. Do you agree with Alexander Hamilton's assessment of the judiciary as the "least dangerous branch"? Are there circumstances in which judges are more likely to be dynamic policymakers? Why or why not?
2. Why do you think that the U.S. Supreme Court enjoys such high levels of public confidence? Do you think that this confidence is deserved, based on what you know about judging?
3. How hard should it be to amend the U.S. Constitution? Are state constitutional systems right to give the public a more direct role in the amendment process? Why or why not?
4. Do you think that school desegregation would have occurred more rapidly in the South if the U.S. Supreme Court had issued a stronger order in *Brown II*? How else could the Supreme Court have managed the implementation of its decision in *Brown*?

KEY TERMS

implementing population
interpreting population
consumer population
secondary population
dynamic court model
positivity bias
diffuse support
specific support
republican schoolmaster

vertical issues
lateral issues
veto point
constrained court model
backlash thesis
initiative amendment
direct initiatives
indirect initiatives
judicial federalism

FURTHER READING

Canon, Bradley C., and Charles A. Johnson. 1999. *Judicial Policies: Implementation and Impact*. Second edition. Washington, DC: CQ Press.
Rosenberg, Gerald N. 2008. *The Hollow Hope: Can Courts Bring About Social Change?* Second edition. Chicago: University of Chicago Press.
Hall, Matthew E. K. 2011. *The Nature of Supreme Court Power*. New York: Cambridge University Press.

NOTES

1. The definition of judicial impact is from Gerald N. Rosenberg, *The Hollow Hope: Can Courts Bring About Social Change?*, second edition (Chicago: University of Chicago Press, 2008), 4.

2. Brown v. Board of Education of Topeka (Brown I), 347 U.S. 483 (1954).

3. Id., at 495.

4. Brown v. Board of Education of Topeka (Brown II), 349 U.S. 294 (1955), at 301.

5. Id., at 300–301.

6. The framework for describing groups responsible for interpreting and implementing court decisions is from Bradley C. Canon and Charles A. Johnson, *Judicial Policies: Implementation and Impact*, second edition (Washington, DC: CQ Press, 1999).

7. *See* J. W. Peltason, *58 Lonely Men: Southern Federal Judges and School Desegregation* (Champaign: University of Illinois Press, 1971).

8. James L. Gibson and Gregory A. Caldeira, *Citizens, Courts, and Confirmations* (Princeton, NJ: Princeton University Press, 2009), 3.

9. Data are from the Gallup organization, available at http://www.gallup.com/. For years in which public support was measured multiple times, data are from the first week of September to maintain comparability. It should be noted that public approval ratings are not ideal measures of legitimacy because they capture both institutional loyalty as well as attitudes about particular decisions. *See* Gregory A. Caldeira and James L. Gibson, "The Etiology of Public Support for the Supreme Court," *American Journal of Political Science* 36 (1992): 635.

10. James L. Gibson, Gregory A. Caldeira, and Vanessa Baird, "On the Legitimacy of National High Courts," *American Political Science Review* 92 (1998): 344.

11. James L. Gibson and Gregory A. Caldeira, "Has Legal Realism Damaged the Legitimacy of the U.S. Supreme Court?," *Law & Society Review* 45 (2011): 213.

12. James L. Gibson, Milton Lodge, and Benjamin Woodson, "Losing, but Accepting: Legitimacy, Positivity, and the Symbols of Judicial Authority," *Law & Society Review* 48 (2014): 840.

13. Bush v. Gore, 531 U.S. 98 (2000).

14. James L. Gibson, Gregory A. Caldeira, and Lester Kenyatta Spence, "The Supreme Court and the US Presidential Election of 2000: Wounds, Self-Inflicted or Otherwise?," *British Journal of Political Science* 33 (2003): 555.

15. Anke Grosskopf and Jeffrey J. Mondak, "Do Attitudes toward Specific Supreme Court Decisions Matter? The Impact of Webster and *Texas v. Johnson* on Public Confidence in the Supreme Court," *Political Research Quarterly* 51 (1998): 633–54.

16. *Compare* Brandon L. Bartels and Christopher D. Johnston, "On the Ideological Foundations of Supreme Court Legitimacy in the American Public," *American Journal of Political Science* 57 (2013): 184–99 (finding that "ideological disagreement exhibits a potent, deleterious impact on legitimacy") *with* James L. Gibson and Michael J. Nelson, "Is the U.S. Supreme Court's Legitimacy Grounded in Performance Satisfaction and Ideology?," *American Journal of Political Science* 59 (2015): 162–74 (disputing these findings).

17. Jeffery J. Mondak, "Institutional Legitimacy, Policy Legitimacy, and the Supreme Court," *American Politics Quarterly* 20 (1992): 457; Valerie J. Hoekstra, "The Supreme Court and Opinion Change: An Experimental Study of the Court's Ability to Change Opinion," *American Politics Quarterly* 23 (1995):

109; Rosalee A. Clawson, Elizabeth R. Kegler, and Eric N. Waltenberg, "The Legitimacy-Conferring Authority of the U.S. Supreme Court: An Experimental Design," *American Politics Research* 29 (2001): 566; James L. Gibson, Gregory A. Caldeira, and Lester Kenyatta Spence, "Why Do People Accept Public Policies They Oppose? Testing Legitimacy Theory with a Survey-Based Experiment," *Political Research Quarterly* 58 (2005): 187.

18. Lamb's Chapel v. Center Moriches Union Free School District, 508 U.S. 384 (1993).

19. Valerie J. Hoekstra and Jeffrey A. Segal, "The Shepherding of Local Public Opinion: The Supreme Court and *Lamb's Chapel*," *Journal of Politics* 58 (1996): 1079.

20. Id., 1096.

21. *See also* John Zaller, *The Nature and Origins of Mass Opinion* (New York: Cambridge University Press, 1992).

22. Matthew E. K. Hall, *The Nature of Supreme Court Power* (New York: Cambridge University Press, 2011).

23. United States v. Texas, 579 U.S. ___ (2016).

24. Michael D. Shear, Nicholas Kulish, and Alan Feuer, "Judge Blocks Trump Order on Refugees; Confusion at Airports Ends with a Partial Stay Favoring Detainees," *New York Times*, January 29, 2017, A1.

25. *The Federalist*, No. 78 (Alexander Hamilton) in *The Federalist Papers*, ed. Clinton Rossiter (New York: New American Library, 1961).

26. Gerald N. Rosenberg, *The Hollow Hope: Can Courts Bring About Social Change?*, second edition (Chicago: University of Chicago Press, 2008).

27. Rosenberg, *The Hollow Hope*, 423.

28. States in the Deep South are Alabama, Arkansas, Florida, Georgia, Louisiana, Mississippi, North Carolina, South Carolina, Tennessee, Texas, and Virginia.

29. Peltason, *58 Lonely Men*, 9.

30. *See* Michael W. McCann, "Reform Litigation on Trial," *Law & Social Inquiry* 17 (1992): 715 (reviewing *The Hollow Hope*); Michael W. McCann, *Rights at Work: Pay Equity Reform and the Politics of Legal Mobilization* (Chicago: University of Chicago Press, 1994); Michael W. McCann, "Causal versus Constitutive Explanations (or, On the Difficulty of Being So Positive . . .)," *Law & Social Inquiry* 21 (1996): 457; Susan Lawrence, "Review," *American Political Science Review* 86 (1992): 812 (reviewing *The Hollow Hope*); *and* Jonathan Simon, "'The Long Walk Home' to Politics," *Law & Society Review* 26 (1992): 923 (reviewing *The Hollow Hope*).

31. Rosenberg, *The Hollow Hope*, 151, 154.

32. McCann, "Reform Litigation on Trial," 727.

33. Michael J. Klarman, *From the Closet to the Altar: Courts, Backlash, and the Struggle for Same-Sex Marriage* (New York: Oxford University Press, 2012); "Backlash from *Roe v. Wade* Continues to Shape Public Discourse, Says Klarman," *Harvard Law Today*, March 25, 2013, available at http://today.law.harvard.edu/backlash-from-roe-v-wade-continues-to-shape-public-discourse-says-klarman/.

34. Michael J. Klarman, "How *Brown* Changed Race Relations: The Backlash Thesis," *Journal of American History* 81 (1994): 118.

35. Id., 82.

36. Charles H. Franklin and Liane C. Kosaki, "Republican Schoolmaster: The U.S. Supreme Court, Public Opinion, and Abortion," *American Political Science Review* 83 (1989): 751.

37. John Hanley, Michael Salamone, and Matthew Wright, "Reviving the Schoolmaster: Reevaluating Public Opinion in the Wake of *Roe v. Wade*," *Political Research Quarterly* 665 (2012): 408; Mary Ziegler, "Beyond Backlash: Legal History, Polarization, and *Roe v. Wade*," *Washington and Lee Law Review* 71 (2014): 969.

38. *See* Robert J. Hume, *Courthouse Democracy and Minority Rights: Same-Sex Marriage in the States* (New York: Oxford University Press, 2013).

39. Delaware is the only state that does not permit citizens to vote on amendments directly.

40. Hume, *Courthouse Democracy*, 170.

41. Baehr v. Lewin, 852 P.2d 44 (Haw. 1993).

42. Goodridge v. Department of Public Health, 798 N.E.2d 941 (Mass. 2003); In re Marriage Cases, 43 Cal. 4th 757 (2008); Kerrigan v. Commissioner of Public Health, 289 Conn. 135 (Conn. 2008); Varnum v. Brien, 763 N.W.2d 862 (Iowa 2009).

43. Matthew E. K. Hall, "The Semiconstrained Court: Public Opinion, the Separation of Powers, and the U.S. Supreme Court's Fear of Nonimplementation," *American Journal of Political Science* 58 (2014): 352.

44. Id., 364.

TEXT ANALYSIS

Federalist 78 (1788)

In Federalist 78, *Alexander Hamilton characterizes the judiciary as the "least dangerous branch" because it possesses "neither force nor will, but merely judgment." Do you agree with Hamilton's characterization of courts as constrained institutions? In what circumstances might the "mere" judgment of courts be a source of strength for the judiciary?*

To the People of the State of New York:

. . .

Whoever attentively considers the different departments of power must perceive, that, in a government in which they are separated from each other, the judiciary, from the nature of its functions, will always be the least dangerous to the political rights of the Constitution; because it will be least in a capacity to annoy or injure them. The Executive not only dispenses the honors, but holds the sword of the community. The legislature not only commands the purse, but prescribes the rules by which the duties and rights of every citizen are to be regulated. The judiciary, on the contrary, has no influence over either the sword or the purse; no direction either of the strength or of the wealth of the society; and can take no active resolution whatever. It may truly be said to have neither force nor will, but merely judgment; and must ultimately depend upon the aid of the executive arm even for the efficacy of its judgments.

This simple view of the matter suggests several important consequences. It proves incontestably, that the judiciary is beyond comparison the weakest of the three departments of power; that it can never attack with success either of the other two; and that all possible care is requisite to enable it to defend itself against their attacks. It equally proves, that though individual oppression may now and then proceed from the courts of justice, the general liberty of the people can never be endangered from that quarter; I mean so long as the judiciary remains truly distinct from both the legislature and the Executive. For I agree, that there is no liberty, if the power of judging be not separated from the legislative and executive powers. And it proves, in the last place, that as liberty can have nothing to fear from the judiciary alone, but would have every thing to fear from its union with either of the other departments; that as all the effects of such a union must ensue from a dependence of the former on the latter, notwithstanding a nominal and apparent separation; that as, from the natural feebleness of the judiciary, it is in continual jeopardy of being overpowered, awed, or influenced by its co-ordinate branches; and that as nothing can contribute so much to its firmness and independence as permanency in office, this quality may therefore be justly regarded as an indispensable ingredient in its constitution, and, in a great measure, as the citadel of the public justice and the public security. . . .

Some perplexity respecting the rights of the courts to pronounce legislative acts void, because contrary to the Constitution, has arisen from an imagination that the doctrine would imply a superiority of the judiciary to the legislative power. It is urged that the authority which can declare the acts of another void, must necessarily be superior to the one whose acts may be declared void. As this doctrine is of great importance in all the American constitutions, a brief discussion of the ground on which is rests cannot be unacceptable.

There is no position which depends on clearer principles, than that every act of a delegated authority, contrary to the tenor of the commission under which it is exercised, is void. No legislative act, therefore, contrary to the Constitution, can be valid. To deny this, would be to affirm, that the deputy is greater than his principal; that the servant is above his master; that the representatives of the people are superior to the people themselves; that men acting by virtue of powers, may do not only what their powers do not authorize, but what they forbid. . . . It is not otherwise to be supposed, that the Constitution could intend to enable to representatives of the people to substitute their will to that of their constituents. It is far more rational to suppose, that the courts were designed to be an intermediate body between the people and the legislature, in order, among other things, to keep the latter within the limits assigned to their authority. . . .

Nor does this conclusion by any means suppose a superiority of the judicial to the legislative power. It only supposes that the power of the people is superior to both; and that where the will of the legislature, declared in its statutes, stands in opposition to that of the people, declared in the Constitution, the judges ought to be governed by the latter rather than the former. They ought to regulate their decisions by the fundamental laws, rather than by those which are not fundamental. . . .

If, then, the courts of justice are to be considered as the bulwarks of a limited Constitution against legislative encroachments, this consideration will afford a strong argument for the permanent tenure of judicial offices, since nothing will contribute so much as this to that independent spirit in the judges which must be essential to the faithful performance of so arduous a duty. . . . This independence of the judges is equally requisite to guard the Constitution and the rights of individuals from the effects of those ill humors, which the arts of designing men, or the influence of particular conjunctures, sometimes disseminate among the people themselves, and which, though they speedily give place to better information, and more deliberate reflection, have a tendency, in the meantime, to occasion dangerous innovations in the government, and serious oppressions of the minor party in the community. . . .

That inflexible and uniform adherence to the rights of the Constitution, and of individuals, which we perceive to be indispensable in the courts of justice, can certainly not be expected from judges who hold their offices by a temporary commission. Periodical appointments, however regulated, or by whomsoever made, would, in some way or other, be fatal to their necessary independence. If the power of making them was committed either to the Executive or legislature, there would be danger of an improper complaisance to the branch which possessed it; if to both, there would be an unwillingness to hazard the displeasure of either; if to the people, or to persons chosen by them for the special purpose, there would be too great a disposition to consult popularity, to justify a reliance that nothing would be consulted but the Constitution and the laws. . . .

Upon the whole, there can be no room to doubt that the convention acted wisely in copying from the models of those constitutions which have established good behavior as the tenure of their judicial offices, in point of duration; and that so far from being blamable on this account, their plan would have been inexcusably defective, if it had wanted this important feature of good government. The experience of Great Britain affords an illustrious comment on the excellence of the institution.

Publius. [Alexander Hamilton]

CASE ANALYSIS

Brown v. Board of Education of Topeka (Brown II), 349 U.S. 294 (1955)

Instead of ordering an immediate end to school desegregation in the South, Chief Justice Earl Warren ordered school districts to integrate with "all deliberate speed." Why do you think that Chief Justice Warren chose this mandate instead of other, stronger alternatives? Is it appropriate for judges to think about implementation when they are making decisions?

CHIEF JUSTICE WARREN delivered the opinion of the Court.

These cases were decided on May 17, 1954. The opinions of that date, declaring the fundamental principle that racial discrimination in public education is unconstitutional, are incorporated herein by reference. All provisions of federal, state, or local law requiring or permitting such discrimination must yield to this principle. There remains for consideration the manner in which relief is to be accorded.

Because these cases arose under different local conditions and their disposition will involve a variety of local problems, we requested further argument on the question of relief. In view of the nationwide importance of the decision, we invited the Attorney General of the United States and the Attorneys General of all states requiring or permitting racial discrimination in public education to present their views on that question. The parties, the United States, and the States of Florida, North Carolina, Arkansas, Oklahoma, Maryland, and Texas filed briefs and participated in the oral argument.

These presentations were informative and helpful to the Court in its consideration of the complexities arising from the transition to a system of public education freed of racial discrimination. The presentations also demonstrated that substantial steps to eliminate racial discrimination in public schools have already been taken, not only in some of the communities in which these cases arose, but in some of the states appearing as *amici curiae*, and in other states as well. Substantial progress has been made in the District of Columbia and in the communities in Kansas and Delaware involved in this litigation. The defendants in the cases coming to us from South Carolina and Virginia are awaiting the decision of this Court concerning relief.

Full implementation of these constitutional principles may require solution of varied local school problems. School authorities have the primary responsibility for elucidating, assessing, and solving these problems; courts will have to consider whether the action of school authorities constitutes good faith implementation of the governing constitutional principles. Because of their proximity to local conditions and the possible need for further hearings, the courts which originally heard these cases can best perform this judicial appraisal. Accordingly, we believe it appropriate to remand the cases to those courts.

In fashioning and effectuating the decrees, the courts will be guided by equitable principles. Traditionally, equity has been characterized by a practical flexibility in shaping its remedies and by a facility for adjusting and reconciling public and private needs. These cases call for the exercise of these traditional attributes of equity power. At stake is the personal interest of the plaintiffs in admission to public schools as soon as practicable on a nondiscriminatory basis. To effectuate this interest may call for elimination of a variety of obstacles in making the transition to school systems operated in accordance with the constitutional principles set forth in our May 17, 1954, decision. Courts of equity may properly take into account the public interest in the elimination of such obstacles in a systematic and effective manner. But it should go without saying that the vitality of these constitutional principles cannot be allowed to yield simply because of disagreement with them.

While giving weight to these public and private considerations, the courts will require that the defendants make a prompt and reasonable start toward full compliance with our May 17, 1954, ruling. Once such a start has been made, the courts may find that additional time is necessary to carry out the ruling in an effective manner. The burden rests upon the defendants to establish that such time is necessary in the public interest and is consistent with good faith compliance at the earliest practicable date. To that end, the courts may consider problems related to administration, arising from the physical condition of the school plant, the school transportation system, personnel, revision of school districts and attendance areas into compact units to achieve a system of determining admission to the public schools on a nonracial basis, and revision of local laws and regulations which may be necessary in solving the foregoing problems. They will also consider the adequacy of any plans the defendants may propose to meet these problems and to effectuate a transition to a racially nondiscriminatory school system. During this period of transition, the courts will retain jurisdiction of these cases.

The judgments below, except that, in the Delaware case, are accordingly reversed, and the cases are remanded to the District Courts to take such proceedings and enter such orders and decrees consistent with this opinion as are necessary and proper to admit to public schools on a racially nondiscriminatory basis with all deliberate speed the parties to these cases. The judgment in the Delaware case—ordering the immediate admission of the plaintiffs to schools previously attended only by white children—is affirmed on the basis of the principles stated in our May 17, 1954, opinion, but the case is remanded to the Supreme Court of Delaware for such further proceedings as that Court may deem necessary in light of this opinion.

It is so ordered.

Glossary

advisory opinion: a judicial answer to a legal question that is presented outside of a regular case or controversy; in federal law, advisory opinions are prohibited by Article III of the Constitution

affirmance deference: the deference given by an appellate court to a trial court's findings of fact

aggressive grant: a judge's agreeing to review an otherwise unmeritorious case because it is a good vehicle for advancing the judge's policy preferences

amicus brief: see "amicus curiae"

amicus curiae: a "friend of the court" filing by an individual or interest group who is not otherwise a party to a case

appellate jurisdiction: the cases and controversies that courts may review on appeal, after an initial proceeding below

attitudinal model: a theory of judicial behavior that holds that judges are motivated by their personal ideologies and values

backlash thesis: a theory of judicial impact that holds that court decisions primarily mobilize the opponents of decisions

bargaining statements: suggestions made by other judges on the same court to revise a majority opinion; can also take the form of threats to withhold support unless changes are made

behavioralism: a methodological approach to political science that holds that our ability to understand and predict political events is improved through systematic observation and analysis of human behavior

campaign finance (CF) scores: measures of state judicial ideology that are based on the preferences of the contributors to judicial election campaigns

case method: a method of legal instruction in which students use inductive reasoning to discover the legal principles that rationalize case outcomes

certiorari petition: a request that a higher court review the proceedings of a lower court

certiorari, writ of: an order from a higher court directing a lower court to submit case records to a higher court for review

concurring opinion: a judge's separate expression of support for the majority opinion, often seeking to clarify or expand upon the rationale described in the opinion; see also "special concurrence"

confirmation bias: a tendency for people to give more weight to evidence that supports conclusions or outcomes they already favor

constitution: a framework of government, typically establishing fundamental principles of organization and human rights

constrained court model: a theory of judicial impact that holds that courts are incapable of producing major policy change

consumer population: the people who make use of judicial policies

contested election: an election with multiple candidates on the ballot

counter-majoritarian difficulty: the dilemma that occurs when unelected judges invalidate the policies of elected branches of government

critical mass theory: an approach to social background theory that holds that a minority group must reach a minimum size within a population before group characteristics gain expression

defensive denial: a judge's declining to review an otherwise worthy case to prevent an unfavorable decision on the merits

departmental theory: an alternative to judicial review that holds that each branch, or "department," of government is capable of determining the scope of its own powers; under this theory, government power is checked by the democratic process

dependent variable: a phenomenon about the world that a researcher is trying to explain, usually with reference to variation in another, independent, variable

difference theory: an approach to social background theory that holds that judges who share certain traits or experiences think about legal problems differently from other judges

diffuse support: public support for an institution, as opposed to its policy output

direct initiative: a form of initiative by which citizens can propose policies for a public vote without having to submit the proposal to the state legislature for approval

dissenting opinion: a judge's separate expression of disagreement with the result and rationale described in the majority opinion

docket: the calendar of cases that a court decides in a year

double jeopardy: to be tried twice for the same offense; in criminal law, the practice is prohibited by the Fifth Amendment to the U.S. Constitution

dynamic court model: a theory of judicial impact that holds that courts are capable of producing major policy change

electoral connection: the link between elected officials and their constituents; often recognized as a primary influence on the behavior of government officials

empirical statement: a description of what is

fluidity: changes in how judges intend to vote; occurring after an initial conference vote but before the decision is announced

GHP scores: measures of the ideologies of federal judges, based on the preferences of appointing presidents and home-state senators; named for the scholars who developed them, Michael Giles, Virginia Hettinger, and Todd Peppers

Greenhouse Effect: a judge's motivation to receive favorable coverage in the press; named for former *New York Times* Supreme Court reporter Linda Greenhouse

horizontal judicial review: the power of courts to evaluate the policies of coequal institutions, such as when the U.S. Supreme Court reviews actions by Congress or the president

hypothesis: a testable implication of a theory, typically involving the relationship between at least two variables

ideal point: the location, in ideological space, where a judge would prefer to set policy

impeachment: an accusation of misconduct against a government official; in federal law, impeachment is for "high crimes and misdemeanors"

implementing population: nonjudicial actors who have the responsibility for putting court decisions into effect

independent variable: a phenomenon hypothesized to explain variation in the dependent variable

indirect initiative: a form of initiative by which citizens can put policies on the ballot for a public vote, but only after submitting the proposal to the state legislature for approval

ineffective assistance of counsel: legal representation that falls below objective standards of reasonableness and affects the outcome of the proceedings

initial selection: see "judicial selection"

initiative amendment: a constitutional amendment that the public proposes, usually via a petition drive, and subsequently votes on; common in state constitutional systems

instrument-choice strategies: judges' efforts to make their policies appear more persuasive to other actors without modifying the contents of the policies

intermediate scrutiny: a legal standard of review requiring policymakers to show that their policies are substantially related to important government interests

interpreting population: the lower-court judges who interpret court decisions and decide how to apply them to other cases and controversies

judicial activism: judges' overextension of their power or lack of appropriate deference to other branches of government

judicial federalism: the dual system of constitutional adjudication, in which state judges rely on their own state constitutions to consider legal claims, frequently to provide more generous rights protections than under federal law

judicial retention: the process by which judges are kept in office

judicial review: the power of courts to evaluate the policies of other government actors

judicial selection: the process by which candidates are initially chosen for judgeships

judicial self-restraint: a philosophy of judging that holds that judges should play a modest role and uphold legislative policies whenever possible

jurisprudential regime: a legal framework established by a landmark precedent

lateral issue: a judicial policy that is implemented by nonjudicial actors

legal formalism: a view of judging, characteristic of the nineteenth century, that considers judicial decision making as a mechanical process with right and wrong answers to legal questions

legal model: a theory of judicial behavior that holds that legal principles influence judicial behavior

legal realism: a view of judging, developed at the turn of the twentieth century, that considers judicial decision making as a discretionary process in which judges make law based on their values

legitimacy: a measure of institutional loyalty that captures the public's willingness to support the institution beyond its satisfaction with the policies of the moment

litigant status: a measure of the relative resources and advantages that litigants have; typically, private individuals rank low and the government ranks high

living constitution: an approach to judging that holds that constitutional language should be interpreted based on what people think the words mean today

majority opinion: on a multimember court, the opinion that receives the support of a majority of the judges for both its result and rationale

mandatory appeals: cases that come to higher courts on a nondiscretionary basis

Martin-Quinn scores: dynamic yearly estimates of the U.S. Supreme Court justices' policy preferences, based on their voting behavior

median voter theorem: a theory that holds that case outcomes can be explained with reference to the ideology of the median, or middle, judge on a tribunal

mediating variable: a variable that explains the causal linkage between two other variables; also known as an intervening variable

merit selection: a system of judicial selection in which a nonpartisan commission nominates a slate of qualified candidates for judicial vacancies

minimum winning coalition: the fewest votes needed for a majority; typically, five votes on the U.S. Supreme Court and two on the U.S. courts of appeals

Missouri Plan: the original merit selection system, first adopted by Missouri in 1940, which combines the nomination of judicial candidates by a nonpartisan commission, appointment by the governor, and retention by popular retention elections

morality policies: public policies that engage moral values; known for their technical simplicity and their capacity to elicit strong opinions

motivated reasoning: a process by which a person's values shape his or her interpretations of facts and evaluations of competing claims

natural law: principles inherent in nature, reason, or the divine

nonpartisan election: an election in which party labels do not appear on the ballot

normative statement: a description of what should be

one-shotters: litigants who rarely participate in the legal system

operationalization: the process of putting a variable in a form that can be measured

originalism: an approach to judging that holds that constitutional words and phrases should be interpreted based on what people understood the words to mean when they were written

original jurisdiction: the cases and controversies that may originate in a tribunal

panel effects: on multimember courts, the impact that judges have on the behavior of other judges on the same panel

partisan election: an election in which party labels appear on the ballot

party-adjusted ideology (PAJID) scores: measures of state supreme court ideology based on a judge's party affiliation and the preferences of the judge's appointers

petitioner: the party who brings a dispute to an appellate court, usually because of a loss below, and generally listed first in the case title (e.g., in *Roe v. Wade*, the petitioner is *Roe*)

playing for rules: a legal strategy, practiced by repeat players, by which litigants seek to establish the most favorable precedents for themselves moving forward

playing the odds: a legal strategy, practiced by repeat players, by which litigants seek to maximize their chances of winning in court more often than not, even if it means not winning every case

plurality opinion: on a multimember court, an opinion that receives the most votes from the members of the majority coalition, but not enough to command a majority of the court as a whole

policy: an authoritative directive from a government institution

policy-choice strategies: judges' substantive modification of the contents of their policies to win the support of other actors

political science: a discipline interested broadly in power, or "who gets what, when, how"

positive law: man-made rules, such as statutes, legal precedents, and constitutional texts

positivity bias: the public's tendency to think about judicial decision making as a principled process worthy of respect

precedent: an authoritative holding by a court

precedential voting: behavior that signals judges' support or acceptance of precedents, especially precedents the judges originally opposed

preemptive accommodation: a judge's writing an opinion in a way that anticipates the goals and preferences of the other members of the majority coalition

preferential voting: behavior that signals judges' commitment to their sincere policy preferences, particularly when judges continue to reject precedents that they originally opposed

professionalization: a measure of an institution's capacity to generate and evaluate information

public mood: a composite measure of the public's support for government programs across a range of domestic policy issues

qualitative methods: methods of inquiry that draw upon interviews, archival research, field work, and other nonquantitative methods to test hypotheses

quantitative methods: methods of inquiry that test hypotheses by using statistics to analyze data

rational basis test: a legal standard of review requiring policymakers to show that their policies are rationally related to legitimate government interests (see also "strict scrutiny" and "intermediate scrutiny")

recusal: the withdrawal of a judge from a case because of bias or the appearance of bias

regulation: a rule promulgated by an administrative agency

reliability: an indicator of whether a measurement produces consistent results each time it is used

repeat players (RPs): litigants who participate frequently in the legal system

representational theories: approaches to social background theory that suggest that judges identify with litigants who have similar traits or experiences

republican schoolmaster: the capacity for courts to change public opinion

respondent: the party who is brought to an appellate court, usually by the petitioner, and generally listed second in the case title (e.g., in *Roe v. Wade*, the respondent is *Wade*)

retention election: an election in which voters decide whether to keep a single candidate in office

retention of judges: see "judicial retention"

roll-off: voters' casting of incomplete ballots, such as when they vote for governor but not other races on the ballot

Rule of Four: a convention on the U.S. Supreme Court whereby justices put a case on the docket when four of them support review

secondary population: parties who are not directly affected by a court's decision but have a stake or interest in the outcome; may include the public at large, the media, interest groups, and other government officials

Segal-Cover scores: measures of the ideologies of U.S. Supreme Court justices, based on the judgments of editorial writers at the time of nomination

selection of judges: see "judicial selection"

senatorial courtesy: a tradition in the Senate to decline the nomination of federal judicial candidates opposed by a home-state senator from the president's party

separation-of-powers model: a subset of the strategic model that examines judicial accommodation of other government actors, especially the president and Congress

social background theory: a theory of judicial behavior that holds that personal background characteristics (e.g., gender, race, work experience) influence judicial behavior

solicitor general: the government officer who is responsible for arguing the federal government's cases in the U.S. Supreme Court

special concurrence: a judge's separate expression of support for the result reached by the majority opinion but not the rationale

specific support: public support for an institution's policies, as opposed to the institution itself

standing: a legal status that establishes a litigant as an appropriate party to file suit

stare decisis: respect for precedent; literally translated as "to stand by things decided"

statute: a policy created by a legislature

strategic model: a theory of judicial behavior that holds that judges modify their behavior in response to other actors on and off the court

strict scrutiny: a legal standard of review requiring policymakers to show that their policies are narrowly tailored to compelling government interests

theory: a collection of statements or principles intended to explain phenomena

validity: an indicator of whether a measurement represents the concept being studied

vertical issue: a judicial policy that a lower court can implement directly

vertical judicial review: the power of courts to evaluate the policies of subordinate institutions, such as when the U.S. Supreme Court reviews state court decisions that involve federal law

veto point: a stage in the policy process in which a proposal can be blocked

writ of certiorari: see "certiorari, writ of"

Index

Note: Page numbers in bold indicate the first appearance of key terms. Page numbers in italics indicate textboxes. Page numbers followed by "f" or "t" indicate figures and tables, respectively.